D0028203

The Origins *of* the
Cuban Revolution
RECONSIDERED

[ENVISIONING CUBA]

LOUIS A. PÉREZ JR., EDITOR

[SAMUEL FARBER]

The Origins *of* the Cuban Revolution

RECONSIDERED

The University of North Carolina Press | CHAPEL HILL

Designed by Heidi Perov and set in Adobe Garamond and Futura

Manufactured in the United States of America

The paper in this book meets the guidelines for permanence and durability of the Committee on Production Guidelines for Book Longevity of the Council on Library Resources.

Library of Congress Cataloging-in-Publication Data

Farber, Samuel, 1939–

The origins of the Cuban Revolution reconsidered / by Samuel Farber.

p. cm.—(Envisioning Cuba)

Includes bibliographical references and index.

ISBN-13: 978-0-8078-3001-7 (cloth : alk. paper)

ISBN-10: 0-8078-3001-1 (cloth : alk. paper)

ISBN-13: 978-0-8078-5673-4 (pbk. : alk. paper)

ISBN-10: 0-8078-5673-8 (pbk. : alk. paper)

1. Cuba—Politics and government—1959– 2. Cuba—History—Revolution, 1959—Causes. 3. United States—Foreign relations—20th century. 4. United States—Relations—Cuba. 5. Cuba—Relations—United States. I. Title. II. Series. F1788.F328 2006

972.9106'4—dc22

2005020671

Portions of this work appeared earlier, in somewhat different form, in "The Cuban Communists in the Early Stages of the Cuban Revolution: Revolutionaries or Reformists?," *Latin American Research Review* 18, no. 1 (March 1983): 59–83, copyright © 1983 by the University of Texas Press, all rights reserved; and *Revolution and Reaction in Cuba, 1933–1960: A Political Sociology from Machado to Castro* (Middletown, Conn.: Wesleyan University Press, 1976), and are reproduced here with permission of the publishers.

cloth   10 09 08 07 06   5 4 3 2 1

paper   10 09 08 07 06   5 4 3 2 1

[C O N T E N T S]

[A C K N O W L E D G M E N T S]

I am grateful to Professor Sherry Warman and the staff of the Interlibrary Loan Department of the Brooklyn College Library for their valuable assistance in obtaining the materials necessary for my research. I also thank the Professional Staff Congress (American Federation of Teachers Local #2334) and the City University of New York for a PSC-CUNY Award for release time from teaching that helped me to finish this project.

I owe special gratitude to a number of people who have criticized and commented on partial and complete drafts of the manuscript while it was in preparation: César Ayala, Mel Bienenfeld, Adolfo Gilly, Dan Labotz, Corey Robin, and Francisco Sobrino. I owe special thanks to Thomas Harrison, whose editorial assistance played an important role in the development of this project.

I am deeply indebted to an anonymous reader for the University of North Carolina Press who provided me with very valuable criticisms and insightful comments. Professor Louis A. Pérez Jr. read my entire manuscript as a reader and adviser to the University of North Carolina Press and made numerous penetrating and useful criticisms. He also made himself available for several very helpful telephone consultations. I thank him for his generosity and graciousness. I am solely responsible for the views expressed in this book.

This project could not have been carried out without the invaluable and unstinting editorial guidance and support of Elaine Maisner, senior editor at the University of North Carolina Press. I thank her warmly. I am thankful as well to Ellen Goldlust-Gingrich and Ron Maner, respectively copyeditor and project editor for this book.

I give special thanks to my stepson, Daniel Marks, for his technical help in preparing this manuscript for publication. To my wife, Selma Marks, I owe eternal gratitude not only for her detailed criticisms but also for her limitless support, patience, and endurance.

Major Events in Cuban History, 1868–1961

1868–98	Cubans wage war against Spain during most of this period.
1898	Battleship *Maine* explodes in Havana harbor, and the United States declares war on Spain. Subsequent peace treaty makes Cuba a U.S. protectorate.
1901	Platt Amendment is attached to the Cuban constitution, granting the United States the right to intervene in Cuban affairs.
1902	Cuba is officially declared independent, although Platt Amendment restrictions on its sovereignty remain.
1903	United States and Cuba ratify and enact reciprocal trade agreement.
1906–9	United States intervenes in Cuba (second time).
1917–22	United States intervenes in Cuba (third time).
1925–33	Gerardo Machado rules as dictator.
1933	Machado dictatorship is overthrown on August 12. On September 4, Sergeant Fulgencio Batista leads revolt with the support of civilian revolutionaries. Ramón Grau San Martín becomes provisional president. U.S. government, which had been actively intervening in Cuban politics both before and after Machado's overthrow, does not recognize Grau government.
1934	Batista, with U.S. support, removes Grau's nationalist government. Platt Amendment is officially abolished,

although United States retains in perpetuity a naval base in Guantánamo Bay. Cuba and the United States sign new reciprocal trade agreement.

1934–40   Batista, as head of the army, controls Cuba through puppet governments.

1940   New Cuban constitution is adopted.

1940–44   Batista rules Cuba as constitutional president.

1944–48   Grau, leader of the Auténtico Party, serves as president.

1948–52   Auténtico leader Carlos Prío Socarrás succeeds Grau as president.

March 10, 1952   Batista overthrows Prío in military coup.

July 26, 1953   Attack on Moncada barracks fails, and the Castro brothers and many followers are imprisoned.

May 15, 1955   Batista decrees political amnesty, and the Castro brothers, their followers, and other political prisoners are released from prison.

December 2, 1956   The *Granma* lands in Oriente Province, bringing Fidel Castro and his followers from Mexico.

March 13, 1957   Attack on Presidential Palace by Directorio Revolucionario fails.

April 9, 1958   General strike fails.

July 1958   Batista army offensive against rebels in Oriente Province fails.

January 1, 1959   Batista flees Cuba, and 26th of July Movement rebels take over.

May 1959   Agrarian reform law is enacted.

October 1, 1959   Unofficial Soviet envoy Aleksandr Alekseev arrives in Cuba to establish direct link between the Soviet Union and Cuban government.

February 4, 1960	Soviet leader Anastas Mikoyan arrives in Cuba and signs trade treaty with Cuban government.
March 1960	U.S. government adopts systematic covert action plans to overthrow Cuban government. Plans had been in preparation since late 1959.
May 1960	Fidel Castro achieves complete control of Cuban press and mass media. Soviet Union and Cuba resume full diplomatic relations.
June–July 1960	U.S.-owned oil companies refuse to process Soviet oil and are then expropriated by Cuban government. Dwight D. Eisenhower abrogates Cuban sugar quota.
August 1960	Castro undertakes large-scale expropriation of U.S.-owned property in Cuba.
October 1960	Full-scale U.S. economic blockade of Cuba begins. Cuban government carries out large-scale expropriation of Cuban capitalists.
January 1961	United States breaks diplomatic relations with Cuba.
April 15, 1961	U.S. government organizes bombing of Cuban airfields.
April 16, 1961	Fidel Castro declares "socialist" character of Cuban Revolution.
April 17, 1961	U.S.-sponsored invasion of Cuba fails after a few days of fighting in central Cuba.

The Origins *of* the Cuban Revolution

RECONSIDERED

[INTRODUCTION]

Almost half a century after its triumph, the rapid evolution of the Cuban Revolution from a multiclass antidictatorial political movement to "socialist revolution," as Fidel Castro officially declared in April 1961, remains a puzzle. Why did it occur? What was the revolution's true character? Experts, observers, and even those intimately involved have put forth conflicting answers.

This is an opportune time to reassess the course taken by the Cuban Revolution. The inevitable passing of Fidel Castro from the scene is likely to open a substantial process of change in Cuban Communism as it is presently constituted. That process in turn will foster a need for ideological legitimation and encourage a reexamination of Cuban history, particularly the history of the revolution. The various ideological and political currents contending for hegemony in the Cuban transition are certain to find an echo in the differing historical interpretations of the Cuban Revolution that are likely to emerge. A variety of existing trends will feed these currents: the ideological change if not deterioration that the Castro regime has experienced since the early 1990s; the growth of Cuban neoliberal economic thought, which has found an echo in such places as the publications of the Association for the Study of the Cuban Economy, headquartered in Washington, D.C.; and the Cuban hard Right's longstanding tendency to praise if not idealize the prerevolutionary Cuban republic, a tendency that is now being echoed by newer center to center-right publications such as the influential *Encuentro de la Cultura Cubana*.[1] The alternative perspective presented in this work of historical synthesis will challenge the conventional views common among both supporters and opponents of the present Cuban government and will contribute to a broad discussion and reevaluation of Cuba's recent history.[2]

This reassessment has been stimulated and greatly facilitated by new information that has recently become available. This includes the U.S.

government's release of previously classified documents from its Cuba archives. Most important for my purposes are the edited volume published by the U.S. State Department in 1991[3] and the primary materials contained in the Confidential State Department Central Files for the years 1955 to 1959 made available by University Publications of America.[4] Historians Aleksandr Fursenko and Timothy Naftali have analyzed Communist Party and government documents relevant to Cuba that had been previously classified by the Soviet authorities.[5] At the same time, a growing biographical and narrative literature has been published in Cuba, illuminating the ideas, activities, and background of revolutionary leaders and activists.[6]

One of the most important claims made by observers of the Cuban Revolution, particularly those on the liberal Left, is that the policies pursued by the Eisenhower and Kennedy Cold War administrations pushed Fidel Castro and his government into the arms of the Soviet Union and Communism. This still widely held view of the Cuban road to Communism makes two critical assumptions: that the United States could have adopted alternative policies and that the revolutionary leaders were merely reacting to U.S. policies regarding the Cuban Revolution. The reexamination of this matter raises important questions regarding Cuban and U.S. history and broader issues pertaining to the weight of politics and ideology compared to objective socioeconomic factors.

While it is conceivable that the United States could have adopted alternative policies, the United States related to Cuba as it did to other Latin American countries. U.S. policies were consistent with the preservation of Cuba's subordinate relationship to the United States. The U.S. government pursued a clear set of interests in Latin America and limited what it would tolerate. For those who claim that the United States could have acted in a substantially different way toward the Cuban Revolution, U.S. support for the Bolivian Revolution of 1952 provides a revealing comparison, posing the important question of what price the Bolivian Revolution had to pay in exchange for U.S. support. Declassified State Department documents also provide an opportunity to analyze the roles played by U.S. investors and the U.S. government in responding to the Cuban government and illuminate the decision-making power of the State Department relative to other federal agencies, such as the National Security Council, as the relations between Cuba and the U.S. became polarized and headed toward confrontation.

While conservatives argue that the Soviet Union and the "old" pro-Moscow Partido Socialista Popular (PSP, the Cuban Communist Party) infiltrated and played a subversive role in the Cuban Revolution, many leftists contend that these forces were reluctant, timid reformist supporters if not sclerotic opponents of a radical Cuban revolution. Against both views, I argue first that the Soviet Union pursued the logic of state interests both in Cuba and elsewhere and second that the leftist dichotomy between reform and revolution is an inappropriate tool for understanding Soviet international behavior.

When Fulgencio Batista fell, the Soviet Union did not consider Cuba a high priority because it ascribed little importance to Latin America and considered the region part of the U.S. sphere of influence. The 1954 overthrow of the Arbenz government in Guatemala merely reinforced this view.[7] Although the Soviet Union did not initially have any great expectations about the radical potential of the Cuban Revolution, Soviet leaders took advantage of certain opportunities opened by the revolutionary process to strengthen forces friendly to their interests. Newly released information from Soviet archives shows that the Soviet Union became involved early on. For example, the Soviets decided to help organize and establish—along with Raúl Castro, Che Guevara, and the old Cuban Communists—the Cuban state security organs less than four months after the revolutionary victory.[8]

The Soviet attitude toward the Cuban Revolution changed in the fall of 1959. Sensing that the revolution was beginning to move in a direction favorable to their interests, Soviet leaders pressed the Cubans to take a more radical course. The October 1959 arrival of unofficial Soviet envoy Aleksandr Alekseev marked an important point in the alliance between Castro and the Soviet Union that developed rapidly in the following year. Other more immediate factors contributed to greater Soviet involvement, including the perception, widely shared across the world, that the Soviet Union's strength was growing in relation to that of the United States. Moreover, the conflict and competition between the Soviets and China in an increasingly polycentric international Communist movement caused support for Cuba to become an important issue. Such competition allowed Fidel Castro to retain some autonomy while committing himself to a close alliance with the Soviet Union and demanding membership in the Communist camp through the transformation of Cuban society into a one-party state with an almost totally nationalized economy. The Soviet

Union, probably fearing the economic burden and political cost of an escalation of its conflict with the United States, resisted Cuba's full incorporation into the Communist camp despite encouraging Cuba's break with the United States. This situation highlights the Soviet Union's incoherent or perhaps cynical strategy toward Cuba.

Similarly, the leftist dichotomy between reform and revolution is also an inappropriate tool for understanding the old Cuban Communists. The PSP kept pace with Castro's radicalization of the revolution. From a programmatic point of view, during the first few months of 1959, the PSP was significantly more anticapitalist than was Castro. However, with the passage of the May 1959 agrarian reform law, Castro's anticapitalism began to catch up with that of the PSP, and by the fall of 1959, the gap had closed; Castro would soon become even more anticapitalist than the PSP. But even when the PSP was tactically more cautious than Castro, it always supported his measures. The PSP also played an important role at the beginning of the revolutionary process as a kind of Cuban government lobbyist in Moscow. The PSP's analyses, programs, and plans of action, although not at all comparable to the decisive role played by Fidel Castro, significantly contributed to the creation of a political climate that facilitated and may have influenced Castro's choice of Communism. However, the PSP did not play a revolutionary role in the same sense that Castro did because it followed the logic of an organizational machine, seeking to attain maximum political gains at the least possible risk and expense.

The revolutionary leaders acted under serious external and internal constraints but were nevertheless autonomous agents pursuing independent ideological visions. These leaders made choices, including selecting the Communist road for the Cuban Revolution. Prerevolutionary social and political conditions facilitated the rise to power of a fairly autonomous political leadership with a great deal of freedom from internal class pressures.[9] My analysis, with its emphasis on the agency of Cuba's revolutionary leadership, challenges some previously held views of the revolution. Thus, my approach differs from the line of analysis that, while rejecting the notion that the Cuban Revolution resulted primarily from U.S. hostility, nevertheless views the development of Cuban Communism as a virtually automatic, predetermined response to objective economic, social, and political conditions as understood and acted upon by men whose guerrilla experience conditioned them to act as realistic revolutionaries to survive.[10]

The question of the relative weight of objective and ideological factors in the development of the Cuban Revolution leads to an analysis of the political and ideological milieu in which Fidel Castro and his close associates developed their politics. This version of Cuban populism remained intent on radicalizing the population while ensuring that the revolutionary process remained under the leaders' tight control. In turn, this specific type of populism was compatible and had an elective affinity with the Soviet model of socialism adopted in the early 1960s. Thus, I also differ from those who acknowledge the agency of the Cuban revolutionary leaders but mischaracterize their politics. Some scholars, for example, have acknowledged the autonomy of Fidel Castro and his circle but have reduced the scope and specificity of the Cuban Revolution by broadly and vaguely characterizing it as "radical nationalism."[11] The particular evolution of the Cuban Revolution shows that it differed significantly from the politics of radical nationalists in Cuba's past as well as from radical nationalist revolutions in the Third World.

In contrast with those who see the development of the Cuban Revolution as virtually inevitable given the island's economic, social, and political reality, the predominant view among Cuban Americans in South Florida is that Cuba did not need a radical social revolution because it was one of the four most economically developed Latin American countries in the 1950s. All it needed, in this view, was a few reforms, most of them political. Accordingly, Communism could not have developed based on internal Cuban needs and must therefore have been entirely the result of willful, even conspiratorial, actions external to the island's "natural" development. In contrast with this view, many defenders of the Cuban regime, particularly abroad, have characterized the Cuba of the 1950s as a typical Third World underdeveloped country, ignoring critical distinctions about the very different levels of development that have existed within that broad category.

The Cuba of the 1950s remained far from European and North American levels of development; however, numerous measures ranked it well above Bolivia, Haiti, and other such Western Hemisphere countries. Cuba at this time constituted a classic case of uneven economic development. The contradictions of capitalist economic crisis (for example, the state regulation provoked by the economic depression of the 1930s) and the organized working class's relative success in defending itself against the effects of such crises had brought the country to a state of economic stagnation, notwithstanding some limited economic growth that took place in the middle part of the decade. This stagnation made the revolutionary road a possibility grounded on Cuban realities that did not need to be artificially imposed on the society through conspiratorial means.

This book deals with unresolved issues and problems pertinent to the early, rapid development of the Cuban Revolution from an antidictatorial, multiclass political revolution to Communism. I have focused tightly on what I view as the key issues affecting the early years of the revolution and the preceding republican period and therefore have not discussed at length other important issues—for example, the histories of women and of race relations in Cuba.

I have organized the chapters around these questions while trying to maintain some chronological order and clarity. Chapter 1, centering mainly on developments before the revolution, discusses whether the economy could have contributed to the creation of a political climate favorable to a radical social revolution. Chapter 2 approximates an understanding of Fidel Castro's politics by looking at the populist political background from which he emerged and which he eventually transcended. Chapter 3 analyzes the development and implementation of U.S. policy toward the revolution and the degree to which it could have differed substantially in the face of revolutionary challenge. Chapter 4 looks at developments inside Cuba during the late 1950s and in that sense provides a Cuban domestic counterpart to my analysis of U.S. policy in that critical period. Chapter 5 discusses the important role played by the Soviet Union and the old Cuban Communists in the revolutionary process. The epilogue brings together the book's various themes and briefly reflects on the likely future context in which the topics discussed in this book will acquire a new importance as well as on the significance of the Cuban Revolution.

CHAPTER ONE

The Prerevolutionary Cuban Economy

Progress or Stagnation?

Did the economic conditions prevailing in Cuba during the 1950s encourage the development of a political climate conducive to a radical social revolution?

The incomplete and frustrated 1933 revolution took place in the midst of a world depression that severely affected the Cuban economy, but, on the eve of the 1959 revolution, the economic situation had certainly improved. Cuba then had the fourth-highest per capita income in Latin America, after Venezuela, Uruguay, and Argentina. Ranking thirty-first in the world by the same indicator, Cuba was wealthier than most "underdeveloped" countries.[1] Average per capita income is, however, not necessarily a reliable indicator of general economic development: in 1953, Cuba also ranked fourth in Latin America according to an average of twelve indexes covering such items as percentage of labor force employed in mining, manufacturing, and construction; percentage of literate persons; and per capita electric power, newsprint, and caloric food consumption.[2] Eugene Staley, the chief economist of the International Bank for Reconstruction and Development (IBRD, the predecessor of the World Bank) mission that investigated the Cuban economy in 1950, classified it as part of an intermediate group of nations that fell in between the highly developed and underdeveloped groups. Staley grouped Cuba with such countries as Chile, Poland, Hungary, and Spain.[3]

Cuba had enjoyed significant postwar prosperity. Sugarcane producers in Asia and beet growers in Europe were only beginning to recover from war destruction and could not yet compete with Cuban sugar exports. This boom allowed liberal but corrupt president Ramón Grau San Martín (1944–48) to proclaim that during his administration every Cuban had "five pesos in his pocket." (One peso was worth one dollar.) By 1950, world sugar production had recovered from the effects of the war, and postwar Cuban prosperity had come under threat. However, with the outbreak of the Korean War, sugar prices went up, thus saving Cuba from an economic downturn, although only for a few years.[4]

On closer inspection, however, it becomes clear that the postwar boom had merely returned the Cuban economy to the predepression days of the 1920s. Thus, as the IBRD's 1951 *Report on Cuba* pointed out, Cuba's per capita income of about three hundred dollars per year was only slightly above that of the early 1920s.[5] Cuba's most important economic breakthrough had taken place from 1900 to 1925, right after Spain was forced to abandon the island in 1898 and the United States made Cuba into a de facto economic and political colony. During this period, the productive basis for Cuba's relatively high economic standing in Latin America had been established. With a U.S. capital investment in the island that amounted to $750 million by 1925,[6] Cuba was producing seventeen times as much sugar in 1925 as in 1900. But as the *Report on Cuba* also explained, the Cuban economy had made relatively little progress since then.[7]

IMPERIAL DEVELOPMENT IN CUBA

While the origins of Cuba's sugar monoculture went back to the 1790s, the entry of U.S. capital and political influence at the end of the nineteenth century and beginning of the twentieth century marked a qualitative new stage in the island's economy and polity. Because the U.S. sugar industry in Cuba required huge expanses of land for the cultivation of cane—with sugar companies competing with each other for the acquisition of land— the industry destroyed small and midsized landed property holdings and created a proletarianized labor force, not all of which would always find work as wage laborers in the sugar industry. The remaining small and medium-sized rural proprietors remained subject to the sugar mill owners, most of them North American, particularly if as cultivators of sugar they had to accept the prices and conditions imposed by the sugar capitalists.[8] Much of this phenomenon resulted from the massive economic destruction that the Cuban guerrilla war against Spain—and heavy Spanish reprisals against the Cuban rebels—had created in the Cuban countryside.

The undercapitalized nonsugar sector faced particularly great obstacles in recovering from this terrible experience.

Later, as the 1920 speculative bubble known as the "dance of the millions" was followed by the crash of the sugar market at the end of that year, Cuba's sugar and banking sectors entered into crisis. Many sugar proprietors were unable to honor their mortgage payments and were forced to sell under very unfavorable conditions. The National City Bank took control of more than fifty sugar mills in the summer of 1921,[9] thereby increasing overall U.S. control of Cuban sugar production.

Viewed strictly from the perspective of the U.S. economy, this economic breakthrough can be seen as another vivid example of capitalist accumulation that recognizes no national boundaries. In that sense, there was nothing special or unique about the growth of U.S. sugar investment in Cuba. When viewed from the perspective of the Cuban economy, the expansion of the period 1900–1925 signified the integration of the Cuban economy into the U.S. economy. From a Cuban perspective, this was not just capitalism but also imperialism.

THE RECIPROCITY TREATIES BEFORE AND AFTER THE DEPRESSION

The Platt Amendment and other forms of explicit U.S. political control over Cuba constituted a key element of the imperial relationship between the two countries. Less attention has been paid, however, to an important economic/political device that survived the Platt Amendment and played at least as important a role in subjecting Cuba to U.S. control: the various reciprocity and other economic treaties in force, in various forms, from 1902 until the early 1960s. These treaties cumulatively cemented Cuba's role as a sugar export economy to the U.S. market and as an importer of U.S. manufactured goods.

The first reciprocity treaty was signed in 1902 and ratified and enacted in 1903, shortly after the adoption of the 1901 Cuban Constitution and the Platt Amendment and the inauguration of the Cuban republic on May 20, 1902. Cuban sugar received a 20 percent tariff reduction in the United States, while U.S. imports received tariff reductions ranging from 25 to 40 percent. As the Cuban economy recovered from the disastrous effects of the war against Spain and massive U.S. foreign investment in sugar created the biggest economic boom the island has ever experienced, Cuban consumption of U.S. imports grew, effectively displacing other suppliers, particularly those from Europe. For their part, Cuban sugar exports to the United States, controlled by U.S. sugar capitalists, increasingly dominated the sugar market in that country. By 1911, Cuba's sugar exporters not only filled the U.S. market's needs but sold their surpluses on the international market, mostly in Europe. This tendency reached its peak during World War I with the destruction of the European sugar industry. Cuban production further expanded during this period of the "fat cows," culminating in the inflationary bubble of 1920 that was followed by the crash of 1921.[10]

THE WORLD DEPRESSION AND AFTER

The world depression that began in the late 1920s devastated the Cuban economy. Moreover, the sugar-based Cuban economy had a much harder time recovering from the depression than did the economies of some other countries. Although the Cuban government implemented a tariff reform in 1927 that encouraged some import substitution of light consumer goods, as Cuban economic historian Julio Le Riverend has pointed out, this limited reform could be realized only by respecting, on the whole, the exceptional advantages that had previously been conceded to U.S. products. The reform was more effective in substituting articles of European origin than those from the United States, but it remained limited in its effect because purchases from Europe had declined as a result of the rising importance of American imports in Cuba. Nevertheless, after 1927, Cuba's production of eggs, poultry, meat, shoes, butter, cheese, and condensed milk, which had been neglected because of sugar's growing dominance, went up at the same time that the import of those products declined. This phenomenon accompanied the strong worldwide protectionist tendencies of the 1920s and 1930s.[11]

Cuba's big economic growth in the early part of the century had been based, to a considerable degree, on sugar exports' unrestricted access to the U.S. market. This changed in 1934, when the Platt Amendment was abolished and the United States and Cuba signed a new reciprocity treaty. That treaty, which continued the pattern of Cuban reliance on sugar, turned out to be more unfavorable for the island republic than the earlier agreement. In the 1902 treaty, Cuba had granted 20 to 40 percent tariff reductions on 497 U.S. products in exchange for a preferential 20 percent tariff for sugar and tobacco; in 1934, however, Cuba granted 20–60 percent tariff reductions on 480 products while ending up with a smaller share of the U.S. consumption of sugar, rum, and tobacco. The most important change was that while the 1902 treaty favored only 241 classes of merchandise (52 percent) with preferential treatment ranging from 25 percent to 40 percent, the 1934 treaty gave tariff concessions between 25 and 60 percent to 406 categories of merchandise (63 percent of the total).[12] While the reduction of tariffs on sugar and other primary products encouraged the growth of those sectors in Cuba, the increased competition from North American imports dealt a serious blow to efforts to diversify the Cuban economy. Thus, from 1933 to 1940, the U.S. portion of Cuba's imports increased from 54 to 77 percent.[13] Therefore, while in the aftermath of the world depression nationalist governments in Mexico and other Latin American countries embarked on a protectionist tariff policy to encourage import substitution, Cuba, as a direct result of the reciprocity treaty, had no such option.

To make matters worse for Cuba, the U.S. Congress approved the Jones-Costigan Act just before the new reciprocity treaty went into effect. This law replaced tariffs with quotas as the means of protecting U.S. domestic sugar producers. The U.S. secretary of agriculture now had authority to assign quotas to all sugar producers, domestic and foreign, on the basis of the secretary's estimation of national sugar needs. While Cuba had derived some slight benefit from the lowered tariffs in the 1934 reciprocity treaty, the country initially was harmed by the quota system, which was based on the participation of sugar producers in the U.S. market between 1931 and 1933. Under the impact of the 1930 protectionist Hawley-Smoot Act, the Cuban share of the U.S. market during those three years was the smallest that Cuba had at any time. Cuban sugar production and exports to the United States did increase throughout the 1930s but did not return to the level of the 1910s and early 1920s.[14] As a result of the limits set by the new law, Cuban sugar, whether controlled by Cuban or U.S. capitalists, could no longer compete with U.S. producers on an economic basis. Conversely, the price for the sugar that Cuba was allowed to sell in the United States was usually above that of the world market.[15] In sum, these changes spelled the end of the days when Cuba, in free competition with sugar from the United States and other foreign producers, could export as much sugar as the U.S. market could consume, creating a much more unfavorable and asymmetrical economic situation for Cuba than had prevailed from 1902 to 1934. This new greater power asymmetry between Cuba and the United States was further reinforced by the fact that Cuba's sugar quota under the 1934 Jones-Costigan Act was unilaterally determined by the U.S. Congress rather than being the outcome of bilateral trade negotiations between the two countries.

During World War II, many of Cuba's sugar competitors suffered considerable war damage, but the benefits of that situation for Cuban sugar were significantly diminished by an agreement signed by Cuba and the United States. Cuba, as a war ally of the United States, agreed to sell its sugar to its North American neighbor at fixed prices for the duration of the conflict. During this period, Cuba produced 20 million tons of sugar, but the price paid by the United States remained below world market prices, meaning that the island failed to obtain an increase in income proportionate to the rising levels of sugar production and exports.[16] According to estimates made by Jorge Domínguez, real per capita income in Cuba remained the same in 1945 as in 1938, although significant variations had occurred within this period.[17] As the war created difficulties in transportation between Cuban and U.S. ports, Cuba planned to develop a small merchant marine to transport sugar to nearby ports in Florida and Louisiana and to bring home industrial raw materials and finished products. This plan, initiated by Cuba's Junta de Economía de Guerra de Cuba (War Economy Board), provoked an official note from the U.S. government objecting in advance to any future efforts to reduce the amount of cargo carried between the two countries by the U.S. merchant marine. The note also contained veiled threats of economic reprisals if such a situation came to pass.[18]

The U.S.-Cuban trade system established in 1934 remained basically unchanged with the 1948 passage of the U.S. Sugar Law, which continued the quota system allocating U.S. sugar imports to sugar-exporting countries and remained in force when U.S.-Cuban relations ended in 1961. The year 1948 also witnessed the foundation of the General Agreement on Tariffs and Trade (GATT), with both Cuba and the United States as founding members and with Cuba as host for the first part of the founding conference that concluded later that year in Geneva, Switzerland. The multilateral GATT agreement required Cuba to sign a new bilateral exclusive agreement with the United States. Neither GATT nor the new Cuban-

U.S. agreement affected in any way the U.S. Sugar Law or the tariff preferences given to U.S. products in Cuba. Under the new arrangements, if Cuba gave to a third country the same tariffs given to a U.S. product, Cuba had to "compensate" that U.S. product with additional advantages. Nevertheless, Cuba benefited to some extent from GATT, granting some tariff concessions to Great Britain and expanding economic relations with that country as well as with other states such as Canada and Germany. Consequently, in the 1950s Cuba became somewhat less dependent on the United States for exports, negotiating sugar sales with a number of countries, including Japan, France, West Germany, the United Kingdom, Canada, and the Netherlands. Even the Soviet Union bought 182,000 tons of Cuban sugar in 1958. Ironically, these non-U.S. sales enabled Cuba to finance its substantial trade deficit with the United States during the 1950s.[19]

INTERNAL STRUCTURE OF
THE SUGAR INDUSTRY

Many of the Cuban economy's problems inhered in the way in which the country's sugar industry developed in the first half of the twentieth century. The prevailing "sprout" (*retoño*) system of sugar cultivation probably doubled the amount of land required for this crop, an extensive exploitation that was possible only because of the abundance of suitable land and the failure to significantly develop alternative crops. A relatively small proportion of farm acreage was dedicated to other crops despite the economic drain caused by food imports, the existence of high rural unemployment, and the existence of abundant cultivable land.[20] During the prerevolutionary period, demand and consequently prices for land remained low.[21] The fluctuations of the international sugar market dictated that some lands be held in reserve for the expansion of sugar production when exports increased. However, as agricultural economist Andrés Bianchi has pointed out, the amount of land kept in reserve exceeded what could be justified by unstable sugar demand. According to Bianchi, from 1953 to 1956 the maximum absolute variation of the area planted with cane represented only about one-fourth of the amount of reserve land held by the sugar mills.[22]

This enormous waste of land and of opportunities for agricultural diversification was made possible by the great concentration of land in the latifundia system throughout the first half of the twentieth century. As the sugar industry greatly expanded in the early part of that century, so did the development of large sugar estates, especially in eastern Cuba. At the same time, what had originally been in the late nineteenth century an important group of middle-class landowners became increasingly dependent on the mill owners. The small and medium-sized sugar landlords (*colonos*) had no alternative but to produce according to the prices and conditions determined by the companies. As a result, by the time of the depression, small and medium-sized landed property holdings had declined, as had the number of *colonos*. Moreover, the rural proletariat grew, and its members had no option but to sell their labor power to the sugar mills when they were hiring. Despite the predepression labor shortage, most of the rural population remained unemployed during the "dead" nonsugar season.[23]

In the two decades after the depression, the Cuban sugar industry entered a period of long-term relative decline. Only one sugar mill was built between 1926 and the Cuban Revolution in 1959. By 1955, most of the sugar industry had mechanized the clearing and preparation of land for sugarcane and, in part, the transport of cane to the mills.[24] However, the overall lack of technical improvements and significant new capital investments led to a situation in which Cuba, although the leading producer and exporter of sugar, came to lag behind almost all of the main sugarcane-producing countries in cane yield per hectare. Although this deficiency was somewhat overcome by the high raw-sugar content of Cuban cane, thus reducing the differential in raw-sugar yield per acre, Cuba occupied a secondary position in this area as well.[25] The excessive capacity built during the 1920 sugar boom and the lack of substantial growth in the international sugar market discouraged significant capital expansion in the industry. These factors combined with the limited modernization that had occurred to reduce potential employment, and the size of the sugar industry's agricultural workforce barely changed even though the country's population grew significantly through the 1940s and 1950s. In 1928, the sugar industry employed 339,362 persons; in 1937, 361,172; in 1940, 350,077; in 1952, 353,660; and in 1955, 351,037.[26] The length of the *zafra* (sugar season) gradually shrank from approximately 300 days at the beginning of the twentieth century to an average of 210 days in the 1920s, 104 days in the 1930s, and 95 days in the postwar period, with the resulting growth of seasonal unemployment.[27]

Unevenness lies at the heart of capitalist development in at least two major ways: first, different economic sectors (e.g., textiles, railroads) within any given capitalist economy typically develop at different times, rhythms, and tempos; second, different national capitalist economies begin their development at significantly different times. Whether a country is an early or late-developing capitalist country has a major impact on the process of economic development. As the first industrial capitalist country, Britain could take the time to go through a series of developmental stages from the putting-out system of cottage industry to fully mechanized industry. Such was not the case for the later capitalist development of countries such as Germany and Japan and particularly for Russia and countries that many years later came to be known as the Third World. In particular, given the existence of international competition and world trade, late-developing capitalist countries could not go through the various stages of development that Britain had experienced. The late-developing countries had to begin with competitive, state-of-the-art industrial installations—whether in steel, electronics, or any other sector of production—that were at least as if not more advanced than existing plants in economically developed countries. Thus, for example, in the latter part of the twentieth century, brand-new Brazilian, Korean, and Japanese steel plants were usually more efficient than U.S. plants as a whole, since the latter necessarily consisted of a mixture of new, middle-aged, and altogether obsolete plants. The creation of these new plants required huge amounts of capital, precisely the factor of production that was most likely to be scarce in the countries attempting to industrialize. This helps to explain why—aside from foreign investment—nation-states have tended to play a much bigger role in the economic development of late-developing capitalist countries than in those that developed earlier. Given weak native capitalist classes, these states were often the only national entities capable of amassing such large amounts of capital, and they played a major role in assisting and protecting these nascent industries through a variety of means ranging from technical assistance to tariff protections.[28] In addition, economic crises, including those provoked by the failure of native industry to compete successfully in the international market, often encouraged further state regulation if not the outright nationalization of industry.

Uneven development also played an important role in the relations among the imperial powers. Relatively late industrializing countries such as Germany and Japan quickly became rivals of the established imperial capitalist powers such as Britain, France, and the United States. In fact, Japan and Germany's unusual aggressiveness (Germany's European expansionism and colonial policy in Africa and Japan's colonial policy in Korea and the rest of Asia) can at least partly be explained as a function of their arrival after the older imperialist capitalist powers had already appropriated most of the colonial booty. Instead of becoming imperial subjects of the already established powers, Germany and Japan became imperial rivals of Britain, France, and the United States. This was obviously not the fate of dozens of countries in the world that fell under the control of the big capitalist powers, whether in the open colonial form adopted by the European powers, mostly in Asia and Africa, or the less open economic form adopted by the United States, mostly in Latin America.

The uneven development of capitalism is also critical to understanding the growth of mass aspirations and expectations in countries that have not yet reached a high level of industrial development. Modern means of communication are, other things being equal, relatively easier to extend and disseminate than means of production and distribution. As a result, the expectations for consumption may rise faster than the means to satisfy them if viewed not from the perspective of the potential productivity and ability of the world economy as a whole to satisfy these expectations but from the perspective of a world divided between have and have-not nation states. This gap, in turn, may under certain conditions stimulate the militancy of working-class and popular movements and nation-states' efforts to regulate and control those movements.

UNEVEN DEVELOPMENT IN CUBA

These theoretical perspectives on imperialism and uneven development are helpful in seeing the big picture regarding Cuba's society and economy prior to the 1950s. In particular, taking the long view helps us to understand the strikingly uneven modernity that characterized Cuban society on the eve of the revolution.

The dramatic growth of sugar production at the beginning of the twentieth century had profound demographic and cultural effects on Cuba's population. For many years, Cuba experienced substantial immigration.

As a result of a serious labor shortage, no fewer than 1.28 million immigrants entered the island from 1902 to 1930. Taking into account the fact that many immigrants returned to their countries of origin, Cuba's population is estimated to have grown by six hundred thousand as a direct result of immigration during this period. Approximately one-third of these immigrants were black workers from the Caribbean, primarily Haitians and Jamaicans. Spain accounted for most of the remainder, with a large proportion coming from Galicia, Asturias, and the Canary Islands. (Cuba also had a significant Chinese community dating back to the mid–nineteenth century as well as small Jewish and Arab communities.) The white Spanish immigrants were considered permanent residents and were greatly preferred, with the Cuban government extending subsidies to that group in 1906 and 1911. Although black workers received only seasonal status, many remained in the country permanently despite their precarious legal situation and the substantial expulsions that took place during the 1930s.[29]

As a result of this immigration, the considerable growth of a multiracial working class, and other changes that took place in the early part of the twentieth century, Cuba acquired some of the characteristics of a frontier society, particularly in the rapidly growing east. This trait, in addition to the relatively shallow implantation of the Catholic Church, which has been heavily white, urban, and middle class in composition, and the weakness of class oligarchies and traditional army rule confirmed by the 1933 revolution[30] prevented the formation of the rigid cultural class hierarchies common in the rest of Latin America. Of course, plenty of class and racial inequality existed, as did poverty, but these phenomena were not accompanied by the degree of social and cultural submission and deference found in other Latin American societies. The plantation culture fostered by the sugar industry considerably loosened the ties between workers and employers. The culture of traditional ties and obligations of precapitalist Latin America was replaced by the impersonality inherent in wage labor and collective trade union militancy. At the level of popular culture, irreverence and the rejection of pomposity and arrogance were strengthened as important features of the Cuban national character. There was no worse sin than being a *pesado*, literally a heavy but used colloquially as an untranslatable term with connotations of humorlessness, dullness, tiresomeness, pomposity, and conceit.

The explosion in sugar production also stimulated growth in transportation, communications, energy production, and construction, thereby contributing to the country's economic development and modernization in cultural as well as economic terms. In addition to significant improvements in sanitation and health and educational levels, this period witnessed the creation of a modern working class and the expansion of the Cuban bourgeoisie. Thus, while there is no doubt that sugar monoculture constituted a form of seriously distorted economic development, the assumption of Cuban dependency theorists such as Francisco López Segrera that prerevolutionary Cuba experienced only economic growth rather than economic development (i.e., rising economic activity without significant change in the economic structure of underdevelopment) is either tautological (all economic activity not fitting a schematic, predetermined model is defined as mere growth) or false.[31]

Historically, Cuba's railroad development was closely related to sugar production, which was usually conducted in mills surrounded by extensive sugarcane fields. Thus, on November 19, 1837, Cuba became the world's seventh country to inaugurate railroad service, doing so more than a decade before its Spanish colonial masters.[32] By 1950, Cuba's network of railways, although poorly maintained, was equivalent to nearly 3.4 kilometers per thousand people, compared with slightly over 2.4 kilometers per thousand people in the United States. Of these railways, 72 percent were private lines operated principally to convey cane from the fields to the mills, and even the public service railways were closely related to the sugar industry.[33] By the 1950s, Cuba lacked good secondary farm-to-market roads, but the Central Highway, built in the 1920s and in need of upgrading, provided relatively advanced transportation and communication for almost the entire length of the 785-mile-long island.[34]

Cuba was also unusually advanced in the field of communications. The telegraph was introduced in 1851, just seven years after the first line was built in the United States. The first cable went into operation in 1867, shortly after the completion of the North American cable. Telephone service began in 1899, only eleven years after the first commercial exchange was established in the United States. In 1910, Havana became the first city in the world to use an automatic telephone system on a multiexchange basis.[35] In fact, Ernesto "Che" Guevara argued that Cuba's relative advancement in communications and other technical matters allowed for the centralized control of some enterprises, thereby facilitating state economic planning.[36]

By the early 1930s, commercial radio and with it popular music had become an important vehicle for the considerable cultural homogenization of the island, as did the introduction of commercial television at the beginning of the 1950s. In this light, it is not difficult to explain Cuban workers' desire "to reach a standard of living comparable with that of the American worker,"[37] aspirations rooted in the conditions of late-developing capitalist countries exposed to existing consumer standards in the economically developed world.

Cuba's peculiar economy, class and racial ambiance, and political developments helped to create what was by Latin American standards a relatively advanced, secular, and socially liberal society. In 1917, married women gained the right to administer and dispose of their property and to make public and private property contracts.[38] No-fault divorce was legalized in 1918, and women's suffrage was decreed in 1934 and came into effect in the elections of 1936, not too long after women in advanced industrial countries acquired the right to vote.[39] Between 1929 and 1933, 19 percent of Cuba's university students were women, as were 27 percent of those enrolled in U.S. universities.[40] While abortion remained formally illegal in Cuba until well after the 1959 revolution, it was relatively safe and inexpensive, at least in urban areas, and was widely practiced with minimal interference from the police and legal system. Although homosexuals encountered much intolerance, the phenomenon resulted from the relative backwardness of civil society rather than from legislation: systematic government discrimination against gays was an innovation of the revolutionary period. If modern medicine was not more universally utilized in the country, it was because of grossly inadequate coverage, particularly in the countryside, not primarily because of any cultural obstacles or rejection by the majority of the population.

STANDARD OF LIVING

The Cuba of the 1950s, as indicated earlier, ranked relatively high among Latin American countries in terms of per capita income and means of transportation and communication. In addition, Cuba also ranked high in terms of several other Latin American standard-of-living indexes. Only Mexico and Brazil had a higher number of radio sets per capita (Cuba had one for each 6.5 people), and Cuba ranked first in the number of television sets and telephones (one per twenty-five and thirty-eight inhabitants, respectively), newspaper readership (one copy per eight persons), and automobiles (one for every forty inhabitants). According to the 1953 Cuban census (the last count before the 1959 revolution), 76.4 percent of the population could read and write, a level that trailed only Argentina (86.4 percent), Chile (79.5 percent), and Costa Rica (79.4 percent). Cuba ranked behind only Argentina and Uruguay in the number of persons per medical doctor and average food consumption.[41]

However, this apparently positive picture was misleading in a number of fundamental respects. First, the country's stagnation and lack of economic diversification did not augur well for the future of living standards. As Dudley Seers has pointed out, if the degree of dependence of the national product on sugar had continued through the 1960s and 1970s, sugar production would have had to rise to 7 million tons in 1961–65 and to well over eight million tons in 1971–75, with no deterioration in the terms of trade, for Cuba to maintain the economic status quo of the 1950s.[42] Given the gradual acceleration of population growth, which reached 2.5 percent a year in the late 1950s, while the labor force was growing by at least as much, it is no wonder that in 1957 the rate of unemployment was 16.4 percent, with an additional 17.1 percent underemployed. For the entire period of the republic (1902–58), the number of jobs grew only 39 percent as much as the size of the employable population.[43] Approximately 50,000 young people entered the labor force every year. Thus, while approximately 150,000 new job seekers entered the Cuban economy between 1955 and 1958, only 8,000 new jobs were created in industry despite the fact that foreign investment was growing.[44]

Most importantly, the national indexes of living standards hid dramatic differences between the urban (57 percent of Cuba's population in 1953) and rural areas (43 percent) and especially between the capital city, Havana (21 percent of Cuba's total population), and the rest of the country. Sixty percent of physicians, 62 percent of dentists, and 80 percent of hospital beds were in Havana.[45] The 1953 census showed that 28 percent of all radio receivers, 43.8 percent of television sets, and 64.5 percent of refrigerators in the country belonged to people living in the capital. The *habaneros* also owned 62.7 percent of the country's automobiles and 76.8 percent of the telephones.[46] The differences between the capital and the rest of the country can be explained in terms of their occupational distribution. With practically the whole impoverished rural proletariat living outside of the capital and with 50 percent of the country's industry concentrated in Havana, 20.6 percent of the metropolitan labor force was employed in industry, 6.2 percent worked in transport, and 6 percent worked in construction. For the country as a whole, by contrast, 15 percent of the labor force was employed in industry, 4.3 percent worked in transport, and 2 percent worked in construction. The government bureaucracy was also heavily concentrated in the capital, as were disproportionate amounts of the import and export trade, media, communications, and other business activities. Thus, 42 percent of the Havana labor force was involved in services and 18 percent in commerce, whereas in the rest of the country these economic activities accounted for only 13 percent and 9 percent of the labor force, respectively.[47] These findings suggest that a considerable proportion of the country's economic surplus was diverted from the countryside to Havana and the other major cities. However, this does not mean that urban workers were not exploited, particularly given the pressure exerted on urban wage levels by rural-urban migration and large-scale urban unemployment. Widespread and very troubling urban poverty resulted, although they did not reach the depths and extent found among rural workers and peasants.

The most thorough and up-to-date account of rural living conditions before the 1959 revolution appears in a survey conducted by the Catholic association at the University of Havana during 1956–57.[48] This study found that while the rural working population constituted 34 percent of the national population, it received only 10 percent of the national income.[49] Rural working people spent 69.30 percent of their income on food, 10 percent more than had been required to maintain a minimal diet in 1934.[50] Whereas in 1953 the rate of illiteracy for the Cuban nation as a whole was 23.6 percent and the rate for Havana was only 7.5 percent, 43 percent of the rural population could not read or write, hardly surprising in light of the survey's finding that 44 percent of these rural working people had never gone to school, compared to only 26 percent of the urban population.[51] Nutrition was also found to be poor and unbalanced, depending heavily on the consumption of rice, beans, and roots and very little meat, fish, bread, or even fruit.[52] Diseases caused by lack of clean water and proper hygienic facilities were common, while only 8 percent of the rural people surveyed received free medical care from government institutions. More than 80 percent of the survey's respondents declared that their only access to medical care was through fee-charging medical practitioners.[53] The study also found that 63.96 percent of these rural inhabitants had neither indoor nor outdoor plumbing, 88.50 percent had to obtain water from a well, and only 7.26 percent of dwellings had electricity.[54] In contrast, the 1953 census had found that among urban dwellings, 61.7 percent had either indoor or outdoor plumbing, 76.6 percent had either indoor or outdoor running water, and 87 percent had electricity.[55]

Another important gap existed between Cuba's white and black populations. While the pattern of racist practices differed from that prevailing in the United States in that North American racism more heavily emphasized spatial segregation, Cuba experienced plenty of racial discrimination, as demonstrated by patterns of employment, education, income, and health, among other indexes.[56]

REACTION TO UNEVEN IMPERIAL DEVELOPMENT IN CUBA

By the late 1950s, despite its modest degree of economic diversification and periods of relative prosperity often associated with war conditions abroad, Cuba remained an essentially monoculture economy relying heavily on a declining sugar industry. In turn, a sugar industry highly dependent on unstable world market prices and the unilaterally determined U.S. sugar quotas created an economic culture of uncertainty. The massive and chronic unemployment that resulted from the short sugar crop reinforced this uncertainty and seriously disappointed popular expectations and aspirations for a better life. Economic discontent, frustration, and lack of hope marked the Cuban psyche even in times of relative economic growth, such as the post–World War II period.

These characteristics of the Cuban economy substantially affected Cuban workers' behavior. The virtual elimination of noncapitalist subsistence relations of production and the relatively advanced means of communication and transportation had created an urban and rural working class that was modern in certain fundamental respects. Cuban workers were generally sober, were quick to learn, and had a healthy dose of self-respect. Punctuality, low absenteeism, and other forms of industrial discipline had taken hold.[57] The urban and rural working class was also fairly heavily unionized (approximately 50 percent in the 1950s) and militant. Because of the economic instability, substantial unemployment, and even insecurity regarding pensions and retirement,[58] workers, urban and rural, prioritized employment security in their union and political demands. The 1957 study of the rural population found that 73.46 percent of those interviewed thought that the solution to their problems was more employment opportunities, ranking that option above all others, including improvements to schools, roads, and hospitals.[59] This perspective explains why Cuban legislation subsequent to the 1933 revolution made it difficult to fire workers and almost closed the country to the employment of foreigners, even as technicians.[60] Cuban workers, far more often than not, usually opposed mechanization in such industries as tobacco manufacturing, not out of some abstract opposition to technological progress but because of their well-founded fear that the jobs lost to mechanization and automation would not be replaced by new unionized jobs. This approach constituted rational behavior in light of the existing alternatives. In addition, worker militancy had raised the cost of Cuban labor so that it was expensive by Latin American standards.[61]

The prevailing climate of economic uncertainty also affected Cuban capitalists. A rentier mentality affected large sections of the moneyed classes and discouraged risk taking and entrepreneurship. The IBRD's 1951 *Report on Cuba* pointed out that Cuban banks had considerable liquidity and that Cuban capital savings showed a marked tendency to go abroad or to be hoarded for real estate investment or speculation at home. This phenomenon was related to a lack of confidence in the country's economy and to an aversion to tying up funds for significant amounts of time that logically led to a lack of desire to invest in industry.[62] Not surprisingly, the general economic instability, coupled with worker militancy and capitalist economic conservatism, led to state regulation and intervention that became quite important in prerevolutionary Cuba, as it did in many other less developed capitalist countries. This process reached a high point after the 1933 revolution resulted in significant social legislation and the establishment of a Cuban version of the welfare state and the loss of at least some of the Cuban capitalists' direct political power in exchange for the preservation of their economic rule.[63] State regulation of the sugar industry had already begun in the 1920s but reached its high point with the Ley de Coordinación Azucarera (Law of Sugar Coordination) approved on March 3, 1937. Thus, when the Cuban revolutionary leadership nationalized the sugar lands and mills in 1960, it took over an industry in which the Cuban state, with input from representatives of mill owners, *colonos,* and labor unions, already regulated prices and total production, the allocation of production among the existing 161 mills, and workers' wages.

The 1937 law and other sugar legislation also responded to the concerns and political pressures exerted by the primarily white rural middle class, which had found extensive ideological support among influential intellectuals such as Ramiro Guerra and the population at large for the claim that this class most authentically represented *Cubanía* (Cubanness). Thus, the law also put into effect measures protecting the rights of the small and medium-sized *colonos*, thus restraining the process of their elimination by bigger holdings.[64] However, the security earned by these sugar growers led, in light of the logic of a competitive capitalist agriculture, to economic irrationalities. Thus, the law established land rents paid by the growers at 5 percent of milled sugar output, regardless of cane prices. Although a major rise in the price of an agricultural commodity competing with sugar would seem to have led sugar growers to shift their land to more profitable uses, the fact that these sugar *colonos* had permanent tenure—as long as they met their sugar quota and paid their rents—made it unlikely that they would have been tempted to plant other crops even if they were significantly more profitable.[65]

A parallel situation developed in relation to the workers' struggle against exploitation by the mill owners. The 1937 law and subsequent legislation required that sugar workers be paid the same minimum wage during the sugar harvest as during the dead season. Thus, the wage rates that the sugar companies would have had to pay for the planting of subsidiary crops throughout the rest of the year were legally fixed at the level prevailing in the most productive sector of agriculture during the period of peak demand. While this legislative concession made perfect sense from a humanistic and working-class point of view, it violated the logic of the capitalist marketplace. As a result, investment in agricultural diversification became less attractive to the sugar capitalists, the people with the largest financial resources and best farmland in Cuba, and may have contributed to unemployment in the countryside.[66]

Worker militancy also led to increased state regulation of labor relations in the sugar and other industries. After the late 1930s, the state exercised a great deal of paternalism with regard to the unions and attempted to influence their internal affairs. The Ministry of Labor became a crucial institution in settling all sorts of external and internal trade-union affairs, and many labor conflicts were ultimately settled by the binding arbitration of ministry functionaries, with political pressure from both capitalists and workers affecting the outcome. By the late 1940s, this governmental trend had become so dominant that the *Report on Cuba* even thought it to be more important than collective bargaining.[67] This period also saw great competition between Communist labor leaders, who had just been forcefully expelled from many of their union positions as the Cold War began to affect internal Cuban politics, and the Auténtico labor factions that had just been installed in office by party leaders controlling the national government. Many of the resulting labor conflicts were prolonged, and the Auténtico governments were occasionally forced to use the tool of "intervention": a government functionary would take over the enterprise and administer it while the owners retained their entitlement to ownership rights and benefits. Employers strongly disliked this kind of intervention, although the U.S. Commerce Department recognized that Cuban government economic activity had been largely regulatory rather than operational and represented a response to social and economic problems rather than to ideology.[68] Other economic reforms were carried out throughout the late 1940s and early 1950s, increasing the Cuban government's role in the economy with the creation of the Cuban National Bank and subsequent establishment of the peso as sole legal tender and establishment of important credit institutions such as BANFAIC (the Banco de Fomento Agrícola e Industrial de Cuba, or Cuban Bank for Agricultural and Industrial Development).[69]

Government actions designed to quiet if not fully satisfy popular discontent often negatively affected the normal functioning of the capitalist market. Thus, for example, the depression-era mortgage moratoria decreed by the Cuban government in 1933, 1934, and 1940 seriously impacted interest rates and other aspects of mortgage lending in rural and urban properties.[70] In June 1949, President Carlos Prío of the Auténtico Party decreed the lowering of electricity rates to their 1944 level. In less than a month, the U.S.-owned Cuban Electricity Company canceled its plans to modernize and improve its power plants and blamed the action on the rate reduction.[71] Labor militancy and popular discontent stimulated by the unfulfilled expectations of the postwar period undoubtedly placed the Prío administration in a very difficult position and unquestionably contributed to its eventual overthrow by Batista in 1952. As *Business Week* perceptively assessed the situation,

As Cuban labor gets more and more politically aware, the government is backed even farther into a corner. . . . If [Prío] grants labor's demands, say for a wage increase, he risks boosting sugar production costs to the point where Cuba will be partially priced out of the world market. But if he can't keep the workers' standard of living within the political safety zone, he will be tossed out of office willy-nilly. . . . There is no doubt that Cuban labor has put management—particularly foreign management—in a tough spot. . . . The frequency with which recent strikes have been settled in favor of the workers' claims is a sign of the times. And it is significant that most settlements in the past couple of years have resulted from special government decrees.[72]

In sum, Cuba's uneven development led to contradictions in the conditions and consciousness of its working class. The fluctuations in foreign capital investment and state regulation responding to economic crises and working-class militancy led to a stagnating economic system that in turn fostered and protected the organization of industrial and agricultural workers and raised their cultural level and consciousness but also limited their ability to make greater economic and social gains. The Cuban working class's cultural and political level and its knowledge of the standard of living of the Cuban upper and middle classes and of North American society gave it economic, social, and political aspirations that could not be met by a Cuban economy caught in the contradictions of monoculture, foreign economic domination, and state regulation.[73]

This situation also led the IBRD's 1951 *Report on Cuba* to use the idea of a "vicious circle" to describe and analyze the quandary in which Cuba's economy and society found itself in the middle of the twentieth century. Using the notion of vicious circle as its leitmotif, the IBRD's highly influential analysis called attention to the phenomenon of a stagnant and unstable economy that created resistance to improvements in productivity, yet such improvements represented an important way to create a more progressive, more stable economy.[74] The study contained numerous recommendations for how to break the vicious circle and bring about economic progress, but many of these recommendations, written from the perspective of the mainstream economics of the time, failed to offer any consideration of conflicting class interests in Cuban society. Apparently based on the assumption that in the end the market always corrected itself and produced the greatest happiness for the greatest number, the IBRD proposed that if sugar wages continued to be tied to sugar prices, wages should be allowed to move downward as well as upward; that somewhat lower wages should apply to additional, supplementary employment during the dead season and to new types of production introduced in the sugar mills;[75] that the Cuban public should be prepared to pay more for better phone service;[76] that the provincial agricultural schools should no longer offer free tuition but should charge at least some token fees;[77] and that any future agrarian reform should not give away the land to the peasants at no charge.[78] Last but not least, the report complained that Cuban workers' economic education had probably been in the hands of "class-struggle" doctrinaires. In response, the IBRD economists recommended voluntary cooperation among labor, management, and workers with the goal of introducing a number of substantial changes such as the end of job tenure and its replacement by the system of dismissal wages in use in other Latin American countries.[79]

The *Report on Cuba* unquestionably captured the need for substantial changes to enable the Cuban economy to grow and modernize but implicitly recommended a fairly radical break with the vicious circle in a clear laissez-faire capitalist direction. Otherwise, the report warned, "social tension will grow, with the danger that some form of dictatorship would arise to 'solve' the country's problems."[80] As one would expect, the drafters of the report failed to ask themselves whether the particular changes they were advocating could have been brought about by anything other than a right-wing dictatorship, and an extreme and ruthless one at that.

The vicious circle concept inadequately captured the problems of the Cuban economy by ignoring how these problems constituted contradictions systematically rooted in the nature of semideveloped Cuban capitalism. First, Cuba, like most late-developing capitalist countries, had a regime of state economic intervention that created, in capitalist terms, economic distortions. Second, Cuban workers, again like those in many other late-developing capitalist countries, tended to be more militant, encouraged both by the existence of an interventionist state and the example of greater worker success in the advanced economies, while the Cuban capitalist economy's ability to satisfy this militancy remained low. Third, Cuba, with an economy that was both late developing and subject to the needs of imperialism, maintained some of these distortions in response to the international capitalist marketplace (i.e., the significant and some-times large fluctuations in the price of sugar) as well as in response to the demands of workers.[81]

As long as the fundamental structural dimensions of a Cuban mono-culture economy continued to exist, reinforced by reciprocity treaties and other imperialist measures, the vicious circles would continue to repro-duce themselves. Thus, the vicious circles existed not because some real economic problems elicited a set of mistaken and avoidable policies but instead because of profound contradictions inherent in the nature of the Cuban economy in the first six decades of the twentieth century. As men-tioned earlier, state intervention and regulation were hardly unique to the Cuban economy and were common features of latecoming capitalist countries, particularly in the less industrialized parts of the world.

A PARTIAL ATTEMPT TO BREAK THE "VICIOUS CIRCLES"

In March 1952, General Fulgencio Batista took power through a military coup d'état, bringing to an end a twelve-year experiment in constitutional democratic government. The coup was made possible by the political and moral crisis of corrupt Auténtico rule and by the labor militancy and other forms of social unrest that had been openly expressed during the democratic interlude. Although the Batista dictatorship worsened the country's problems, it did attempt to reduce if not completely break the vicious circles by implementing a few of the policy changes favored by employers and the IBRD mission.

However, Batista was no Augusto Pinochet. Unlike the Chilean dicta-tor of the 1970s, Batista's relationship with the upper classes was based not on solid, organic ties but on a temporary convergence of interests. Batista's corruption, extreme even by the standards of the corrupt 1940s, and his opportunistic, nonideological brutality eventually alienated those moneyed Cubans who had originally accepted and even welcomed his return to power in 1952. As Robin Blackburn has aptly described, Batista's regime occupied a precarious social position:

> The Batista machine was politically isolated, since it possessed
> no real roots in local class formations. It was thus forced to make

such internal alliances as it could, within the limits set by the U.S. international and economic policy of the period. The dictatorship remained, of course, the guarantor of the capitalist order in Cuba, but this was because of the context external to it, not because of its class content or ideological orientation. Within the limits of this context, its policy was purely opportunist.[82]

Moreover, the Cuban working class had not been so weakened by the military takeover as to allow for the success of a Chilean style antilabor offensive had Batista been tempted to follow such a course of action. Therefore, instead of undertaking a frontal offensive, the Batista regime whittled away at labor's power, curtailing civil liberties and turning the top members of the labor bureaucracy into the regime's collaborators. As a result, the number of strikes was greatly reduced, but relatively few legislative changes were made to diminish labor's legal and social position. A 1956 report by the U.S. Department of Commerce prepared to provide "basic information for United States businessmen" noted that the labor situation had improved materially in 1953–55.[83] Indeed, "interventions," or operational takeovers of enterprises, which had grown in number from twenty-five under the Auténtico Grau San Martín administration (1944–48) to sixty-five during Prío's administration (1948–52), almost disappeared during the Batista dictatorship.[84] Batista's government introduced the shipment of sugar in bulk and increased the use of the *despido compensado* (compensated layoff). As the country's political situation worsened, Batista instituted giveaway programs to encourage foreign investment. Near the end of his rule, he even raised the rates charged by the U.S.-owned telephone company, something other administrations—and even Batista himself—had previously not dared to do.

The prolongation of sugar prosperity induced by the Korean War reached its peak with the record 1952 crop. However, the period immediately after Batista's coup coincided with a decline in the international sugar market, a major cause of Cuba's subsequent serious economic recession. From 1952 to 1953, per capita income in Cuba fell by 18 percent as a result of a drop in production and the deterioration of the terms of trade. This economic relapse almost neutralized the growth of the postwar period, as per capita income dipped to near the 1945 level.[85]

By 1954, the gradual but steady government and employer attacks on the Cuban working class's gains since the 1933 revolution were beginning to make themselves felt. The 1954 *Economic Survey of Latin America* pointed out that labor's share of the country's net income had fallen from 70.5 percent in 1953 to 66.4 percent during 1954. Furthermore, on the whole, the average wage rate had decreased. Other sectors were barely able to absorb the workers left idle by the sugar decline, and salaries and wages decreased 4 percent between 1953 and 1954.[86]

Growing political discontent eventually led the Batista dictatorship to implement policies to improve the economic situation, even if only temporarily, through the 1954 Social and Economic Development Plan. Central to this plan was the policy of compensatory expenditures based on the Keynesian concept that public expenditures had a multiplier effect on the growth of national income. While the plan gave lip service to the goals of agricultural diversification and industrial development, its real goal was to promote expenditures in wages and salaries to compensate for the disastrous effects of the decline in sugar production. At the same time, the plan created opportunities for the enrichment of public officials and their business associates.[87]

The new economic strategy led to a partial recovery that began in 1955 and reached its peak two years later, when the estimated growth of the gross product in real terms surpassed 8 percent, at least in part as the result of a rise of sugar prices in the international market.[88] The improvements were small, however, and the economy did not approach the strength that it had enjoyed during the period of postwar prosperity. Serious chronic unemployment continued to plague the country: as the *Economic Survey of Latin America* pointed out, "during the relatively prosperous interval between May 1956 and April 1957, 16.4 percent of the labor force" was unemployed.[89]

THE BASES FOR GROWTH IN THE LATE 1950S

The economic growth that occurred during the late 1950s did not constitute a major departure from the relative stagnation or at best slow growth that the Cuban economy had been experiencing since the depression.[90] Taking into consideration that population growth had accelerated in the 1950s at the rate of 2.5 percent a year, in 1958 per capita real income remained about the same as in 1947.[91]

U.S. capital had long been withdrawing from sugar. Whereas in 1939 U.S. investors controlled 55 percent of Cuba's sugar production, that number had fallen to 40 percent by 1955.[92] Moreover, North American investors were also becoming relatively less interested in agriculture. The Batista dictatorship's probusiness climate encouraged some new U.S. investments in petroleum and mining, electricity generation, telephone communications, and tourism.[93] In 1958, U.S. investment in Cuba amounted to slightly over $1 billion. While investment in agriculture rose from $203 million in 1950 to $265 million in 1958, investment in petroleum grew from $20 million to $90 million, investment in mining shot from $45 million to $180 million, and investment in public utilities escalated from $271 million to $394 million during the same period.[94]

This renewed U.S. investment was coupled with Batista's policy of public works. Thus, out of the total bank credits conceded by the Batista dictatorship at the end of September 1957, only 6.1 percent were destined for agriculture and 29 percent for industry, while 62 percent were assigned to such relatively unproductive public works projects as the construction of a tunnel under Havana Bay. As a United Nations report pointed out, this public investment "had not been accompanied by an adequate expansion in the productive capacity of agriculture and industry or by any marked improvement in employment figures."[95]

Some diversification had taken place in the Cuban economy: for example, large-scale, specialized rice production had risen from 118.2 metric tons in 1951 to 256.8 tons in 1957 before declining somewhat to 225.9 tons in 1958.[96] Nevertheless, sugar remained king. The obstacles encountered by Cuban rice production constitute a telling case study of the imperial subjection of the Cuban economy. By the mid-1950s, Cuban domestic production was satisfying 52 percent of domestic demand at the expense of rice grown in the United States. U.S. rice growers protested, and the U.S. Department of Agriculture supported them and implied that the Cuban sugar quota might be reduced. In response to this threat, Cuban sugar and commercial interests lobbied to defend the sugar interests, thus opposing economic diversification. As a result, Cuban state banks failed to provide credits to expand rice cultivation, and the Cuban government formally agreed to import rice from the United States to protect the preferential treatment of sugar. Between 1955 and 1959, Cuban rice imports grew by much more than domestic production, and the proportion of national consumption satisfied by domestic production shrank by 5–7 percent.[97] Thus, in the mid-1950s, the percentage of total exports represented by sugar and other cane products was higher than it had been immediately before and during World War II.[98]

The policies implemented following the 1954 plan had high economic costs. Public debt rose to $788 million in 1958, and the country experienced a growing balance-of-payments deficit. Cuba's international reserves fell dramatically from $500 million when Batista took power in 1952 to only $100 million when he was overthrown at the end of 1958.[99] The modest degree of diversification that had occurred during the 1950s did not substantially alter the basic character of a one-crop economy with massive unemployment, particularly during the eight to nine months of the nonsugar season. The growth of domestic and especially foreign investment under Batista, which had brought about a degree of economic diversification in manufacturing, mining, and commerce, resulted from the creation of an attractive climate of investment through such means as suppressing the union movement's autonomy, repressing strikes, and government giveaways (for example, raising the rates charged by the foreign-owned telephone monopoly).

In spite of all the spending, much of it on unproductive activities, during the last years of the Batista dictatorship, the regime failed to achieve its political aims. By late 1956, political rebellion began to grow rapidly, showing few signs of diminishing as a consequence of the relative upturn in the economic cycle. By and large, however, the political dynamic of the dictatorship's repression and opposition to it constituted the main factors in increasing resistance to the regime during those years when temporary economic improvements occurred.

The prevailing view among Cuban exiles in Florida and elsewhere is that the prerevolutionary Cuban economy was sound and had a bright future. An early, typical expression of this attitude can be found in a massive treatise published under the direction of economist José R. Alvarez Díaz, who had served as treasury minister under Carlos Prío. According to this study, Cuba's 1940–58 economic development "was really extraordinary," and the causes of Cuba's problems lay not "in any lack of economic development" but "in the lack of a sufficient political and social consciousness and maturity."[100] Thus, conservative exiles typically perceive only economic development before the revolution, just as supporters of the current Cuban regime, particularly those such as Francisco López Segrera who follow the dependence school, perceive only economic underdevelopment in prerevolutionary Cuba.

Both of these camps have self-serving and distorted views. In reality, the prerevolutionary Cuban economy featured contradictory, uneven development. On the eve of the 1959 revolution, the fundamental problems outlined by the IBRD's 1951 *Report on Cuba* remained essentially unsolved. The contradictions or vicious circles of the primarily stagnant economy ruled by King Sugar continued to prevail. The relatively ineffectual attempts to break the contradictions or vicious circles coming from the social and political Right had not effected any major changes in Cuba's economic reality.

The failure of the reformist generation of the 1930s to resolve the contradictions or vicious circles of economic instability and stagnation, let alone to achieve full national sovereignty, created a widespread sense of popular dissatisfaction, frustration, and betrayal. In that sense, a large majority of the population had the potential to support radical solutions to Cuba's problems. However, the popular majorities did not necessarily possess such radical, let alone "socialist," political consciousness at the time Batista's dictatorship was overthrown on January 1, 1959.

As far as Fidel Castro and the members of the radical and politically conscious circles close to him were concerned, the profound problems of Cuba's economy and society and the failure of the previous reform efforts made the revolutionary road a possibility grounded in Cuban realities. In that sense, the revolutionary road turned out to be a conscious choice compatible with both the objective need to eliminate the contradictions of the Cuban economy and potential popular support for radical social transformations.

CHAPTER TWO

Fidel Castro and the Cuban
Populist Tradition

THE ROOTS OF CUBAN POPULISM

The Cuban economy's problems had helped to create a widespread sense of popular dissatisfaction and frustration that made a large majority of the population potentially open to supporting radical solutions to Cuba's problems. But what, if any, radical solutions would be presented to the Cuban people had not yet been determined.

Fidel Castro's political ideology before he came to power remains unclear to this day despite the Cuban leader's claim that he had been a supporter of or at least strongly influenced by "Marxism-Leninism" before the revolution. If this statement is true rather than an after-the-fact attempt to legitimize his membership in the Communist world, it would lend credence to the idea that he was involved in a conspiracy to bring Communism to Cuba, as his conservative detractors have long alleged. It would also mean that the contention that he was "pushed" into the arms of the Soviet Union and Communism, as many of his North American liberal and radical defenders have maintained, is unfounded. Absent a smoking gun of new documentation that may come to light after Fidel Castro and his close associates pass from the scene, we can rely only on the available evidence to attempt to understand the roots of Castro's politics.

A good place to start is to examine a Cuban and Latin American political tradition that has been often downplayed if not ignored: populism. Observers frequently apply the model of West European and North American political experiences to Cuba and attempt to find in that country familiar political currents: conservatives, Communists, social democrats, or U.S.-style liberals. However, these political currents do not accurately portray Cuba's political universe, which evolved in response to a variety of historically grounded issues and needs.

In his massive study of revolution and revolutionaries, James H. Billington has identified a political division that became established in Europe in 1830–48 and that distinguished what he called national and social revolutionaries. As Billington put it, the national revolutionaries were interested in establishing new nations with a cultural unity that would erase class divisions. The social revolutionaries were instead aiming at the abolition of classes, which would eliminate national borders. Giuseppe Mazzini, the leader of Young Italy, was a typical national revolutionary, while Auguste Blanqui and Filippo Buonarroti represented the social revolutionary tradition in 1830s France. Important philosophical differences also existed between these two traditions, as Billington explained:

> The conflict between national and social revolutionaries was, in
> essence, between Romanticism and rationalism: the nationalists'
> emotional love of the unique and organic against the socialists'
> intellectual focus on general laws and mechanistic analysis. The
> nationalists saw revolution as a "resurgence" (the Italian *risorgi-
> mento* or even "resurrection" (the Polish *zmartwychwstanie*) of
> an individual nation. Social revolutionaries saw it as an extension
> of the scientific universalism of the Enlightenment. If revolu-
> tionary nationalists were often poets like Petofi in Hungary and
> Mickiewicz in Poland celebrating the uniqueness of their vernacular
> idiom, social revolutionaries like Blanqui tended to view them-
> selves as educational theorists teaching universal principles.[1]

These two political traditions help us to understand certain key figures and stages in the formation and development of Cuban political thought. If we look back to the high point of the Cuban struggle for independence, in the 1890s, we find the critical figure of José Martí, a poet, writer, journalist, and patriot known as Cuba's founding father. Even though one or possibly two generations of Cuban patriots preceded and influenced Martí, he was and remains the source from which Cuban political factions of every kind—whether right-wing exiles in Miami or Fidel Castro and his political and cultural apparatus—claim their moral and political legitimacy.

Such widely divergent political currents have claimed Martí's legacy because he was, to a significant extent, concerned with issues that have traditionally preoccupied social revolutionaries, even though his political roots lay mainly in the national revolutionary tradition. Martí's campaigning and fund-raising among Cuban exile tobacco workers in Tampa and Key West in the 1890s brought him into close contact with the "social question," because the milieu of Cuban exile tobacco workers was strongly influenced by the class struggle orientation of anarchist trade unionism. As historian Joan Casanovas has shown, this experience pushed Martí's politics to the left.[2]

Martí was affected by blacks' and poorer whites' major role in the struggle for Cuban liberation that culminated in the third and final Cuban war of independence (1895–98), which was fought in a far more socially inclusive manner than were previous Cuban uprisings. Martí responded to this development, even if his color-blind political approach is open to criticism. He also spent many years in New York in the 1880s and 1890s as a political exile, becoming familiar with as well as sympathetic to the period's social struggles. His life "within the entrails of the monster," as he put it, also deepened his understanding of the perils that the United States posed for a future independent Cuba. However, it does not follow that Martí became a socialist, much less a Marxist. Although he sought a society without privilege and dominant classes, two Martí scholars, Manuel Pedro González and Iván E. Schulman, have demonstrated that "Martí did not go beyond the borders of democratic individualism, whether in the economic or political order. If he condemned excessive or ill-gotten riches or the exploitation of the helpless, he also defended [the] possession [of wealth] when it was the product of honest effort without detriment to the proletariat."[3] Finally, strong elements of stoicism and romanticism also featured prominently in Martí's thinking and subsequently became fixtures in the Cuban populist tradition that sometimes regarded firm dedication, sacrifice, and heroism as self-sufficient virtues in the harsh sphere of political action, particularly revolutionary action.

THE TWO WINGS OF THE CUBAN LEFT

The opposition to the Machado dictatorship in the early 1930s also shows a division that in some limited but revealing ways is reminiscent of Billington's distinction between national and social revolutionaries. One tradition was most typically represented by the Cuban Communist Party, founded in 1925 and following the lead of the Communist International, which was undergoing its rapid Stalinization. Cuban Communists were strongly oriented to the working class and played a major role in organizing its members into unions. But the Communist International's so-called Third Period line, an ultraleft policy imposed by Moscow from 1928 to 1934, required Communists to direct their main attacks at social democrats, who were denounced as "social-fascists." Since Cuba had no social democrats, the party took a stance of sectarian opposition to student and populist nationalist groups, which represented the other tradition. Cuban populism, even in its most left-wing versions, usually addressed itself to an amorphous "people" and spoke of conflicts between the poor and the rich rather than workers and employers. The small, "just and fair" employer would also be included among the people. Policy and program were not characteristic or strong points of Cuban populism. More important was the personal commitment of the populist militants, who often saw themselves as engaging in exemplary acts that would set a standard and arouse the masses to militant action. As the key line in the Cuban national anthem states, "morir por la patria es vivir [to die for the fatherland is to live]." In this tradition, winning is not the only or even main aim of struggle; it is better to go down fighting than to stay alive and submit to oppression.[4]

In late 1933, as a result of the successful revolution against the Machado dictatorship, Cuban populists found themselves running a short-lived nationalist and militant reform government. This government constituted a highly unstable coalition. President Ramón Grau San Martín led the reform nationalists in the center. On the right was Colonel Fulgencio Batista (whom the new revolutionary government had recently promoted from sergeant). Antonio Guiteras, the nationalist and socialist minister of the interior, led the Left as the most radical member of the cabinet. The Communists refused to support this government even though it was engaged in a life-and-death struggle for survival in the face of the Roosevelt administration's refusal to grant diplomatic recognition. A few months earlier, the Communists had already aroused hostility within the opposition when they favored calling off the August 1933 general strike against Machado in exchange for some trade union organizational gains.

This was the origin of the major split within the Cuban Left that would come to an ostensible end only with Fidel Castro's founding of the united

Cuban Communist Party in 1965. On one side of the split was again a Stalinist Cuban Communist Party, which never became a large mass party in the manner of the French, Italian, and Indonesian Communist parties but was nevertheless based on the organized working class. As we shall see in chapter 5, which discusses the relationship between the Soviet Union and the Cuban Communists, the Cuban Communists allied with Batista in the late 1930s in exchange for the government's granting the party official control of the trade unions. At the height of their political influence, with an average support of 7 percent of the electorate, the Communists obtained representation in Batista's cabinet in the early 1940s and maintained a small but visible presence in the Cuban Congress throughout most of that decade. The Cold War, however, brought a substantial decline in the party's influence.[5] Communist decline was not limited to the party's electoral fortunes; it also involved the party's trade union influence, particularly after the party was forced from the control of the central trade union federation in the late 1940s. In addition, the party's subordination to the Soviet Union, which had been somewhat of an asset in the days of the wartime alliance against Nazism, became a definite liability.

As a result of their association with Batista and other conventional politicians, the Cuban Communist leaders, although by and large personally honest, associated themselves with *politiquería* (unprincipled and corrupt political wheeling and dealing). This *politiquería* was highly disdained by idealistic young Cubans who became increasingly disillusioned and frustrated by the corruption of the reformist and nationalist leaders of the 1933 revolution who were elected to office in 1944 and served until 1952. The left-wing nationalists failed to maintain a stable, organized political tendency. Batista's army killed Guiteras in 1935, and many of those who had sided with him turned into political gangsters, engaging in armed conflict over political spoils, a development that was later encouraged by President Ramón Grau San Martín (1944–48). Grau cleverly eliminated potential left-wing populist nationalist pressure (the anti-imperialist element of Grau's reform current had disappeared) by encouraging competition for political spoils, thereby stimulating violent struggles among the various groups of nationalist and populist origin. At this time, in the mid-1940s, Fidel Castro graduated from a distinguished Catholic high school and entered the University of Havana law school.

The political gangs of the 1940s—organized remnants of the populist and nationalist militants of the 1930s who had become demoralized—were, to be sure, an extremely decayed expression of the populist political culture. Unlike the Communists, the populist milieu was not strongly oriented toward the trade union movement. It also was not hostile to the union movement, but since the populist political culture saw the people and the nation as the central entities, it did not prioritize the unions in its political action. This populist tradition approached the social question from the perspective of a nationalism that, in the spirit of Martí, aspired to have broad popular appeal among those lacking advantages and privileges rather than to develop a class-based point of departure. Castro was following the populist tradition when he defined what he meant by "the people" in *History Will Absolve Me*: "When we speak of the people, we do not mean the comfortable and conservative sectors of the nation that welcome any regime of oppression, any dictatorship, and any despotism. . . . [W]e mean the unredeemed masses to whom everything is offered but nothing is given except deceit and betrayal."[6]

If it is true, as some observers have claimed, that the theoretical level of the Cuban Communists was low by international Communist standards,[7] it was high compared to the Cuban populist milieu and the country's political world as a whole. This is evident in the biographies of forty-one Cuban generals published under the auspices of the Castro government in 1996. Only five of these generals have political roots that can be traced to the prerevolutionary Communist Party. Few had any significant political education when they joined the rebel army as rank-and-file soldiers in the late 1950s. One general stated that at the time "he had no solid convictions, but a little sense of adventure and of indignation against the assassinations and beatings that people suffered in Santiago de Cuba." Another said that he had told Fidel Castro that he was joining "for an ideal" but that he did not know what those words meant: he had heard the expression and figured it was a good thing. A third general stated that before joining the rebel army, he had participated in high school student strikes but had had no revolutionary consciousness. Another general, a black Cuban, had a more developed sense of injustice, as indicated by his remark that when he joined the rebel army, he had "no economic possibilities and no political knowledge, but a clear concept of racial, religious and economic discrimination." Another explained that Fidel and Raúl Castro later taught him whatever he knew about socialism. Along the same lines, one general stated that when he joined the rebel army, he had no political ideas but was attracted by the fact that the leaders identified with the aspirations of the peasants in their pronouncements. This perspective, in addition "to the dreams of adventure that all young people have in the face of the heroic," caused him to join the rebels.[8]

At its best, the Cuban populist milieu encouraged the study of Martí's works, but in a worshipful fashion designed to extract maxims and quotations bearing on appropriate moral and political behavior rather than in a respectful yet critical spirit. Martí's ideas and actions provide an invaluable example of moral and political integrity. However, Cuban populism has treated him as the infallible source of knowledge for all conceivable political and human problems, notwithstanding the fact that Martí wrote for and about a late-nineteenth-century Cuba that differed substantially from the Cuba of the mid–twentieth century. In contrast, even the crude Stalinist Marxism[9] of the Cuban Communists was superior in its analytical power and overall comprehension of society to the fragmented and sometimes intellectually incoherent views of Cuban populism. If nothing else, the Stalinist Marxism of the Communists was modern and had some discernible connection, even if rudimentary, to an informed and intellectually disciplined approach to social reality.

Cuban populism generally failed to understand the relationship between politics and society. Yet populists were generally better able than Communists to grasp the principal issues at stake in a particular political situation. In a sense, the light intellectual baggage of populist nationalism posed far less of an obstacle to an engagement with political reality than did the dogmatic schematism of the Cuban Communists and their subordination to the dictates of Soviet foreign policy. These often proved to be crippling handicaps for the Cuban Communists, who were likely to find themselves trapped in rigid Stalinist categories as well as in their organizational dependence and political commitment to the Soviet bloc.

Fidel Castro's unquestionable tactical genius comes from this populist background. It can be appreciated in comparison with the Cuban Communists as well as in contrast to Argentinean nonparty Communist Ernesto "Che" Guevara. Guevara, unlike Castro, often failed to recognize the practical political necessities produced by specific historical conjunctures. He could not understand, for example, and opposed Castro's very effective tactic during the guerrilla war of freeing prisoners after taking away their weapons.[10] Castro understood, as Guevara did not, that this tactic made a great deal of sense when facing a mercenary and demoralized army with no social or political support from the population at large. Even more striking was Guevara's colossal political error of proposing that the rebels rob banks to finance their operations. When this proposal was rejected by the urban leadership of the 26th of July Movement, Guevara took it as a sign of their social conservatism.[11] He seemed unaware that from the mid- and late 1940s to the early 1950s, Cuba had gone through a period of political gangsterism. Many of the earlier revolutionaries had degenerated into gangsters, carrying out violent activities, including bank robberies such as the 1948 armed assault on the Havana branch of the Royal Bank of Canada. Any involvement in similar actions would have brought back memories of that dark period and been extremely damaging, particularly since Castro had been associated with those groups in his student days. Using such tactics would have made it easy for the Batista-controlled press to argue that the revolutionaries were just bringing back the bad old days.

Cuban populism was far more politically militant than Cuban Communism but tended to be more conservative on social issues. Populists, however, glorified action and denigrated theory as if the two were necessarily opposed. As indicated earlier, they were very influenced by Martí's emphasis on sacrifice, dedication, and selflessness on behalf of the fatherland. Cuban populism stressed the heroic and glorified adventure in the sense of exciting and dangerous actions as well as unusual and romantically stirring experience. This approach was connected to the long-established tradition of armed struggle going back to Cubans' various nineteenth-century wars against Spanish colonialism.

POPULIST VALUES:
PRECAPITALIST AND MODERN

Populist political culture combined modern traits with others rooted in a Hispanic and precapitalist tradition, including a great emphasis on the concept of honor. Honor is a many-sided social and historical phenomenon that in egalitarian and humanist terms has positive and negative consequences. In recent years, however, honor has been viewed in mostly negative terms. Thus, for example, Cuba scholar K. Lynn Stoner perceptively notes that honor has been the "cornerstone of social consciousness" in prerevolutionary and revolutionary Cuba but then goes on to view it merely in terms of the male leaders' dependence on public adulation and uncontested loyalty and ultimately as a cult of death. Following the analysis of Glen Dealy, Stoner continues to describe honor as depending on "individual male status within a group of potential competitors."[12] William Ian Miller, another author Stoner cites, draws primarily from the Icelandic sagas, viewing honor as the core values and behavior one would expect from the likes of members of the Mafia, southern slave owners, and medieval lords—men who take strong and often violent exception to even the most trivial offenses and are strongly motivated by envy and status, even in very small matters.[13]

There is, however, another side to honor, associated with the values of dignity,[14] self- and mutual respect, courage, resistance to arbitrary power, integrity, and adherence to an internalized code of public, political morality. Most important, this "honorable" behavior, although obviously rooted in social mores, is inner-directed and is not viewed by the actor primarily as a means of obtaining outside approval or in terms of a market-type relationship where a one-for-one exchange of homage or services is expected in return. This type of honorable behavior is essential to the notion of solidarity, or "doing the right thing" in support of others without any expectation of immediate or equivalent returns. Of course, these notions of honor and solidarity reflect a social, long-term notion of the Golden Rule: others will do for you as you did for them.

Although usually thought of in terms of appropriate behavior for men, little intrinsic connection exists between the moral and political virtues associated with honor and masculinity as such, as is illustrated by the October 1958 response of rebel leader Camilo Cienfuegos to a Masonic lodge in central Cuba that had expressed concern about an army sergeant captured by the rebels:

> Your petition is unnecessary, because under no condition would
> we put ourselves at the same moral level as those we are fighting.
> . . . We cannot torture and assassinate prisoners in the manner
> of our opponents; we cannot as men of honor and as dignified
> Cubans [*Cubanos dignos*] use the low and undignified procedures
> that our opponents use against the people and against us. The spirit

of nobility and chivalry inculcated in each one of our soldiers, with respect for prisoners and for the military, is the reason why more than seven hundred of them, after twenty-three months of struggle against the tyranny, find themselves today in the bosom of their families.[15]

Cienfuegos's pride in the rebel army's prisoner policy contrasted with the different position adopted on the same question by the more cosmopolitan, nonpopulist Guevara. The notion of honor was closely associated, as indicated earlier, with other highly appreciated values such as integrity, dignity, and loyalty to a cause,[16] which were in turn part and parcel of a strong sense of membership in a highly politicized society. This politicization was national, not the localism of voluntary associations and neighborhood issues that sometimes is defined as political in the United States. Cuban politicization resulted from a variety of factors, including the relative compactness and cultural homogeneity of Cuban society and the overwhelming dependence on sugar, a product that had been, particularly since 1937, highly regulated by the state.

Mixed with the values of precapitalist origin were strongly held ideas of solidarity not with family, church, or other traditional sources of loyalty but with thoroughly modern public collectivities such as students, workers, the Cuban nation, and Latin America. The typical Cuban populist took all of these values, whether modern or Hispanic, quite personally. In this sense, the political was indeed personal, while the personal, in the sense of private morality and customs, was perceived as being outside the public, political realm.

In his analysis of the 1989 Chinese student movement, sociologist Craig Calhoun stresses the importance of honor as a motivator of the students' willingness to take serious risks. Calhoun argues that the transformation of Western culture over the past several hundred years has made honor a less important category and that this phenomenon may be related to differences in radicalism and risk taking in social movements.

Calhoun also contrasts the logic of guilt and innocence with the logic of honor. The logic of guilt and innocence may, for example, excuse a political prisoner who, under the extreme pressures of torture, provides information about comrades. The prisoner's sense of self as a person, however, may be deeply damaged by the revelation, even if the prisoner knows that the action was forced. According to Calhoun, the logic of honor is at work here.[17] It is also clear that resistance under extreme negative conditions is tantamount to heroic conduct, a key feature of the Cuban populist tradition.

Of course, the revolutionary leaders could and did manipulate the positive aspects of honor for other ends. Thus, in the summer of 1959, Fidel Castro declared that it would be "hardly honorable" to attack the Communists to avoid being accused of being a Communist. Thus, Castro portrayed the issue as a matter of not picking on the weak to humor the strong (that is, the United States) or to satisfy the prejudices of many Cubans.[18] This was, however, a clever maneuver by Castro to distract attention from the main issue at hand, which was not primarily a matter of attacking the Communists (although many undoubtedly wanted him to do so) but instead a matter of his failure to be clear and straightforward about his politics.

To be sure, in the Cuban context, honor was inevitably combined with sexism. As a result, women usually did not play central leadership roles in the struggle against the Batista dictatorship, perhaps partly because the Cuban women's movement, a vital force in the 1920s and 1930s, had significantly declined by the 1950s.[19] Nevertheless, machismo unquestionably was an important cause of the exclusion of women from certain revolutionary activities. While this exclusion was by no means absolute, women were generally confined to such traditional roles as nursing, providing shelter, fund-raising, and other auxiliary chores. Consistent with Latin American social patterns, many female leaders were relatives of the top revolutionary leaders, as in the cases of Vilma Espín and Haydée Santamaría.[20] Celia Sánchez, Fidel Castro's close associate, was the first woman to participate in armed combat, and in the summer of 1958, women were allowed to form their own Mariana Grajales platoon.[21] In 1960, after the revolutionary victory, all independent women's organizations were disbanded,[22] but this was of course the fate of all independent organizational life in Cuba, as demonstrated by the abolition of the black Cubans' important *sociedades de color*.[23]

Given the Cuban populist worldview's emphasis on the values of heroism, selflessness, and sacrifice, the tendency to suicide among a significant number of leaders of Fidel Castro's government is intriguing. Of course, the revolutionary leaders were products of the culture in which they were formed, including its higher propensity to suicide. (Cuba ranks among the top five countries in the world in suicides and has the highest suicide rate in Latin America.)[24] Thus, many prominent Cubans in exile killed themselves, including former President Carlos Prío Socarrás, publisher Angel Quevedo, and Bay of Pigs commander José Pérez San Román, among others.[25] Nevertheless, the characteristics of political leaders that lead them to kill themselves likely differ from those prevailing among the rest of the population. Although little is known about the specific circumstances, the suicides of these political leaders suggest the applicability of French sociologist Émile Durkheim's analysis of "altruistic" suicide and its strong association with the spirit of renunciation and abnegation often found in institutions such as armies.[26] The important revolutionary figures who committed suicide include former President Osvaldo Dorticós, Haydée Santamaría, Alberto Mora, and Felix Peña; Augusto Martínez Sánchez tried to kill himself but failed. Most of the founding members of the 26th of July Movement came out of the youth wing of the Ortodoxo Party, whose founder and leader, Eddy Chibás, committed suicide in August 1951. Chibás also fought ten duels between 1945 and 1950, a clear indication of the importance of honor in the Cuban political culture of the time.[27]

Populist political culture can be usefully contrasted with the far less important political culture of Cuban Communists, who were at times a persecuted minority and who endured the hardships of a clandestine life, particularly in the late 1950s, when the Communist Party decided to support Castro's rebels. But while definite advantages accompanied the Communists' "objective" view of politics as the outcome of certain impersonal processes and social causation, the disadvantage, in the Cuban context, was a certain loss of heroism and passion, whether in reality or appearance. Educated middle-class Communists also tended to be more sophisticated and less parochial than populists of similar class and educational backgrounds. In addition, the sectarian politics of the party and the long experience of its leadership in the unprincipled and often corrupt wheeling and dealing of electoral activity tended to widen the gap between the political cultures of militant populism and Communism.

GENERATIONAL CONSCIOUSNESS

Another distinguishing feature of Cuban populism was its strong generational consciousness, which developed as the frustrations and failures of political movements became strongly associated with specific age cohorts. The leading members of the generation of the early republic, officially inaugurated in 1902, failed to create a truly independent republic and greatly disillusioned those who eventually became the young revolutionaries of the 1933 generation. They in turn wallowed in corruption after obtaining power in the mid-1940s and thereby disillusioned the new young revolutionaries of the "Generation of the Centenary," named after the one hundredth anniversary of José Martí's 1853 birth.[28] The revolutionaries' tendency to see themselves as belonging to a distinctive generation was considerably reinforced by intellectual currents, influential in Cuba and Latin America in the first half of the twentieth century, that saw young people as the main carriers of nonconformity and innovation. This was an important component of the thought of turn-of-the-century Argentinean writer José Ingenieros as well as of his Uruguayan contemporary José Enrique Rodó. Besides praising the powers of youth, Rodó emphasized the role of spiritual idealism, which he contrasted with the utilitarianism and materialism he attributed to North American culture. His lengthy essay, *Ariel*, one of the most influential Latin American writings of the early twentieth century, was widely read in prerevolutionary Cuba.

The corruption of the revolutionary generation of the 1930s after achieving power from 1944 to 1952 constituted an important factor in bringing about a shift in Cuban populism. As open anti-imperialist politics became limited to the Cuban Communists[29] and as the working-class political radicalism of the 1930s declined, the road was opened to a militant but somewhat classless democratic populism. In the late 1940s, Ortodoxo leader Chibás coined the slogan "Vergüenza contra Dinero [Honor or Integrity against Money]"[30] and rejected *politiquería*. The Ortodoxo Party refused to make electoral pacts with the corrupt traditional political parties (even though it was much less strict in admitting certain traditional politicians and even big landowners into its own ranks). In social terms, the Ortodoxos endorsed a vague and moderate version of land reform, but this plank was not central to the party's activity. Instead, it became involved in agitating against the U.S.-owned public utilities, such as the electricity and telephone companies, and in formulating proposals for nationalizing them. Chibás served a brief term in jail on charges of contempt of court when he accused some judges of having been bribed by the Cuban Electricity Company (a subsidiary of Bond and Share).[31] Nevertheless, Chibás supported the United States in the Cold War but refused to join the McCarthyite attacks against the Cuban Communists. Although the Ortodoxos supported the idea of a welfare state and provided political support for many strikes, they were not a class-based party and did not advocate a radical restructuring of Cuban society. They attracted the professional middle classes as well as many young students and urban and rural workers sickened not only by the corruption of national politics but also by the corruption and bureaucratization of the majority of the unions. This young Ortodoxo milieu became the principal source of recruitment for Fidel Castro's 26th of July Movement. In the late 1940s and early 1950s, Fidel Castro was a second-rank leader of the party who attempted to form a more socially radical tendency within its ranks.

REJECTION OF *POLITIQUERÍA*

In recent years, a new political current has sought to develop a model of liberal democratic politics for Cuba. Some of its prominent leaders have criticized the intransigent rejection of *politiquería* that constituted the political starting point for many of Cuba's revolutionaries of the 1950s. This liberal current is explicitly antirevolutionary, not just anti-Castro or anti-Communist. Many of the scholars and intellectuals who have taken this view used to support the Castro regime, and proponents have a home in the important high-quality Madrid-based journal *Encuentro de la Cultura Cubana*. The journal occupies the center to center-right of the political spectrum, although not all contributors fit this characterization. This attempt to develop a new form of Cuban political liberalism has included a wholesale revision of Cuban history, sometimes going all the way back to the late nineteenth and early twentieth centuries. Thus, more than a hundred years after their efforts failed, the Autonomistas (those Cubans who, in contrast to José Martí, argued for a program of political reforms short of independence from Spain) are beginning to be viewed more favorably.[32] So has Tomás Estrada Palma, the first president of the republic, whose conservative pro-U.S. stance is retrospectively viewed in a positive light as a precursor of present-day aspirations for national reconciliation.[33] High praise has even been bestowed on Carlos Márquez Sterling, a traditional Cuban politician who participated as a loyal opposition candidate in Batista's fraudulent November 3, 1958, elections. Even after being defeated in what Márquez Sterling himself described as dishonest elections, he nevertheless recommended that the United States renew the sale of weapons and support the Batista regime.[34] Broader intellectual currents that have emerged from the collapse of the Soviet bloc in the late 1980s and early 1990s and that include such representative figures as Poland's Adam Michnik and the Czech Republic's Vaclav Havel have influenced the new Cuban liberals.[35]

Some new Cuban liberals have criticized what they perceive as the intransigence and the moral/political absolutism of twentieth-century revolutionary and reform thought in Cuba, accusing it of having engendered a political climate of intolerance and illiberalism hostile to democracy. One of their targets is the militant impulse against *politiquería*. They equate democratic politics with a give-and-take process, with compromise, and with the presumably inevitable horse-trading of politics. Accordingly, in their view, the reformist and revolutionary rejection of *politiquería* points in the direction of an intolerant absolutism incompatible with democratic politics.

This liberal rejection of the opposition to *politiquería* confuses various phenomena that although often associated with each other are by no means identical. Political compromise or trade-offs are not the same as betrayal or unprincipled political behavior, of course, let alone venality or corruption. Politics may often involve compromise. But there are compromises and there are compromises. We need to ask whether the compromise in question involves fundamental principles. For example, militant and democratic unions with honest leaders often make principled compromises. Very often, this process involves an assessment of the relative strengths of workers and capitalists at any given point in time. Whenever a union is not strong enough in relation to the employers to win everything it wants (a common occurrence), its leaders compromise with employers and settle for less. If the leaders are honest and democratic, they will recommend that the members accept a compromise and explain why no choice exists. The point is to tell the truth to the workers so that they can take stock and learn the lessons available from the situation at hand. Then they will be fully aware of what is going on, organize to be stronger next time, and take control of their fate. As far as revolutionaries making compromises is concerned, what were the 1918 Treaty of Brest-Litovsk with Germany and the New Economic Policy adopted in 1921 but major, king-size compromises made by V. I. Lenin and the Russian Communist Party?

In prerevolutionary Cuba, the opposition to *politiquería* did not involve hard cases of compromises that raised difficult questions of political and moral principles. Neither did those who rejected *politiquería* abstractly reject the transactions or give-and-take of politics, democratic or undemocratic, reform or revolutionary. Instead, they simply repudiated a long history of betrayal and corrupt political behavior in Cuba, particularly after the mid-1940s, and rejected the deeply entrenched view that public office was, more than anything else, a source of unlimited personal enrichment and social mobility. Under Batista's government, those rejecting *politiquería* also insisted on an intransigent opposition to a dictatorial regime that had overthrown by force the country's democratic constitution. As these oppositionists pointed out, the Batista regime's actions had amply demonstrated that it was not interested in peacefully ceding power.

Political corruption was so pervasive in the Cuba of the 1940s and 1950s that it even corroded voluntary nongovernmental organizations, political and otherwise.[36] Thus, the intransigent opposition to *politiquería* in the Cuba of the 1940s and 1950s did not involve making politics "a matter of saints and virgins," as implied by a foremost proponent of the new Cuban liberalism.[37] Opposition to *politiquería* was, rather, a fundamental component of democracy and progressive as well as revolutionary social change.

CLASS, RACE, AND NATIONAL ORIGIN

The populists came from among all Cuban social classes, although less from among the wealthy and the poorest. According to British historian Hugh Thomas, the participants in Fidel Castro's armed July 26, 1953, attack on the Moncada army barracks included accountants, agricultural workers, bus workers, businessmen, shop assistants, plumbers, and students. Nineteen of these men were among those who accompanied Castro when he landed in eastern Cuba on the yacht *Granma* in 1956: although the social composition of this group of eighty-two men varied, more of them had higher education than the Moncada fighters. According to Thomas, both of these groups comprised Castro's loyal followers.[38] Although many of them seem to have been workers by origin or occupation, very few had been active or even involved in trade union or working-class political organizations. The two groups of men were later enlarged in 1957 and 1958 by the recruitment of a couple of thousand peasants in the Sierra Maestra and elsewhere in Oriente Province. These fighters added a new element to the typical urban populist background of the Moncada and *Granma* veterans, although with a handful of important exceptions, the peasant recruits typically had little or no history of previous organized peasant struggles. This was very important in allowing Fidel Castro to mold these men into faithful followers of his caudillo leadership.[39] In any case, an inner circle of "classless" men unattached to the organizational life of any of the existing Cuban social classes became Fidel Castro's political core. Even though some prominent middle-class political personalities went to the Sierra Maestra to join Castro, they never became part of this inner circle, even when Castro's movement achieved clear dominance over the broader anti-Batista opposition.

The populists included a significant number of first-generation Cubans, the children of Spanish immigrants. Their presence in the ranks of the Generation of the Centenary was linked to the huge migration of hundreds of thousands of Spaniards, particularly of peasants from Galicia, Asturias, and the Canary Islands, that took place from 1900 to 1930, when Cuba's population of the county remained below 4 million. Such first-generation Cubans included revolutionary leaders Camilo Cienfuegos, Frank País (both of whose parents were Spanish Protestants), Abel and Haydée Santamaría, Faustino Pérez, and Fidel and Raúl Castro. At least 22 percent of the forty-one Cuban generals whose biographies were published in the previously mentioned volume had at least one parent born abroad. Aside from one general whose parents were born in China, all the other foreign-born parents were Spaniards. (Several generals did not mention their parents' nationalities.) This is particularly remarkable because the overwhelming majority of these generals came from the easternmost Oriente Province, where they had originally joined the rebel army. Spanish immigration had a greater impact in the western half of the island, where Havana is located.[40]

The case of Camilo Cienfuegos, the most important rebel leader after the Castro brothers at the time of the January 1, 1959, victory, is of particular interest in this context. Cienfuegos was born in 1932 into a humble—although not extremely poor—working-class family. He exemplified the quintessential native, male, urban Cuban with his sense of humor, great interest in dancing and baseball, good looks, love of women, and overall joie de vivre. Both of his parents were Spanish immigrants. His father, Ramón, who espoused left-wing politics, worked as a tailor in a men's shop in central Havana, a member of a relatively poor but employed stratum of the Cuban working class. Ramón Cienfuegos had the craftsman's typical sense of self-respect, an attitude that should be distinguished from upwardly mobile persons' search for respectability in the United States and many other economically developed countries. As Ramón Cienfuegos recalled, "Only decent people entered my household. Neither runners for the illegal lottery [boliteros] nor lazy people, nothing like that. Camilo grew up in that kind of environment. I remember that at the time of the Spanish Civil War, he went out with us, even though he was a child, to raise money for the Spanish Republic."[41]

Camilo Cienfuegos studied sculpture at art school but had to drop out to help with his family's finances. He went to work in the store where his father was employed, starting as a janitor and messenger and eventually becoming a salesman. His older brother, Osmani, had graduated from the School of Architecture at the University of Havana, where he joined the Communist Party. In the 1950s, Camilo migrated to the United States, working illegally for a couple of years before leaving for Mexico, where in 1956 he joined Castro's expedition. Cienfuegos began as a rank-and-file member of the force but distinguished himself in the Sierra Maestra and eventually became one of the most popular leaders of the rebel army. However, Cienfuegos remained less politically sophisticated than the Castro brothers as well as Che Guevara. Cienfuegos died in October 1959, the presumed victim of a plane accident, according to the Cuban government's version of the event. His body was never found, and the government's account of what happened has never been conclusively proven or disproven.

The heavy presence of the children of Spanish immigrants was only one of the factors that determined the disproportionately white character of the populist movement. As stated earlier, although populism cut across social classes, it was much less representative of the poles of Cuban society, the rich and the very poor. Even after slavery was abolished in Cuba in the 1880s, the black Cuban population remained greatly over-represented among the very poor. In addition, in part because of Martí's strong ideological influence, Cuban populist and nationalist thought was color-blind—that is, it failed to recognize the special oppression of black Cubans. Consequently, populists rarely went out of their way to recruit blacks as such. The traumatic impact of the "race war" of 1912—really a massacre of Cuban black people—also played a role in delegitimizing race as a topic worthy of open political discussion. This was reflected in the generally progressive Constitution of 1940, which raised to constitutional principle laws that had been on the books even before 1912 and that explicitly forbade political parties organized around racial criteria. Thus, Cuban nationalist populism did not for the most part explicitly address the specific needs of Cuban blacks or mulattoes, who in the 1940s and 1950s were officially estimated at about 30 percent of the Cuban population.

By contrast, the Cuban Communists attempted to recruit blacks and to address issues of direct concern to them. This, like every other aspect of Communist politics, was subject to changes in the Moscow party line (e.g., whether or not to advocate the recognition of a "black belt" nation in Oriente Province) and to the domestic politicking the party conducted with its political partners of the day. Nevertheless, a significant proportion of the Communist leadership was black (including Blas Roca, Lázaro Peña, and Salvador García Agüero), and black Cubans formed a significant part of the party's membership. While blacks were an important group within the party, however, Communists were not as important within the Cuban black population as a whole. There, the five hundred local branches of the *sociedades de color* (black self-help social clubs) constituted by far the principal form of black self-organization.[42]

THE ROLE OF RELIGION

The Roman Catholic Church played an important role in the overthrow of several Latin American dictators of the 1950s, including Colombia's Gustavo Rojas Pinillas, Argentina's Juan Perón, and Venezuela's Marcos Pérez Jiménez. Such was not the case in Cuba. The Catholic hierarchy and the heavily Spanish regular clergy were politically conservative and went along with the dictatorship; Cardinal Manuel Arteaga of Havana even congratulated Batista after the general's successful coup d'état and was photographed with him on many occasions.[43] Nevertheless, when hostilities reached a boiling point in 1958, the church called on Batista to bring peace through the establishment of a commission on harmony and the formation of a government of national unity.[44] These Catholic efforts failed, and the church hierarchy lost its opportunity to play an important role as a mediator.

Among Cuban Catholics, members of the secular clergy and of the laity were much more involved in the opposition to the Batista dictatorship. This was particularly true of the Catholic Worker Action and Catholic Worker Youth organizations and of well-known Catholic intellectuals such as Andrés Valdespino and Angel del Cerro.[45] Nevertheless, none of these groups and individuals significantly influenced the course of the revolution.

This was not surprising. Cuban Catholicism was politically weak for reasons deeply rooted in Cuban history. The church had supported Spanish colonialism during the Cuban struggles for independence. The great majority of the Cuban independence leaders were Masons, and if they were not strongly anticlerical, they at the very least favored a strict separation of church and state, the policy adopted by the new Cuban republic in 1902. In addition, the weakness of the Cuban oligarchy significantly diminished the church's influence. The church was also disadvantaged by the fact that most priests were Spanish[46] and that the parishioners were mostly white, urban, and middle and upper class. Most peasants and rural workers had little contact with Catholic churches and priests. Although the great majority of the population was nominally Catholic, only a small proportion of Cubans actively practiced the Catholic religion.[47]

Cuban Protestants, who constituted only 4 to 6 percent of the Cuban population during the 1950s, faced a somewhat different situation.[48] The Protestant clergy seem to have been more sympathetic to Fidel Castro than their Catholic counterparts.[49] Moreover, a significant number of important revolutionary leaders had roots in Cuba's various Protestant denominations, most notably Frank País, who came from a family that was active in the Baptist church in Santiago de Cuba. His father was a well-known pastor, and an older half-sister became one of the country's most important Protestant leaders.[50] Other prominent revolutionary leaders with Protestant affiliations included Faustino Pérez and leading urban underground fighters Marcelo Salado and Oscar Lucero, both of whom were killed by the Batista police. For a time, former Presbyterian seminarian Mario Llerena acted as a spokesperson for the 26th of July Movement in the United States.[51] Several other revolutionary leaders taught at or attended Protestant high schools or elementary schools.[52]

The presence of Cuban Protestants among the revolutionary leaders and activists may be partly explained in terms of the social bases of Cuban Protestantism. According to Marcos A. Ramos, a historian of Protestantism in Cuba, "Protestantism . . . never reached the aristocracy. Its schools penetrated the middle class, even the upper middle class. But the average Protestant belongs to the poor class or the lower middle class."[53] Thus, the social bases of Protestantism significantly overlapped with the social bases of Cuban populism. In addition, until the 1930s, a sort of unofficial alliance existed between Masons and Protestants because most early Cuban pastors were active Masons.[54] This historic connection may suggest a certain outsider status to Protestantism in relation to the traditional Catholicism of the ruling class. Nationalists seem not to have resented Cuban Protestantism's historic connection to the parent churches in the United States;[55] however, the most significant feature of Cuban Protestantism in the political context of the 1950s may well have been the puritan cast of Protestant values[56] and their elective affinity with the Cuban revolutionary populism of the period, particularly the radical populist rejection of corruption and *politiquería*.

FIDEL CASTRO AND THE POPULIST POLITICAL CULTURE

Fidel Castro does not seem to have had strong political interests before he matriculated as a law student at the University of Havana in 1945. He was then eighteen years old[57] and had just graduated from the Jesuit Belén (Bethlehem) High School. This was an elite school where the great majority of the students were the children of affluent white Catholic families. While in high school, Castro seems to have been most interested in basketball and other sports, although on one occasion, he spoke at a "scientific-pedagogic debate" on the Belén campus, putting forward the school's Catholic position on the relationship between private and public education.[58] According to Castro, his Spanish Jesuit teachers instilled in him the virtues of personal dignity and honor and the willingness to sacrifice.[59] Father Armando Llorente, one of these teachers who knew Castro well during his high school years, noted many years later that he had been "a good student. [He] was not deep, he was intuitive. He has a radar!" In addition, Llorente pointed out, Castro "had the cruelty of the Gallego [a native of the Spanish region of Galicia, birthplace of Angel Castro, Fidel's father]. The Cuban is courtly. The Cuban would give up before he made people suffer. The Spaniard of the north is cruel, hard."[60] This is likely hostile testimony, but it supplements Gabriel García Márquez's observations regarding his friend Castro: "One thing is known with certainty: wherever and with whomever he is, and regardless of how he is doing, Fidel Castro is there to win. I don't believe there is anybody else in the world that is such a sore loser. His attitude toward defeat, even in the minimal acts of daily life, seems to obey a private logic. He doesn't even admit defeat, and he will not have a minute of peace as long as he is unable to invert the terms of the situation and convert defeat into a victory."[61]

The transition to what was then the only university in Cuba must have impressed the young Castro. Although this public university could not have been considered a working-class school, its students were socially more diverse, plebeian, and closer to the realities of Cuban society than anything that Castro could have experienced at the Belén school, and he soon became a student activist of some importance. University politics in Cuba were far removed from the parochial concerns of contemporary students on U.S. campuses and in many ways served as the training grounds for the national political arena. At the time, in the mid- and late 1940s, the university was plagued with political gangsterism, the legacy of the 1933 revolutionaries, some of whom had also fought on the side of the republic in the Spanish Civil War and/or on the Allied side in World War II. These armed gangsters had found a profitable refuge at the University of Havana, where as student leaders they often controlled the sale of books, trafficked in grades, and misappropriated student and university funds.[62]

Fidel Castro developed a relationship with one of the gangster groups, the Unión Insurreccional Revolucionaria (UIR, Insurrectional Revolutionary Union). Like its rivals, the UIR covered itself with a thin ideological veneer—in its case, anarchism. During this period, Castro was accused of the murders of student leader Manolo Castro (no relation) and of university police sergeant Oscar Fernández Caral, in February and June 1948, respectively. The first charge was dropped for lack of evidence and the second because a witness later declared that the police had forced him to accuse Castro of the murder.[63] By the time Castro graduated with a law degree in 1950, he had honed the skills required of a student leader under Cuba's prevailing circumstances. These political skills were of two kinds. One was the ability to develop contact with national politicians to organize protests against, for example, the raising of bus fares, occasions on which the protesting students would burn several buses. The other was the skill of negotiating with professors and administrators about the scheduling and nature of tests. Student politicians were also active in the distribution of study materials to students, sometimes including pirated translations of foreign textbooks. These leaders were also involved in lengthy negotiations with other student politicians regarding the formation of slates for student elections, distribution of student government posts, and the control of the agenda and possible outcomes of student assemblies.[64] To sway students, a successful leader had to be a good orator, mastering the stylized nationalist and populist rhetoric. But he or she also needed the verbal negotiating skills necessary for the wheeling and dealing part of the job, which entailed a lot of informal talking and manipulative double-crossing abilities. At the time, student politicians had to know or pretend to know how to handle guns. In these requirements lie the origins of Castro's reputation as an effective if long-winded orator, a charming although often extremely prolix conversationalist, and a man of armed action.

Castro enrolled in the ill-fated 1947 Cayo Confites expedition, which was supposed to overthrow Rafael Trujillo's dictatorship in the Dominican Republic. The expedition was organized by the Caribbean Legion, a mixed group of idealistic democrats, nationalists, and plain delinquents, and was supported by influential populist and liberal democratic politicians in Cuba, Venezuela, and Costa Rica.[65] When the Cuban army was about to seize the Cayo Confites expeditionaries, Castro claims to have put his athletic abilities to use and escaped by swimming ashore from the small key where the group's boats were anchored. On another occasion, while attending a student congress in Bogotá, Colombia, he became involved in the "Bogotazo," the Bogotá riots that followed the assassination of popular Colombian leader Eliecer Gaitán in April 1948.[66]

Castro was thus a product of the Cuban populist tradition, with its pronounced emphasis on the man of action, the adventurer, in the sense in which I defined it earlier. However, his populist adventurism should be distinguished from voluntarism, a useful term that is part of the Marxist intellectual tradition. Marxism defines voluntarism as the current of thought that affirms the ability of the human will to prevail regardless of material conditions and limitations. But this voluntarism presupposes at least an awareness of such conditions and limitations, even though a voluntarist may argue that they can be overcome with sufficient will and determination. Fidel Castro, was, by his own admission, an economic illiterate. Virtually all of the numerous books he kept in prison after the defeat of the 1953 Moncada attack dealt with literary, historical, political, and philosophical themes.[67] Castro's economic illiteracy was a factor in his later inclination toward gigantic showcase projects (e.g., the disastrous attempt to bring about a 10-million-ton sugar harvest in 1970 and the Ocho Vías, the eight-lane highway traversing much of the country). His ignorance also explains his stubborn resistance, particularly during the early years of the revolution, to the realities that material resources were limited and that an inescapable need existed for strict investment and spending priorities. Conversely, Che Guevara, a revolutionary versed in Marxism but with a strong affinity for the bohemian values that thrive among certain groups in Buenos Aires and other highly developed metropolises, was both a voluntarist and an adventurer in the sense described earlier. At the time, Fidel Castro was simply an adventurer.

Perhaps as a result of his populist political socialization, Castro reputedly is inclined to improvisation and disorganization in his work habits. His younger brother, Raúl, has always lacked Fidel's political radar and rapport with people but is known to be highly disciplined and to have excellent organizational skills. The brothers' political strengths and weaknesses may help us to understand why Raúl joined the youth wing of the Cuban Communist Party in the 1950s while Fidel did not.

The populist political milieu was by no means sealed off from other political and ideological currents. Fidel Castro, like other populists, was exposed to other ideologies. Thus, his statement that in his student days he went to the bookstore at the Communist Party's headquarters in Havana does not by itself indicate that he was then more of a Communist than a populist. Similarly, his clear expressions of sympathy for Venezuela's Acción Democrática government and his attempts to arrange a meeting with that country's president while on his way to Bogotá do not necessarily lead to the conclusion that he was a social democrat.[68] He also seems to have been somewhat more educated and cultured than the typical populist activist. Instead of the anti-intellectual man of action described by some observers,[69] Castro appears to have been an intellectual, although something of a dilettante. To this day, he continues to read voraciously, and after reading several books and articles on a given subject, he is prone to proclaiming himself an expert. This is a common characteristic and would not be a serious flaw except that Castro possesses practically unlimited power. Military tactics and strategy, agricultural and cattle science, and sports are just some of the areas he claims to know well, and on that basis he makes personal, irrevocable decisions with enormous consequences for Cuba's limited resources. In the late 1960s, huge investments were made in Castro's stubborn attempt to develop the F-1 hybrid, which would have crossbred the native zebu with imported Holstein cattle, despite the fact that the project was strongly opposed as thoroughly unviable by the two British specialists Castro had invited to Cuba to advise him.[70] Left-wing French agronomist René Dumont had a similar experience with Castro in the field of agriculture and eventually came under vicious attack by the Cuban leader.[71]

Moreover, Fidel Castro has always held grandiose ambitions of a kind scarcely ever found among Cuban politicians of any stripe. As a young man, he reportedly sympathized with the thesis maintained by Gustavo Pitaluga, a Spanish exile residing in Cuba, in *Dialogue over Destiny* that Cuba had a great destiny, including becoming the leader of a federation of Caribbean states.[72] But Fidel Castro had the misfortune of being born in a relatively small island country with very limited possibilities for playing a major role in world affairs. After achieving power, Castro for a time projected Cuba onto the world stage, but the end of the Cold War greatly diminished the country's international role and forced Castro to severely limit his foreign involvements.

To fully understand Fidel Castro, however, it is necessary to see him not simply as a product of the populist political tradition but also transcending it. Castro's reflections on his political upbringing help to elucidate his politics, even allowing for the inevitable distortions resulting from the effort to justify himself. The most striking features of these recollections are the recurring themes of control and order and Castro's ideological obsession with organization, always understood in a top-down fashion. These in turn must be placed in the context of the failures of the revolution of 1933 and of subsequent Cuban populist politics. Castro said that as an adolescent he wanted to go to the Belén High School because "I felt more suited to the Jesuit discipline and their behavior in general."[73] Of his participation in the 1947 Cayo Confites expedition, Castro recalled, "There were around 1,200 men in the expedition. It was very badly organized; there were good people, many good Dominicans and Cubans who truly supported the Dominican cause, but also—as a result of too hasty recruiting—delinquents, some lumpen elements and all kinds of others."[74] Of the Bogotazo riots, he remembered that although he had been impressed by how an oppressed people could erupt and by their courage and heroism,

> there was no organization, no political education to accompany that heroism. There was political awareness and a rebellious spirit, but no political education and no leadership. The [Bogotazo] uprising influenced me greatly in my later revolutionary life. . . . I wanted to avoid the revolution sinking into anarchy, looting, disorder and people taking the law into their own hands. . . . [T]he [Colombian] oligarchs—who supported the status quo and wanted to portray the people as an anarchic, disorderly mob— took advantage of that situation.[75]

Castro may have been correct in his diagnosis of what went wrong with the Cayo Confites and Colombian events, but the political lessons he drew from these events were one-sided and heavily weighted toward the need for political order and control from the top.

IS IT POSSIBLE TO HAVE A CONSPIRACY OF ONE?

In his recollections, Fidel Castro indicated that his contribution to the Cuban Revolution consisted of having synthesized the ideas of José Martí with those of Marxism-Leninism. Castro also mentions that he had noticed that the Cuban Communists had been isolated in the late 1940s and 1950s as a result of the prevailing atmosphere of imperialism, McCarthyism, and reactionary politics. He thus concluded, he said, that the Communists had no chance under these circumstances.[76] In the face of all this, Castro recalled,

> I worked out a revolutionary strategy for carrying out a deep social revolution—but gradually, by stages. I basically decided to carry it out with the broad, rebellious, discontented masses, who did not have a mature political consciousness of the need for revolution but who constituted the immense majority of the people. . . . It was

clear to me that the masses were the basic factor—the still confused masses in many cases, prejudiced against socialism and communism; the masses who had received no real political education, influenced as they were from all quarters by the mass media.[77]

According to Castro, he had no mentor and had figured out the political situation by himself, with no political groups or other individuals involved in this process. This statement is corroborated by the fact that neither the Soviet Union nor the Cuban Communists had a clear idea of where Castro was going or where he wanted to go when he took power on January 1, 1959. Even more remarkable was the fact that Guevara, a political sophisticate, spent almost two and a half years working closely with Castro both politically and physically yet did not really know Castro's politics well. Thus, in late 1957, Guevara wondered whether Castro would denounce the Miami Pact, a far-from-radical agreement among all the opposition groups about how to overthrow and build the succession to the Batista dictatorship (see chap. 4). A representative of the 26th of July Movement had been maneuvered into signing the agreement without Castro's authorization, and Castro quickly denounced it. In a farewell letter to Castro written before leaving for the Congo in 1965, Guevara reflected that "my only serious failing was not having had more confidence in you from the first moments in the Sierra Maestra, and not having understood quickly enough your qualities as a leader and as a revolutionary."[78] Nevertheless, even after the Miami Pact question had been resolved to Guevara's satisfaction, he still described Castro as "an authentic leader of the left wing of the bourgeoisie," although he did have "personal qualities of extraordinary brilliance that placed him well above his class."[79] This language clearly suggests that Guevara, who then saw himself as a supporter of the supposedly proletarian Communist camp, did not see Castro as belonging to that same camp.

On some occasions, even Raúl Castro expressed doubts about his brother's political intentions. One such occasion was Fidel Castro's April 1959 trip to the United States at the invitation of the American Society of Newspaper Editors. While in the United States, the Cuban leader softened his tone and disassociated himself from Communism, alarming Raúl, who telephoned Fidel to tell him that there was talk at home that the Yankees were seducing him. Fidel reacted with indignation and repeatedly stated that he knew them too well for that to happen.[80] According to declassified Soviet documents, Raúl Castro briefly considered splitting the rebel movement to convince his brother that he could not govern without the Communists, and Guevara threatened to emigrate if his spring 1959 proposals for a popular militia were not approved at the time.[81] (The militias were created the following fall.)

In fact, Fidel Castro did not use his trip to the United States to sell out, as Raúl Castro had feared. Instead, Fidel carried out a complex political maneuver. He instructed his liberal companions, several of them government ministers, not to request U.S. assistance and to pretend a lack of interest when U.S. officials offered aid. At the same time, he soothed the liberals' unhappiness regarding these instructions by conveying the impression that he was on their side and was waiting for the Communists to make the wrong move before acting against them. He also met privately in New York for more than three hours with famed Central Intelligence Agency agent Frank Bender and convinced him that those were indeed the Cuban leader's intentions.[82]

It would be a mistake to view Castro's shrewd manipulation of the various Cuban social and political forces merely in terms of his personal skills. His manipulative success also owed much to the prevailing situation in Cuba. The liberals and middle classes allowed themselves to be manipulated by Castro during the initial stages of the revolutionary process because they were so politically weak. They hoped that Fidel Castro would protect them from more radical and pro-Communist leaders, including Guevara and Raúl Castro. Fidel's middle-class supporters acquiesced in the postponement of elections and other substantial modifications of constitutional procedures in early 1959, branding this behavior unconstitutional as well as a betrayal only after Castro turned decisively against their material interests. In addition, the nature of populist politics, with its ambiguous class commitments, allowed Fidel Castro, at least for a while, to be different things to different people.

Fidel Castro's political behavior has led some to conclude that the eventual Communist outcome of the Cuban Revolution resulted from a conscious plan developed by Castro and his close associates in collaboration with the leadership of the old Communist Party prior to Batista's overthrow on January 1, 1959. Because this alleged plan was developed in secrecy, it fits the criteria to be labeled a conspiracy whether or not the term is explicitly used. This view still constitutes the commonsense understanding among right-wingers, just as the view that the United States pushed Castro into the arms of Russia and Communism constitutes the commonsense view among liberals and part of the Left, at least in the United States. In 1986, well-known journalist Tad Szulc, who had covered Cuba for the *New York Times* in the late 1950s and early 1960s, published a biography of Fidel Castro that claimed that he had made a secret deal with the old Cuban Communists in mid-1958 (before the victory of the revolution). The deal was subsequently confirmed by the early 1959 establishment of a "secret government" parallel to the official revolutionary government. The purpose of such an agreement between Castro and the pro-Soviet Cuban Communists was to bring about the establishment of Cuban Communism at some future point in the development of the revolutionary process.[83]

Szulc claimed to have based his controversial contentions on interviews conducted with Cuban revolutionary leaders during the 1980s, but his analysis is marred by a number of problems that cast serious doubts on the validity of his thesis. In addition to questionable statements (e.g., referring to Camilo Cienfuegos as a "closet Communist" during the war against Batista),[84] Szulc's use of historical events as evidence for his thesis fails to distinguish between incidents that took place at different times during the revolutionary process. Thus, for example, to cite instances of collaboration between Fidel Castro and leaders and supporters of the Partido Socialista Popular in late 1959 and early 1960 (e.g., the creation of the revolutionary instruction schools for civilians in late 1959)[85] does not constitute evidence in support of a conspiracy established in the pre-revolutionary period. By the time Szulc published his book, scholars had already firmly established that important changes had taken place in the relations between Fidelistas and Communists during the summer of 1959. Most significantly, Szulc made no effort to confront and analyze evidence that might have conflicted with his conspiracy theory. For example, he failed to analyze the frictions that arose among Raúl Castro, Guevara, and Fidel Castro or the frequent clashes that took place among leading elements of the 26th of July Movement and the Communists in at least two very important arenas, the unions and the press, including Fidel Castro's own newspaper, *Revolución*. In addition, neither the pronouncements nor the behavior of the old Cuban Communists and the leaders of the Soviet Union during at least the first nine months of 1959 show, as we shall see in chapter 5, that they regarded Fidel Castro as having entered into a pact with them or being one of them.

Castro was no conspirator, if the term refers to someone who plans a future political strategy secretly with others. Although his behavior and pronouncements involved a great deal of secrecy and deception, he was merely determining in an ad hoc manner the general political direction in which he wanted to go, not pursuing a precise long-term strategy with a previously determined specific goal. This was true at least until the fall of 1959, when he decided to ally with the Soviet Union. Fidel Castro had political designs that he shared with no one. They were pragmatic in the sense that although Castro wanted to make a radical revolution, he left it to historical circumstances, the existing relations of forces and tactical possibilities, to determine specifically what kind of revolution it would be, all along making sure that he would remain in control. Although he did not necessarily foresee membership in the Soviet bloc, he also did not preclude it a priori. Castro's considerable political talents were eminently tactical: that is, he knew how to advance his agenda in a certain general but unspecified leftist political direction by taking advantage of particular political conjunctures and relationships of social and political forces. Moreover, Castro has always resisted subordinating himself to any organizational apparatus. His own ruling Cuban Communist Party was itself fully established and formally founded only in 1965, when virtually all the major social and economic changes in Cuban society had already been carried out under his personal leadership and control. Castro's leadership is strongly reminiscent of the Latin American phenomenon of caudillismo, except that Fidel Castro is a caudillo with political ideas.

FIDEL CASTRO'S REVOLUTIONARY STAGES

Clear evidence indicates that Castro followed his plans for conducting the revolutionary process by stages, although these stages did not necessarily involve an ascending order of radicalism. His approach did not involve a long-term strategic plan but rather a series of tactical adjustments and innovations by an intelligent revolutionary politician. Castro's stages had nothing to do with the way the term has been used in the classical Marxist tradition—that is, to refer to the appropriate revolutionary goals and actions in light of a certain development of the productive forces, class relations, and domestic and international political situations. The Marxist theoretical view is exemplified in the early-twentieth-century debates between the Russian Mensheviks and Bolsheviks regarding the prospects for revolution in Russia. The Mensheviks held that, given the degree of economic development and state of class relations in their country, the revolution would be carried out by the bourgeoisie and thus could not be expected to go beyond the bourgeois, democratic republic stage. Although Lenin and the Bolsheviks agreed that the establishment of a democratic republic was the only possible first stage of revolutionary development in their country, they maintained that the Russian bourgeoisie was not capable of revolutionary action. Consequently, Lenin argued, the Russian working class was the only class capable of leading the democratic revolution. Lenin changed his view in the 1917 April Theses, in which he implicitly adopted Leon Trotsky's idea of the permanent revolution. According to this theory, the working class would not only have to lead the revolution but, having done so, would have to move beyond the bourgeois democratic stage to the socialist stage. However, according to Trotsky, because Russia had achieved only a limited degree of industrialization, the prospects for socialism would depend on the revolution spreading beyond the country's borders to economically developed countries such as Germany. A successful socialist revolution in one or more developed countries would in turn help the Russian revolutionaries in the economic development of their country.

In contrast, Castro's notion of stages was exclusively concerned with the right tactics to follow in a given political conjuncture, with a particular focus on the audience to which he was appealing at any given moment. Castro's stages also reflected his preoccupation with avoiding political isolation and with the need to delay any confrontation that he figured he had little chance of winning. His first stage began with a radical, nonsocialist program subsequently known as "History Will Absolve Me." Castro initially put forward this program at his defense in the trial that took place after his unsuccessful attack on the Moncada barracks on July 26, 1953, long before he had achieved supremacy in the anti-Batista opposition. This speech, later rewritten in prison, along with the "Manifesto no. 1 to the People of Cuba," dated August 8, 1955, and written in Mexican exile shortly after he and his supporters were released from prison under an amnesty granted by Batista's government, constituted the bases for the first radical stage.[86] Although these documents were addressed to the people in general, they were in fact more narrowly directed at the militant anti-Batista students and young workers who had not yet joined his group. Castro sensed that several thousand of these young people were ready to be brought into his nascent movement. Neither of these documents became widely known until after the revolutionary victory.[87]

By the summer of 1957, the situation had changed considerably. Castro had established a base in the Sierra Maestra and was beginning to gain dominance in the anti-Batista coalition, particularly after other efforts to topple the regime ended in failure. By this time, his audience had broadened well beyond the original ranks of young, anti-Batista militants. Castro now sought legitimacy and respectability so that he could earn the confidence of the Cuban middle classes and allay any concerns in Washington, D.C. He achieved a major success along these lines when two highly respected leaders of the opposition, Felipe Pazos, a top Cuban economist and former president of the National Bank of Cuba, and Raúl Chibás, brother of deceased Ortodoxo leader Eduardo Chibás, went to the Sierra Maestra and signed a joint "Manifesto of the Sierra Maestra" with Castro on July 12, 1957.[88] This manifesto, unlike the previously mentioned documents, was published in Cuba's principal magazine, *Bohemia*, during a brief lull between two periods of censorship and was read and widely commented on by hundreds of thousands of Cubans. The manifesto also became the guiding text of the next Castroite stage of the revolutionary process: the formation and consolidation of a politically militant but socially moderate coalition to overthrow Batista and avoid alarming the United States. Castro wrote privately to his confidant, Celia Sánchez, in June 1958 that when the current war ended, a bigger and much longer war would begin against the United States.[89] In public, however, as an example of the social moderation that went hand in hand with Castro's political intransigence, the rebels decreed a mild and noncontroversial agrarian reform law in October 1958. This second stage lasted from 1957 to 1959.

After coming to power, Fidel Castro gradually moved away from the second moderate stage. First, he divided the potentially enormous middle-class opposition at home by taking on different sections of it in turn. The radical rent reduction law of March 1959, reminiscent of the History Will Absolve Me program, negatively affected only a landlord segment of the relatively affluent urban middle and upper classes; the May 1959 agrarian reform law affected a different segment of these same classes; and so on. Even more important, while continually raising the anti-imperialist temperature of the country he tried to postpone the final confrontation with the much more powerful opposition of the U.S. government. In any case, by the spring of 1959 a third stage of the revolution was clearly in the making, again reminiscent of History Will Absolve Me. Before the end of 1960, this stage had ended, with the collectivization of Cuban society along the general, systemic lines of the Soviet bloc and China.

FIDEL CASTRO'S POLITICAL CONTROL

Fidel Castro's notion of stages as tactics was guided in part by his determination to keep as much personal political control as possible. We have already seen how this approach was related to the lessons he drew from the Cayo Confites incident in 1947 and especially the Bogotazo experience in 1948. As early as 1954, Castro wrote to his close friend Luis Conte Agüero,

> *Conditions that are indispensable for the integration of a truly civic movement: ideology, discipline, and chieftainship.* The three are essential, but chieftainship is basic. I don't know whether it was Napoleon who said that a bad general in battle is worth more than twenty good generals. *A movement cannot be organized where everyone believes he has the right to issue public statements without consulting anyone else; nor can one expect anything of a movement that will be integrated by anarchic men who at the first disagreement take the path they consider most convenient, tearing apart and destroying the vehicle.* The apparatus of propaganda and organization must be such and so powerful that it will implacably destroy him who will create tendencies, cliques, or schisms or will rise against the movement.[90]

These strictures evidently were not supposed to apply to Castro, who had the habit of acting on his own and of disregarding agreements made by the 26th of July leadership, even those in which he had participated and to which he had given his concurrence. Such were the complaints made by Carlos Franqui, a leader of the 26th of July Movement, in an October 1958 document addressed to Fidel Castro and the members of the movement's national executive. Franqui also noted that Castro tended not to accept criticism and to react to it by attacking the critic and concluded, "I have observed that many of our meetings are more like a consultation. Or a conversation, almost always the prodigious conversation of Fidel, in which a decision is taken for granted, while hardly ever an agreement is reached that has been amply discussed by all of us. We are all responsible for such situations for both reasons of commission and omission."[91]

The movement guidelines also assumed that Fidel Castro would always be the chieftain. However, in July 1957, Frank País, the national coordinator of the 26th of July Movement with underground headquarters in Santiago de Cuba, wrote to inform Castro that the movement's policies, strategies, and program were going to be under the control of the national directorate. This directorate, País wrote, would have thirteen members; he would designate one delegate, Celia Sánchez, to represent Castro's guerrillas. País also complained that the 26th of July Movement lacked a systematic program and told Castro that there was work in progress to develop one, with several people specifically assigned to write on the racial issue and on economic problems and solutions. País asked Castro to send some suggestions. There is no available record of Castro's response to País's letter, but Castro chose that moment to prepare and sign the joint document with Pazos and Chibás, thereby preempting País's and the task force's programmatic efforts. The timing of Castro's political and ideological coup was particularly significant, since País was known to favor a more socially radical line than that adopted in the Pazos-Chibás-Castro manifesto. País's signature did not appear on this manifesto, and Batista's police captured and killed him on the streets of Santiago shortly thereafter, on July 30, 1957, thereby eliminating the potential confrontation between the two leaders.[92]

THE COST OF "SUCCESS"

Fidel Castro's politics and methods succeeded in the sense that they enabled him to seize and maintain power in Cuba. Central to Castro's functioning was manipulating people and hiding his political agenda, with the purpose of dividing and conquering his actual and potential opponents. However, that does not mean that he was from the beginning a "Communist." Castro's brand of populist caudillismo, detached from any significant institutional ties to Cuba's principal social classes, had an elective affinity with Soviet-style Communism. But only the presence of certain historical circumstances (e.g., U.S. pressures, the widely shared belief in the international rise of Soviet power, and political pressures coming from the Partido Socialista Popular and the group around Raúl Castro and Che Guevara) converted that affinity into choice and commitment. Had Castro confronted a different set of opportunities, pressures, and constraints, he might have steered in a different direction.

Castro's politics are inextricably bound with his caudillismo, by which I mean, among other things, the politics of blindly following the leader. This constitutes a major obstacle to raising the Cuban people's political consciousness and increasing their organizational autonomy. Consciousness and autonomy cannot by definition depend on all-knowing leaders keeping their secret political aims to themselves, so when the time is ripe to defeat the opposition, the leader carries out the aims he has hitherto kept to himself. But these aims do not necessarily correspond to the political consciousness and explicit desires of those he is supposed to lead and represent.

Thus, Castro's tactics have enabled him to manipulate and deceive his working-class and peasant supporters. As a result, the Cuban masses have remained the objects rather than the subjects of history, notwithstanding the political radicalization they may have experienced in the initial stages of the revolutionary process.

[CHAPTER THREE]

U.S. Policy and the Cuban Revolution

What role did external pressures—specifically, Washington's strong opposition to the Cuban revolutionary government—play in Cuba's decision to join the Soviet camp? For a long time, the predominant view among liberals and many leftists has been that U.S. Cold War foreign policy during the Eisenhower and Kennedy administrations was responsible for pushing Fidel Castro and his government into the arms of the Soviet Union and Communism. This approach has shown remarkable endurance among North Americans to the left of the political center as the predominant commonsense explanation of the fate of the Cuban Revolution and its relations with the United States. Such a view clearly implies that the United States could have adopted significantly different policies and that the actions of Cuba's revolutionary leaders can be explained primarily as reactions to the American foreign policy of the time.[1]

Other interpretations have given a great deal more importance to the ideas and actions of the Cuban revolutionary leaders. Thus, for historian Richard E. Welch Jr., Cuban leaders established the main course of the revolution. Welch acknowledges what he sees as the many errors of American policy: U.S. officials placed undue emphasis on cash compensation for American properties expropriated by the agrarian reform law, the Eisenhower administration could have offered economic assistance to the Castro regime rather than waiting for requests that never came, the United States was negligent in patrolling Florida airfields and policing the activities of Cuban refugees, Washington was guilty of pressuring some of its European allies not to sell arms to Cuba on the basis of overstated claims that Havana was inspiring rebel invasions against dictatorial regimes in the Caribbean, and finally the United States exaggerated Communist influence in Cuba during the early period of the revolution.[2] Nevertheless,

Welch finds it "doubtful" that "these errors singly or collectively altered the course of the Cuban Revolution or fundamentally determined the domestic and foreign policies of the Cuban government between January 1959 and March 1960. Possibly they accelerated in a limited way the radicalization of the revolution."[3] While Welch's analysis recognizes the centrality of the Cuban leaders' initiatives and actions in determining the direction taken by the revolutionary process, he seems to assume that in so doing, they somehow diminished the importance of U.S. policy. In other words, he implicitly discarded the possibility that although the Cuban leaders may have been responsible for the revolution's course, the United States still played a major role in the revolution's development.

Part of the problem with Welch's analysis as well as that of many other historians and social scientists is that he restricts his focus to the explicit decisions made and policies implemented, omitting key questions pertaining to the institutionalized power relationships between the United States and Cuba. Such relationships unquestionably express themselves in specific policies, but only an institutional power analysis can determine the relative importance of different kinds of policies and provide knowledge of the systemic and powerful constraints on governmental policy making in general.

Welch identifies various "errors" in the U.S. Cuban policy in the early period of the revolution: some indeed were errors in the sense that alternative courses of action might have been compatible with U.S. interests; others, however, were not errors at all but inflexible policies institutionally determined by the system of U.S. imperial commitments and business needs. For example, the demand for cash payment for expropriated American properties was more institutionally determined than Washington's "negligence" (if it really was negligence) in not patrolling Florida airfields to prevent hostile flights over Cuba near the beginning of Castro's rule. An institutional analysis requires some overall notion of what kind of revolution, broadly speaking, the United States would and could have accepted in the Latin America of the 1950s and 1960s. Thus, if it can be shown that the United States was not willing to accept a radical social revolution, then the actions taken by the revolutionary leaders acquire a different meaning, particularly if their actions represented a well-founded anticipation of what Washington would not allow. These leaders might have opted for the tactic of striking first to compensate for their weakness in relation to the United States and to take advantage of the element of surprise. In this sense, the question of whether Fidel Castro—or, for that matter, Eisenhower and Kennedy—acted first in any given context is of secondary importance, at least as far as the issue of assigning moral and political responsibility is concerned.[4]

WASHINGTON'S POLICIES TOWARD CUBA

With these analytical considerations in mind, we now turn to an analysis of the policies that Washington pursued. First, it is important to consider the historical context, to remind ourselves that U.S. interest in Cuba goes back well into the nineteenth century, when at various times members of several powerful circles spoke of annexing the island.[5] A critical period was the late 1890s, when the Spanish atrocities against the Cuban fighters for independence became grist for the mill of the yellow Hearst press. Hearst's pioneering efforts in mass propaganda facilitated the imperial ambitions of key sections of the American ruling class by manufacturing popular support for the Spanish-American War and subsequent occupation of Cuba, Puerto Rico, and the Philippines. This first occupation lasted four years and ended in Cuba winning nominal independence in 1902 under U.S. control, as guaranteed by the Platt Amendment, which gave the United States various rights, such as the right to maintain military bases in Cuba (eventually reduced to one in Guantánamo). The most important American prerogatives were spelled out in title III, which gave the United States "the right to intervene for the preservation of Cuban independence, the maintenance of a government adequate for the protection of life, property and individual liberty," and in title IV, which ratified and validated "all acts of the United States in Cuba during its military occupancy."[6] The latter provision was quite important because while occupying Cuba, U.S. military authorities had given concessions to U.S. enterprises in various fields, particularly public utilities. Title IV ensured that none of those concessions would be altered or declared invalid by any future Cuban government.

The situation essentially represented de facto if not fully de jure colonialism. For more than three decades, U.S. economic and political control of the island republic was quite open and was often reinforced by actual or threatened military intervention. Foreign domination, in combination with the native class system, produced a political system dominated by two almost indistinguishable political parties, the Conservatives and Liberals, who alternated in office under the leadership of their usually corrupt chieftains. Cuban politicians accommodated themselves to the internal and external status quo, and some had direct ties to U.S. business.

The frustrated revolution of 1933 altered and complicated this arrangement with the eventual development of a Cuban domestic equivalent of the U.S. New Deal, which was enshrined in the democratic and progressive 1940 constitution. However, important parts of this document (e.g., agrarian reform) were never implemented during the period of constitutional rule, which lasted through 1952. As we saw in greater detail in chapter 1, the Cuban state also acquired a major role in the regulation of economic activity. Thus, by 1937, a number of laws, including the Ley de Coordinación Azucarera (Law of Sugar Coordination), had legalized state control of all sugar-producing land, provided for state allocation of quotas to producers and regulation of prices and wages, and established measures protecting the rights of the small and medium-sized sugar farmers (*colonos*). These laws did not apply to nonsugar farmers, who had less legal protection, and to squatters, who had none. These laws of course could not have solved the agrarian problem since they left untouched most of the evils of rural Cuba described in chapter 1.

The post-1933 period could be described as a transition from a de facto colonialism to a neocolonial arrangement. The Platt Amendment was repealed; in exchange, Cuba agreed to lease to the United States the land for the Guantánamo Naval Base in perpetuity, and the two countries signed a trade reciprocity treaty that institutionalized Cuba's sugar monoculture and economic dependence on the U.S. market. U.S. economic power remained formidable, although in a developing partnership with Cuban capitalists who achieved considerable economic power, especially in the boom years during and after World War II. Thus, while in 1939 Cuban sugar capitalists owned only 28 percent of the country's sugar mills, that proportion increased to 45 percent in 1946 and 59 percent in 1955. Similarly, the proportion of total domestically owned deposits in Cuban banks (as distinct from deposits in foreign banks in Cuba) grew from 16.8 percent in 1939 to 60.2 percent in 1955.[7]

Neocolonialism in Cuba meant that U.S. political control became substantially more indirect, coming to depend to a considerable degree on Cuban politicians' willingness to ingratiate themselves and anticipate the wishes of Washington and of U.S. business interests rather than on day-to-day U.S. interference in Cuban political decision making. In spite of the relatively greater independence achieved after 1934, the political maturity and self-reliance of Cuba's political establishment and the economically powerful did not appreciably develop, primarily because these Cubans became accustomed to the idea that they had no need to worry about major social and political threats to their power. The United States would take care of any such threats that arose. This sentiment formed part of a much more generalized attitude among the Cuban people that nothing could be done if the United States did not approve.

During this period, Washington's policy toward Cuba essentially remained one of law and order and business as usual, not significantly different from its policy toward the rest of Latin America. The Cold War context added new political priorities to the long-standing U.S. concern with protecting its economic interests in Latin America and maintaining its geopolitical hegemony on the continent. Washington now had to line up Latin American governments to act in concert and protect the Western Hemisphere against "foreign subversion" from the Soviet Union and the international Communist movement. These governments acquired a new role as faithful clients whose votes could be counted on at the United Nations and other international organizations such as the Organization of American States. In practice, the defense against Communism meant U.S. endorsement of and support for any and all Latin American governments professing anti-Communism, regardless of whether they had been democratically elected or were military dictatorships, a group that included Trujillo in the Dominican Republic, Somoza in Nicaragua, and Pérez Jiménez in Venezuela.

BATISTA'S COUP D'ÉTAT

This political context explains why the United States quickly granted diplomatic recognition to the Batista government, established by a March 10, 1952, military coup d'état that put an end to twelve years of elected, constitutional governments. The constitutional period was rife with governmental corruption and violent conflict among political cliques, but it was generally characterized by open and free political life and by the willingness of labor to strike to strengthen its bargaining power. U.S. and Cuban businesspeople welcomed Batista's return to power after his 1944 electoral defeat, perceiving it as the beginning of a period of stability, law and order, and the reestablishment of labor discipline.[8] Washington supported the dictatorship in a variety of ways, particularly by providing military hardware, supplies, and training. This policy persisted until March 1958, when it became clear that the Batista regime faced a serious crisis and would not survive for long. The total absence of Cuban support for Batista brought about a significantly different relationship of political forces that compelled the United States to withdraw most of its previous support for the dictatorship.

The standard model of a business-as-usual, law-and-order foreign policy was no longer adequate to deal with a rapidly changing and potentially dangerous political situation. After March 1958, the U.S. government shifted to a more finely tuned policy toward Cuba, with the eventual goal of getting rid of the no-longer-reliable Batista while preventing the rise to power of Fidel Castro and his rebel army.[9] The United States suspended arms shipments to the Batista regime, although some loopholes in this policy remained in place, and the U.S. military mission continued to provide its services to Batista's armed forces. From March 1958 until Batista's overthrow on January 1, 1959, the principal issue for Washington was not the claims and rumors about possible links between rebel army leaders such as Raúl Castro and Communism, although these claims were of course hardly reassuring. Nor had the multiclass democratic movement led by the rebel army adopted a clear anti-imperialist, nationalist political posture. Contrary to the claims of many authors,[10] an open and explicit anti-imperialist nationalism became a defining feature of the movement only after the rebel victory. The real issue for the United States in the months leading up to the triumph of the revolutionaries was the fact that the movement led by Fidel Castro was not part of Cuba's traditional political forces and was therefore not a known and tested entity of the sort with which Washington much preferred to deal. The 26th of July Movement was too independent and did not exhibit the reassuring political behavior necessary to earn the U.S. seal of approval. Friction had already occurred, as when Raúl Castro's rebel forces kidnapped several American citizens in June 1958 to protest the Guantánamo Naval Base's assistance to the Batista regime.[11] However, although even at this early date Washington saw Fidel Castro as an unpredictable wild card who could not be counted on to safeguard U.S. interests in Cuba, it does not automatically follow that he was already viewed as a declared anti-imperialist nationalist—let alone pro-Communist—enemy of the United States.[12] For this reason, Washington simultaneously persuaded Batista to resign and helped to organize a military coup aimed at establishing a provisional government and bypassing Castro's rebel forces. The latter part of this plan turned out to be completely unrealistic and was quickly nipped in the bud by the decisive actions of Castro's 26th of July Movement. The most important of these actions was a general strike carried out in the first week of January 1959 that was in part celebration and in part a precautionary move on the part of the revolutionary leadership.

In the end, the struggle against Batista had a denouement that neither the United States nor the rebels had anticipated: the complete collapse of the dictatorship, the Cuban armed forces, and consequently the key structures of the Cuban state. It left the United States surprised and concerned. Less than twenty-four hours before Batista left Cuba, Assistant Secretary of State for Latin America R. Roy Rubottom Jr. told the Senate Foreign Relations Committee, "It has been hard to believe that the Castros alone, that the 26th of July Movement could take over, because they have not had enough broad support in Cuba to do this job by themselves. . . . I would not be happy with Castro solely in command. I cannot quite visualize that at this stage."[13]

U.S. POLICY TOWARD THE CUBAN REVOLUTION IN POWER

Because its preferred solution to the terminal crisis of the Batista regime proved an utter failure, the United States confronted a new constellation of social and political forces inside Cuba. Within the next two years, the island republic witnessed a profound process of revolutionary change that sent relations between the United States and Cuba into a severe crisis and led to a break between the two countries at the beginning of 1961 and subsequently to the failed Bay of Pigs invasion in April of that year.

During this critical period, the institutions in charge of the day-to-day implementation of U.S. foreign policy, such as the State Department and the U.S. embassy in Havana, did not necessarily play the most important roles in making the decisions that shaped this policy. Rather, other parts of the executive branch, especially the National Security Council, the

Central Intelligence Agency (CIA), the Department of the Treasury, and, of course, the president, played the decisive roles. Moreover, these policies were formulated within a political and social context substantially influenced by the views and interests of U.S. business circles and the political climate fostered by the U.S. press and Congress.

In the earliest days of the Cuban Revolution, the U.S. executive branch adopted a stance that could be described as worried vigilance, expressing neither outright sympathy for nor outright hostility to the new Cuban government but rather exerting subtle but steady pressures while maintaining cautious diplomatic-style correctness. Washington expressed a warmer attitude toward the members of the liberal wing of the first revolutionary cabinet (e.g., Felipe Pazos, president of the National Bank of Cuba) precisely because they were, from the U.S. point of view, tested and proven elements that would at least do no damage to fundamental U.S. interests. Philip Bonsal, a career diplomat, replaced conservative pro-Batista U.S. Ambassador Earl E. T. Smith. Bonsal was a sober and moderate figure who had just served as ambassador to Bolivia, in itself an important fact since Bolivia's 1952 revolution represented the most significant social revolution in Latin America since the Mexican Revolution earlier in the century. Thus, Washington probably saw in Bonsal a specialist experienced in helping to influence and control governments rooted in revolutionary upheaval.

The broad principles of U.S. policy toward the Cuban Revolution can be easily discerned and were hardly novel in the Latin American context. First came the defense and protection of the political and juridical conditions necessary for the functioning of private property and capitalism, particularly insofar as U.S. investments in Cuba were concerned. Second came the related but not identical Cold War aim of opposition to Communism, domestic or foreign. Located close to the United States, Cuba is part of Latin America, which was considered the safest and most untouchable U.S. sphere of interest (meaning that it was not thought to be in play in relation to the Soviet Union).

Some differences regarding U.S. Cuban policy continued to exist within government circles, especially during the first five months of 1959. Relatively friendliest, or least hostile, toward the Cuban government was Ambassador Bonsal (whose views will be closely examined later in this chapter). The State Department showed a greater willingness to pressure the Cuban government than did Bonsal but was still relatively circumspect and conscious of public relations, particularly the protection of the U.S. image in Cuba and Latin America. To take an important example, the State Department repeatedly expressed its concern within the inner circles of the Eisenhower administration about the clandestine, hostile flights over Cuba (which increasingly included sabotage) originating in Florida. In a confidential memo sent to the Secretary of State on October 23, 1959, Undersecretary Rubottom expressed this concern, arguing that the flights were highly prejudicial to U.S. relations with Cuba and would give Castro "the one issue which could be sure to rally the Cuban people around him and win the sympathy of other Latin Americans, thus undermining the efforts of all those desiring to bring about in Cuba a more moderate policy and one of increased friendship with the United States."[14] Rubottom's detailed recommendations to end the flights were then endorsed by the secretary of state, Christian A. Herter. On December 30, 1959, Rubottom went further, proposing to Herter that former Batista officials accused of atrocities and engaged in activities against the Cuban government be removed from Florida.[15] The Department of State continued to object to these illegal flights several months later, when U.S. policy toward Cuba had entered a much more aggressive and interventionist phase. Thus, on February 24, 1960, a confidential memo from Deputy Assistant Secretary of State for Inter-American Affairs Lester D. Mallory to Acting Secretary of State C. Douglas Dillon virtually repeated the rationale of the October 23, 1959, memo and made a new set of recommendations to stop them; Dillon approved these new recommendations.[16]

Some of these highly placed functionaries in the State Department, so concerned with their own public relations functions within the overall foreign policy division of labor, apparently failed to understand where U.S. policy was headed in this area. This phenomenon points to the qualitatively diminished weight of normal diplomatic considerations in a critical situation where far weightier interests were at stake. Thus, while Ambassador Bonsal and some State Department officials wrung their hands about air raids originating in the United States, something else was happening in more politically powerful Washington circles. At a December 16, 1959, National Security Council meeting at which Dillon was present, Rubottom was criticized for his views on Cuba, and the attorney general remarked that his department could either be tough or lenient with respect to anti-Castro elements operating in Florida. He added that he needed policy guidance before specific instructions could be given to Federal Bureau of Investigation agents in the Miami area. According to the attorney general, between thirty and forty agents in that area were spending all their time on Cuban affairs, but they were having difficulties because of uncertainty about to whether anti-Castro activities should be permitted. Allen W. Dulles of the CIA commented that the answer depended on what the anti-Castro forces were planning, since the United States could not let the Batista-type elements do whatever they wanted.[17] About a month later, at the January 14, 1960, National Security Council session (that is, before the February 24 Mallory memorandum), with Rubottom in attendance, Eisenhower's assistant for national security, Gordon Gray, asked if U.S. policy included attempting to stop anti-Castro elements from preparing actions against Cuba from U.S. territory. President Eisenhower tellingly responded that "it was perhaps better not to discuss this subject. The anti-Castro agents who should be left alone were being indicated."[18] U.S. laws, including the Neutrality Act, apparently were disregarded when important imperial interests were at stake.

Other elements within governmental circles were much less circumspect and restrained than the State Department. Admiral Arleigh Burke of the Joint Chiefs of Staff always took the hardest line on Cuba. In July 1958, Burke had proposed using U.S. troops to rescue the American hostages held by Raúl Castro.[19] Dulles was unwilling to grant respect to Cuba's leaders, arguing on February 12, 1959, that "the new Cuban officials had to be treated more or less like children. They had to be led rather than rebuffed. If they were rebuffed, like children, they were capable of doing almost anything."[20] Vice President Richard Nixon declared to his fellow members of the National Security Council in December 1959 that "we needed to find a few dramatic things to do with respect to the Cuban situation in order to indicate that we would not allow ourselves to be kicked around completely."[21] However, it is not true that Nixon began advocating the overthrow of Castro immediately after meeting the Cuban leader in April 1959, as Nixon claimed in his 1979 book, *Six Crises*,[22] where he criticized Kennedy's 1960 electoral campaign and misrepresented his own relatively moderate views at the time the interview with Fidel Castro took place.[23] Rather, Nixon took a few months before coming to regard Fidel Castro as a danger. By midsummer 1959, the vice president had begun to urge President Eisenhower and Secretary of State Christian Herter to adopt a more belligerent attitude toward the Cuban government and to consider ways to undermine it.[24]

The U.S. Congress played a very minor role in terms of U.S. government decisions concerning Cuba, as witnessed by the surrender of legislative authority over the Cuban sugar quota to the president. Nevertheless, Congress, animated for the most part by an ideology hostile to revolution and of course to Communism, was quite important in helping to turn public opinion against the Cuban leadership. Before January 1, 1959, only a handful of representatives and senators, the most vocal of which were Charles Porter and Wayne Morse of Oregon and Adam Clayton Powell of New York, had expressed any concern about let alone opposition to the misdeeds of the Batista dictatorship or any sympathy for the opposition. And even this small amount of congressional sympathy for the Cuban revolutionaries diminished further after Batista's overthrow. In fact, Morse quickly turned against the new Cuban government after the executions of Batistianos (discussed later in this chapter) early in 1959.[25] After traveling to Cuba in March 1959, Powell met with two State Department officials in charge of the Office of Caribbean and Mexican Affairs and gave them a very negative report on the situation that included a number of exaggerations and wild charges, among them the claim that the Communists had taken control of the 26th of July Movement newspaper *Revolución* (at the time and for months thereafter one of the principal press organs openly polemicizing against the Communists!). The State Department officer who drafted the report of the interview commented that Powell had been most cordial and disarmingly frank and had admitted "that he had been misled and previously misjudged several aspects of the current Cuban scene. One can speculate that he is about to change horses—among other things."[26]

When scores of Batistiano officials were executed in January 1959, U.S. Representative Wayne L. Hays called for a proscription on tourist travel to Cuba and if necessary a trade embargo. Representative Emanuel Celler of Brooklyn proposed that the issue of the executions be taken to the United Nations. Representative Victor Anfuso of New York stated that Castro was no better than Batista and that the new Cuban leader should study a map of the Western Hemisphere so he could learn the facts of life affecting the Cuban economy. Anfuso threatened to move to drastically curtail the Cuban sugar quota.[27]

Fidel Castro and Congress enjoyed a brief honeymoon during the Cuban leader's April 1959 visit to the United States. Castro appeared before the Senate Foreign Relations Committee and denied any con-

nection with Communism, thereby earning what turned out to be temporary praise and friendship from such legislators as Alabama Senator John
Sparkman and Congressman James G. Fulton of Pennsylvania. Florida's
George Smathers was more cautious, praising Castro as a "good man" but
expressing doubts about others in his government.[28]

But hostilities resumed soon thereafter, in the wake of the Cuban
government's May 1959 agrarian reform law (discussed in more detail
later in this chapter). At this point the most important congressional action of the early phase of U.S.-Castro relations took place in July 1959
when the Senate Internal Security Subcommittee, chaired by Mississippi
Senator James Eastland, openly attacked the Cuban government, taking
U.S. official criticism to a new level. The subcommittee held closed as well
as public hearings featuring testimony by Major Pedro Luis Díaz Lanz,
the former chief of the Cuban air force, who had arrived in Miami on
July 1 on a small boat. Díaz Lanz's testimony was full of charges about
Communist infiltration of the Cuban armed forces and about Castro's
support of expeditions to overthrow other Latin American governments.
These hearings had an important effect on Cuban public opinion and
benefited the Castro government by cementing the developing mass anti-
imperialist consciousness. They also placed the nascent opposition into a
clearly defensive posture, forcing it to distance itself from and even criticize the actions of the congressional committee.[29] By the fall of 1960, even
the most liberal members of the House and Senate appeared to agree that
Castro endangered American security. According to historian Richard E.
Welch Jr., the liberals were ambivalent about how to meet that danger, in
part because they did not want to appear to be left-wing pacifists uncon-
cerned with the demands of national security.[30]

U.S. GOVERNMENT POLICY AFTER THE
MAY 1959 AGRARIAN REFORM LAW

During the early months of 1959, Washington's overall policy assumed
that pressure could still reform the Cuban government and push it toward
friendlier policies concerning U.S. interests, although American policy
makers were not completely united in this orientation. While Washington worried about Cuban leaders' growing anti-imperialism, the fact remained that the new government's radical early 1959 measures (e.g., dras-

tic reductions in rents) had had very little effect on U.S. interests on the island. The important exception was the Cuban government's takeover of U.S.-owned public utilities, but this economic sector had been the expected target of any reform government in Cuba and did not by itself signify a broad offensive against U.S. and other foreign investments. In fact, in early 1959, Ambassador Bonsal even offered technical assistance to the Cuban Ministry of Communications on how to run the telephone company after the government had "intervened."[31]

U.S. policy became much more hostile—based on the conclusion that the Cuban government could not be reformed and thus had to be replaced—shortly after Havana adopted the agrarian reform law in May 1959. Although radical, the law was not Communist because it emphasized land redistribution. While it referred rather vaguely to the creation of some form of cooperatives, it did not even remotely hint that collectivization in the form of state farms would later become Cuba's predominant form of agricultural organization. Nevertheless, the agrarian reform law limited individual ownership to a maximum of 995 acres, and compensation for expropriated property was to be based on the assessed land valuation for tax purposes, which obviously underestimated the true market value. Payments were to be made with twenty-year government bonds bearing 4.5 percent annual interest.

While many important U.S. capital investments in Cuba remained unaffected by the announced agrarian reform, the law nevertheless marked the beginning of a new stage in relations between Cuba and the United States. On June 11, Washington officially responded to the agrarian reform law with a diplomatic note aptly described by U.S. historian William Appleman Williams as "proper, cold, blunt and more than a bit intimidating."[32] This note contained a number of criticisms of the law as well as some subtle threats. However, the greatest emphasis was placed on the demand for appropriate cash compensation. Subsequently, the phrase "prompt, adequate and effective compensation for American properties expropriated in accordance with the accepted principles of international law"[33] became a mantra in U.S. claims against the Cuban government. In any case, the agrarian reform clearly indicated that the Castro government had turned a page as far as Washington was concerned. Harry R. Turkel, director of the State Department's Office of Inter-American Regional Economic Affairs, succinctly summarized the U.S. view: "I interpret our policy during the first six months of the Castro regime as being one of giving him a chance to succeed and in the meantime working to strengthen the moderates around him in the hope that the extreme leftists would be discredited or shoved aside. With the signature of the Agrarian Reform Law, it seems clear that our original hope was a vain one; Castro's government is not the kind worth saving."[34]

Although the first CIA front organization (the Double Check Corporation) was set up in Miami in May 1959,[35] not until the fall of 1959 did military activities began to play a central role in U.S. Cuban policy. From June on, the U.S. government had focused its efforts first on trying to foment and develop an internal opposition inside Cuba rather than merely pressuring Havana, as had been the case earlier in the year, and second on shaping an economic strategy centering on a possible reduction or total elimination of Cuba's share of the U.S. sugar import quota.[36] In Washington, D.C., on June 1, 1959, less than a month after the approval of the agrarian reform law, eleven highly placed officials with such executive government agencies as the White House staff, the Departments of State and Agriculture, and the Council on Foreign Economic Policy held a meeting at which Department of Agriculture representatives, clearly guided by domestic concerns and ignoring imperial priorities, argued that the administration should recommend an extension of the Sugar Act without a change in the existing quotas, notwithstanding recent developments in Cuba. The only change they recommended was granting authority to the president to adjust quotas in case of a sugar shortage, which U.S. critics of the Cuban agrarian reform law predicted would arise as a result of economic disorder and chaos provoked by the measure. Rubottom and Thomas Mann, representing the State Department at this meeting, argued against the agriculture officials. Rubottom maintained that if the Sugar Act were to be extended without change, Castro would interpret the action as a vindication of his prediction that the United States would never reduce Cuba's quota in retaliation for expropriation of American properties. Rubottom wanted to keep the question of the sugar quota open to use it as leverage in obtaining amendments to that law, and he urged that the president receive authority to change the sugar quota for any reason, not just if a shortage of sugar production occurred in Cuba. At the same time, Rubottom did not want Congress to take up the issue of the sugar quotas because he feared that doing so would lead to premature and unwarranted reductions and weaken moderate Cuban forces that supported U.S. efforts to obtain changes in the agrarian reform law.

Mann declared that he could not support a bill that would assure Cuba 70 percent of all U.S. sugar imports for several years while $800 million in U.S. investments was being threatened.[37]

By the fall of 1959, relations between the U.S. and Cuban governments clearly had deteriorated considerably. By November, even Bonsal had given up all hope of influencing or winning over Castro's government. The removal of most liberal ministers from the Cuban cabinet eliminated the one remaining source of optimism for U.S. moderates who had pressed for a change from within the Cuban government. In addition, the forced resignation of anti-Communist President Manuel Urrutia in July 1959 and the less obvious but perhaps most important development—the inability of Ambassador Bonsal and Washington to coax Fidel Castro into negotiating with the United States—contributed to the growing conviction of even the most cautious elements in the U.S. government that the Castro regime had to be removed. The center of gravity of U.S. policy making had now moved to the position that some form of military intervention constituted the only remaining option. As this shift took place, the president, the CIA, and the National Security Council became ever more involved in the direct management of Cuba policy, thereby reducing the State Department's weight and influence. Although a clear hardening toward Havana had taken place in the executive branch, Congress continued to stake out even more extreme positions. Senator Eastland took advantage of his subpoena power as head of the Internal Security Subcommittee to bring a number of right-wing Cuban refugees to testify: they leveled wild charges against the Cuban government. In contrast to these witnesses, the CIA's deputy director general, C. P. Cabell, sounded almost like a liberal when he testified before Eastland's subcommittee that although Communist influence had grown a great deal since Castro had come to power, he did not believe that the new Cuban leader had been a Communist while he was a guerrilla chief fighting Batista or that he was even now a member of the Cuban Communist Party.[38]

By the end of 1959, the U.S. government was beginning to develop a program to get rid of the Castro government through the use of force. That fall, the United States successfully lobbied the reluctant British government not to provide military aircraft to Cuba.[39] In December, the State Department suggested that anti-Castro propaganda become the purview of the CIA, and small-scale lower-level operations in Cuba received official sanction from the CIA director's office. The U.S. government prepared detailed plans to train Cuban exiles for infiltration into Cuba to sabotage sugar mills and other economic targets.[40] On December 10, the Defense Department asked Gerard C. Smith, assistant secretary of state for policy planning, to prepare a policy paper on Cuba on the grounds that the military would sooner or later be called on to help.[41] On December 29, 1959, Livingston T. Merchant, undersecretary of state for political affairs, proposed to General Nathan B. Twining, chairman of the Joint Chiefs of Staff, that representatives of the two entities hold weekly meetings to discuss Cuba and other problems in the Caribbean.[42]

On January 18, 1960, the CIA set up a special task force composed mainly of veterans of the 1954 intervention against the Arbenz government in Guatemala. This task force prepared a wide-ranging attack on the Castro regime.[43] Still, President Eisenhower's mid-February assessment of the existing CIA programs considered them to be too narrow. Eisenhower wondered "why we weren't trying to identify assets for this and other things as well across the board, including even possibly things that might be drastic."[44] Eisenhower might have been influenced by the fact that Soviet leader Anastas Mikoyan had visited Cuba on February 4–13, leading to the conclusion of a new trade agreement between the Soviet Union and Cuba. Finally, on March 16, 1960, a systematic plan of covert action against the Castro regime was put into place and presented to Eisenhower for approval. Although substantial parts of this plan have not been declassified, they clearly included the U.S. creation of a unified Cuban opposition leadership located outside of that country, a shortwave radio station to be located on Swan Island, the carrying out of sabotage and intelligence activities inside Cuba, and the creation and training of an exile paramilitary force, which would take an estimated six to eight months to be ready for action. This was the origin of the invasion force that the United States landed at the Bay of Pigs in April 1961.[45] The CIA also initiated a separate project to assassinate Castro and other top Cuban leaders.[46]

THE DIE IS CAST: U.S. GOVERNMENT POLICY TOWARD CUBA AFTER FEBRUARY 1960

By early 1960, the various wings of the U.S. government were beginning to close ranks in their efforts to overthrow Castro. In a fundamental sense, the die was cast by February 1960, when the Eisenhower administration systematized its various initiatives to get rid of the Castro leadership. A few last-minute attempts to bring about an understanding between the two countries, such as the late January mediation attempted by Julio Amoedo, the Argentinean ambassador to Havana, went nowhere. After the United States began moving in the direction of overthrowing Castro by force, it clearly did not want any mediation efforts to get in the way, although for obvious reasons Washington did not put forward this position for public consumption. The United States also launched a campaign of economic warfare against the Cuban regime. For example, a $100 million loan to the Cuban government by a consortium of Dutch, French, and West German banks was countermanded under considerable pressure from Washington in March.[47]

Cuba established formal diplomatic relations with the Soviet Union in May 1960, the same month that witnessed substantially increased strains between the United States and the Soviet Union as a result of the Soviets downing an American U-2 plane flying over Russian territory. A planned summit meeting between Eisenhower and Khrushchev was canceled as a consequence of this new friction. At the end of the month, the Cuban government notified U.S. oil companies in Cuba that they would have to refine the Soviet oil Cuba was importing. These companies initially were willing to obey the government's orders under protest, but they received instructions from U.S. Secretary of the Treasury Robert B. Anderson not to comply. Anderson also persuaded the British to go along with U.S. policies, and as a result neither the U.S. companies nor the British/Dutch–owned Shell refineries agreed to process the Russian oil. Anderson and the Treasury Department acted without clearing the government's decision with the State Department,[48] an indicator of the marginality of professional diplomacy in these types of situations. On June 29, the Cuban government seized the U.S.- and British-owned refineries and had relatively little difficulty overcoming the technical problems in refining Russian oil, contrary to the dire predictions made by U.S. and British management teams.

A swift round of measures and countermeasures followed the seizure of the oil refineries. On July 6, President Eisenhower suspended Cuban sugar shipments for the remainder of the year, hypocritically claiming that he had done so because the United States could not count on Havana's ability to fulfill the remainder of the 1960 sugar quota. In fact, as Ambassador Bonsal noted later, the suspension of the sugar quota constituted part of the U.S. government's strategy to overthrow Castro, not, in reality, even a reprisal for the Cuban government's seizure of the oil refineries.[49] On July 9, Soviet Premier Khrushchev made the speech in which he, "metaphorically speaking," offered to defend Cuba from any U.S. attack with nuclear weapons if doing so proved necessary. During July, Washington continued to lobby and pressure a number of capitalist countries, particularly in Europe, to eliminate or sharply reduce their economic activities in Cuba.[50] In August, the Cuban government carried out the large-scale expropriation of the rest of the U.S.-owned properties in Cuba; the large-scale expropriation of Cuban capitalists followed in October.

By the fall of 1960, the United States had considerably tightened the economic pressures on the Cuban government: U.S. citizens were told not to travel to Cuba, and countries receiving U.S. aid were advised not to buy Cuban sugar with the money. On October 19, in the middle of a presidential campaign in which John F. Kennedy and Nixon were competing to be tougher on Castro's government, Washington announced what constituted nothing less than a full economic blockade of the island. The Eisenhower administration, acting under the authority of the Export Control Act, prohibited all U.S. exports to Cuba except medical supplies and nonsubsidized food products, exceptions that were soon eliminated.[51] On January 3, 1961, shortly before Kennedy's inauguration as president, the United States terminated diplomatic relations with Cuba.

The long-expected invasion was just now a matter of time. On April 15, three bombers piloted by U.S.-trained and -equipped Cuban refugees took off from Nicaragua in an attempt to destroy the small Cuban air force. The raid caused little damage but alerted the Cuban government to the coming invasion. A day later, speaking at the funeral for those killed in the air raid, Fidel Castro declared that the Cuban Revolution was a socialist revolution. The invasion force arrived at Girón Beach in the Bay of Pigs at on April 17; by the afternoon of April 19, the invaders had been defeated.[52]

BUSINESS, THE STATE, AND CUBA POLICY

U.S. policy toward Cuba in the period 1959–61 also reveals the roles played by the state and business interests in the development and implementation of foreign policy, helping to illuminate the options available to the revolutionary government in dealing with its northern neighbor. By itself, U.S. business could not develop a unified political front or a common strategic and tactical orientation toward Cuba's revolutionary government. The federal government in Washington had to organize business interests and translate the defense of those interests into a coherent political language and the development of sophisticated strategy and tactics. In addition, the government had to do so while keeping in mind general capitalist interests and the pursuit of geopolitical goals in the Caribbean and the Western Hemisphere. In that sense, the executive of the U.S. state was truly functioning, as Marx put it, as the committee for managing the common affairs of the U.S. capitalist class.

The executive branch, particularly the National Security Council, played the central role in the events discussed in this chapter. In that body, the president hammered out the key policies concerning Cuba in collaboration with the intelligence agencies and several other executive departments such as Treasury and State. But while certain differences existed within Washington concerning Cuba, the government's policies were more coherent and more systematic than those of corporate America.

Although events in Cuba interested the U.S. business class as a whole, the U.S. corporations with investments in Cuba were by far the most active in voicing their concerns and complaints to members of Congress, the White House, and especially the State Department. In that sense, they constituted an important source of pressure on the government and particularly on the executive branch, which was in charge of U.S. foreign policy. However, corporations did not play a decisive role in the shaping of U.S. policy toward Cuba in part because they could not put forward a unified and coherent strategy toward the Cuban government.

The most active and vocal U.S. capitalists with business interests in Cuba included Robert J. Kleberg, president of the King Ranch cattle empire headquartered in Texas, and Lawrence Crosby, chairman of the U.S.-Cuban Sugar Council, which represented U.S. sugar capital on the island. After the agrarian reform law was approved, Kleberg became very aggressive and in the summer of 1959 proposed to the president and the State Department a far more confrontational approach to the Cuban leaders than Secretary Herter or President Eisenhower, who followed Herter's advice, was willing to undertake at that moment. Crosby, a more representative businessman in frequent contact with the U.S. embassy in

Havana and the State Department in the U.S. capital, usually followed Washington's policies.[53]

Although Kleberg, Crosby, and other U.S. capitalists with investments in Cuba closely followed events in the island and actively lobbied the U.S. government to protect their interests there, no equivalent movement arose among individuals and organizations representing broader sectors of U.S. capital. One exception was the U.S. Inter-American Council, a business organization representing U.S. investors in Latin America that unanimously adopted a confrontational resolution against the Cuban government at its June 2, 1959, meeting in Chicago. The resolution was communicated to Secretary Herter on July 1, and Rubottom acknowledged receipt of the council's letter on July 29, telling the group that its suggestions and point of view were under detailed study. He promised a full reply "shortly." On October 2, Rubottom sent a formal letter to the council that included a number of generalities about the department's concern for foreign investors and related matters and then merely restated existing legislation suspending U.S. government assistance to foreign governments that did not treat U.S. interests properly.[54]

The relative absence of broad business-class intervention in this situation leads to the conclusion that Cuba had limited importance to U.S. business despite its substantial investments there. This issue remains relevant forty-five years later. American corporations are not as interested in the possibility of investing in Cuba as they are, for example, in China. Important sectors of U.S. capital—particularly midwestern agricultural and food-processing businesses—would like to see an end to the economic blockade of Cuba and would love to invest and trade there even more than they already do. Nevertheless, they have not yet been able and/or willing to summon the political clout to defeat the Cuban American right-wing lobby based in South Florida, the principal power source still defending the blockade.

TENDENCIES AMONG U.S. BUSINESSES IN CUBA

One important tendency among U.S. corporations in Cuba was to respond on the basis of a narrow, short-term vision instead of considering the long-term interests of U.S. business as a whole. This approach was evident in the different ways in which the government, represented by Treasury Secretary Anderson, and oil executives responded to Cuba's demand that U.S.-owned refineries in Cuba process oil from the Soviet Union. The same held true for Harold S. Geneen, the president of the International Telephone and Telegraph Corporation, who as late as December 14, 1959, told Assistant Secretary of State Rubottom that he did not want to speak publicly because he still had Cuban properties that had not been seized by the Cuban government. Geneen consequently adopted a moderate line on the U.S.-Cuban conflict, arguing that he did not favor redistributing the Cuban sugar quota to other countries because such a move would do nothing for Cuba in the long term. Instead, Geneen supported the notion of maintaining the Cuban sugar quota while taxing Cuban sugar imports to compensate those who had lost property in that country.[55] Similarly, although for different reasons, U.S. industrial consumers of Cuban sugar in the United States, including bottlers, bakers, and confectioners, did not support a rapid, dramatic change in sugar legislation in late November 1959 because "the industrial users consider Cuba the most secure source of sugar for the U.S. over the long run, and do not wish to see market stability sacrificed to obtain negotiating leverage on current problems with the Cuban government."[56]

Alongside this narrow, short-range view, U.S. businessmen were also swayed by a certain impressionism and volatility that was not as evident in government circles. Thus, on December 2, 1958, the group of businessmen acting as consultants to U.S. Ambassador to Cuba Earl E. T. Smith took a hard anti-Castro line and proposed that the United States "promote and give full and actual support including arms to a military civilian junta" to prevent Castro from coming to power.[57] Yet on January 6, 1959, just a few days after Batista's overthrow, many of the same people met with Daniel M. Braddock, the second-ranking official at the U.S. embassy (Smith was in the United States). On this occasion, the businessmen were almost enthusiastic about the new Cuban leadership and urged that the United States provide official recognition to the new Cuban government as soon as possible. In fact, group members were more insistent about recognition than were some embassy staff members. As Braddock reported to the State Department, Eugene A. Gilmore, the embassy's counselor for economic affairs, believed that it would be prudent to await further indications of the new government's attitude toward U.S. trade and investment but was nevertheless convinced of the need for immediate recognition after hearing the U.S. businessmen. According to Braddock's dispatch, these men were,

> unanimously of the view that present government was much better than they had hoped for, and that it has broad base of popular support (one previously strong Batista supporter said this was most popular government he had seen in Cuba in his sojourn of more than 30 years). They felt that 26th of July had shown intelligence and discipline in handling situation to date, and that Castro was unquestionably boss in Cuba. [The] group felt that early recognition would assist in strengthening 26th against more radical elements in revolutionary movement, and would possibly assist in curbing possible growth of Communist strength.[58]

Although in this case the businessmen were undoubtedly correct in their assessment of the serious political dangers involved in any further delay of U.S. recognition, it was nevertheless characteristic of the difference between businessmen and the representatives of the U.S. government that Gilmore, the diplomat specializing in economic issues, was more inclined to think in longer, systemic terms.

After the very short lived business enthusiasm for Castro gave way to outright hostility, occasions arose when U.S. investors in Cuba worried about whether the U.S. government might sacrifice their local Cuban-based interests on behalf of policies that would protect the capitalist system as a whole. Thus, in mid-December 1959, as the U.S. government was moving toward an open and full clash with the Cuban government, Crosby and Kleberg were determined that the upcoming sugar legislation should include some provision covering the rights of U.S. investors in Cuba. These investors also worried that high State Department officials might want to take advantage of the existing situation to advance other objectives of U.S. foreign policy, such as spreading the sugar quota among a larger number of countries and bringing the United States into closer compliance with international trade agreements such as the General Agreement on Tariffs and Trade. Crosby in particular believed that the interests of U.S. investors in Cuba should constitute the paramount factor in the new sugar legislation.[59]

As the conflict between Cuba and the United States deepened, U.S.

businessmen in Cuba started to acquire a consciousness of their long-term common interests. This tendency began to crystallize after the agrarian reform law was approved in May 1959 and was accompanied by a marked decline of general U.S. business confidence in the Cuban economy, as indicated by the fall in the demand for Cuban securities.[60] C. Douglas Dillon, at the time undersecretary of state for economic affairs, wrote to Ambassador Bonsal on May 22, 1959, that the law had caused great consternation in government and sugar circles. Crosby called on Assistant Secretary of State for Economic Affairs Thomas C. Mann in Washington and declared the law confiscatory and disastrous to the Cuban sugar industry. Because Bonsal had had extensive conversations in Havana with various representatives of U.S.-owned sugar mills, he was asked to come to Washington for a meeting to discuss the situation with Crosby and others as well as to discuss the question of sugar legislation.[61]

These class-conscious tendencies became more pronounced when relations between the U.S. government and Cuba deteriorated considerably. On September 24, 1959, Bonsal met in Washington with several important State Department functionaries and ten influential sugar industry executives active in Cuba. The meeting revealed a class-conscious position in the form of a domino theory of the impact of Cuban events on other Latin American and economically underdeveloped countries. Thus, Sam H. Baggett, vice president of the United Fruit Company, maintained that agrarian reform in Cuba would have far-reaching effects if it were to become a pattern for other countries in Latin America. Baggett added that if the low valuation of property and payment in IOUs spread, it would force United Fruit out of business. Mann of the State Department referred to growing nationalism worldwide and declared that the United States could not refrain from using such means as it had to protect its interests; otherwise, the United States would have to brace itself for attacks of this nature from every quarter. Finally, B. Rionda Braga, president of the Francisco Sugar Company, argued that if Castro succeeded unchallenged, there would be no respect for contracts throughout the region. W. Huntington Howell, first vice president of the West Indies Sugar Company, agreed with Braga and stated that the situation was desperate: the company was being nibbled to pieces by the Cuban government. John A. Nichols, president of the Cuban American Sugar Company, declared that the agrarian reform formed only a part of the gloomy picture and cited what he described as arbitrary wage increases, decrees lowering utility rates, new tax laws, and general arbitrary treatment. Yet a narrower sectoral approach had not totally disappeared. Lawrence Crosby indicated that the U.S. sugar industry wanted the cane lands to be exempt from the agrarian reform law, although expropriating other lands presented no real problem since U.S. capital was much less involved in nonsugar agricultural pursuits. Crosby was implicitly willing to compromise with the Cuban government if the interests of U.S. sugar capitalists could somehow be protected.[62]

It also became clear at the September 24 meeting that the sugar capitalists were already engaged in an economic boycott. This was the obvious meaning of the prediction made by Philip Rosenberg, president of the Vertientes-Camagüey Sugar Company, that Cuba would have an ample crop in 1960 but a considerably smaller crop in 1961—probably 20 percent less in the case of his company. The reason was simple: his company had stopped fertilization and new planting. He claimed that he did not want to financially support a hostile government and did not want to sit and wait for the executioner's sword to drop. Thus, while Washington was forecasting a sugar shortfall in Cuba on the basis of supposed governmental chaos, the North American sugar owners were making sure this shortfall would occur even before the government actually took over the companies' holdings. On June 29, 1959, Crosby had told the State Department that he seriously doubted reports that the mill owners were not giving advances to *colonos* for fertilizers, cleaning cane fields, and irrigation. Crosby added that his company was planning to continue such advances, "except perhaps for new cane plantings, which will not produce until 1963."[63]

The government bureaucrats who attended the September 24 meeting continued to show greater concern for political appearances than the less politically sophisticated businessmen. When William F. Oliver, president of the American Sugar Refining Company, said that he felt that sufficient sugar could be obtained from various sources other than Cuba should Congress decide to punish Havana through a reduction of the sugar quota, Rubottom and Mann quickly corrected him and pointed out that the United States had not used or desired to use the term "punish" with regard to Cuba.[64]

By mid-1960 the differences of opinion, tactics, and timing that had existed among U.S. businessmen in Cuba and between these businessmen and the U.S. government had disappeared. These forces pulled together along the lines supported and initiated by the president and the National Security Council, the only entities institutionally capable of hammering out a joint strategy and plan of action with careful attention to tactics and timing. On June 30 high State and Commerce Department officials; representatives of sugar, oil, and banking interests active in Cuba; and members of the Business Advisory Council's Committee of Consultants on Latin America attended a meeting in Washington. The Committee of Consultants presented a report on how to deal with Cuba, and none of those in attendance raised any substantive objections. Remarkably, the committee had come up with pretty much the same type of recommendations that Eisenhower and the National Security Council had been elaborating during the previous months, including the suggestions that Washington join with other countries in exposing Cuban government's Communist orientation; that a strong note should be presented to Havana demanding just, adequate, and effective compensation for expropriated U.S. properties; that radio broadcasting to Cuba should be encouraged; that the Cuban situation should be brought before the Organization of American States in consultation with other Latin American countries; that the premium price that the United States paid for Cuban sugar should be eliminated and the president should receive discretionary authority to alter the sugar quotas; that exchange and trade controls should be imposed to eliminate Cuba's dollar income; that aid and encouragement should be given to the Cuban opposition to overthrow the Castro regime; and that a white paper should be published to show how Cuba threatened peace in the hemisphere.[65]

At a minimum, this discussion suggests that had the Cuban government chosen the strategy of making deals with individual U.S. firms or even business sectors such as the oil refineries, this approach probably would not have succeeded. The Cuban government would have needed to convince the U.S. government that in making such deals the revolutionary leaders were willing to recognize the sacrosanct principle of "prompt, adequate, and effective compensation" for seized U.S. properties as well as to give up any plans to break with the United States and ally with the Communist world.

THE CUBAN REVOLUTION AND U.S. SOCIETY IN 1959

We have been examining the roles played by the legislative and the executive branches of the federal government as well as powerful business interests in the development and implementation of U.S. Cuban policy. However, achieving a better understanding of the dynamics of empire requires attending to certain features of the metropolis itself—in particular, how the political climate that provides popular acquiescence if not support to the interests of the dominant business class and its political allies in Washington differs from that of nonimperial societies. One of the most striking features of U.S. political culture is its inability to understand—let alone sympathize with—social revolution. This was especially true of the period that preceded the antiwar and social movements of the 1960s. While the civil rights movement had already come into existence by 1960, it had not yet become a national phenomenon, as it had by 1963, and it had not yet fully developed a radical wing (a process that began in 1960 with the sit-in movement and the activities of Robert Williams and his Monroe, North Carolina, chapter of the National Association for the Advancement of Colored People).

Castro enjoyed broad sympathy in the United States while he was fighting in the Sierra Maestra against the Batista dictatorship, and his struggle was widely understood in liberal-democratic and often romantic terms. For a number of reasons, the radicalization of the revolution after Castro came to power sharply reduced U.S. popular support for the Cuban leader. Nevertheless, a small but active minority supported the Cuban revolutionary leadership and played a significant role in the rebirth of a left-wing movement in the United States. This became evident in the protests against the U.S.-sponsored April 1961 Bay of Pigs invasion.[66] On the one hand, these protests were small and politically ineffective in comparison with the gigantic demonstrations against the war in Vietnam that took place later in the decade or with the anti-imperialist movement at the end of the nineteenth century. The Treaty of Paris—hostile to the interests of the rebels in Cuba and the Philippines—was almost defeated in the U.S. Senate in February 1899, and anti-imperialists managed to stir up a major public discussion in the United States.[67] On the other hand, the movement in support of the Cuban revolutionaries of the late 1950s and early 1960s constituted a significant departure from the virtual absence of public dissent when the CIA launched its 1954 proxy intervention in Guatemala.[68] Nevertheless, in 1962 William Appleman Williams viewed American political culture as fundamentally hostile to revolution: "It has been so long since we had a revolution that we are very much out of touch with that rudimentary feature of political and social reality. This is true even if one views the Civil War, at least in some respects, as a revolution. One hundred years—let alone two centuries—is a long time between revolutions. No other major country in the world has been tucked away in a cocoon for anything approaching that length of time."[69]

The problem was not that the American public had no legitimate reasons for concern about the fate of democracy and civil liberties in Fidel Castro's Cuba but that these legitimate concerns were subordinated to what was at best a tepid, nonmilitant, business-as-usual liberalism that did not question the U.S. empire in any fundamental way. U.S. Cold War liberalism had virtually no legitimacy in the eyes of the one public that counted the most in this context: the great majority of the Cuban people, who were being radicalized and won over by the Castro leadership.

When in the early days of the revolution Congress held outrageous hearings, such as the ones featuring former Cuban air force major Díaz Lanz in June 1959, Ambassador Bonsal and the State Department insisted that they had no control over such right-wing grandstanding because of the separation of powers. However, the average Cuban did not have to be a sophisticated political analyst to realize that such congressional hearings were quite important in helping to create a climate of public opinion justifying U.S. intervention in or reprisals against Cuba.

Bonsal and the State Department also insisted that because the United States had freedom of the press, they were not responsible for whatever unfavorable coverage American newspapers and magazines might provide about Cuba. In fact, the press was even more important than Congress in generating a climate hostile to Cuba. This was especially true of the prominent Luce publications, headed by *Time*, which became nearly obsessed with uncovering any damning fact they could find or invent about Cuba.[70] A number of U.S. journalists, some of them quite influential, such as Herbert Matthews of the *New York Times* and Jules Dubois of the *Chicago Tribune*, had strongly supported Castro before the triumph of the revolution, although Dubois came to oppose the revolutionary leader during his first year in power.[71] Furthermore, as Richard E. Welch Jr. has argued, in January 1959 most of the U.S. media offered cautious approval of the Cuban Revolution. This attitude, according to Welch, was based on a belated recognition of the cruelties and corruption of the Batista dictatorship, the novelty of the bearded Castro as a Latin American political figure, and the Fidelista assurances that they would bring U.S.-style political democracy as well as social justice to Cuba.[72] But that is precisely the point: the U.S. press could muster a degree of sympathy for the Cuban revolutionaries only to the extent that their politics could be understood in terms of the U.S. political system, in which New Deal liberalism constituted the outer limits, on the left, of both the possible and the desirable.

An early test of the ability of the press and public opinion in the United States, including much of liberal opinion, to understand the Cuban Revolution—or any revolution, for that matter—came soon after Batista's overthrow. Starting in January, several hundred Batistiano members of the police and army were executed under widely varying conditions of legal due process.[73] A great hue and cry broke out in the American press and Congress. As Tad Szulc and Karl E. Meyer have described the reaction, "Members of Congress and editorial writers, many of whom had evinced a remarkable stoic detachment about atrocities committed by the Batista dictatorship, were suddenly aroused by the execution of Batista henchmen by revolutionary firing squads."[74] In fact, these executions met with overwhelming approval among Cubans of almost all political inclinations (a reaction that perhaps resembled that aroused by the lynching of secret policemen in 1956 in Hungary). Actually, these punishments constituted an advance on the application of revolutionary justice at other times in Cuban history—for example, during the 1933 revolution. The executions, organized by the new government, prevented informal lynchings. At the very least, torturers and assassins were properly identified, and no innocent bystanders fell prey to the revolutionary settling of accounts. The arrogance and paternalism of the U.S. press and Congress met with wholesale rejection by the great majority of Cubans, who were at the very least suspicious of Americans' sudden interest in the fate of human rights in their country. As Szulc and Meyer have pointed out, two years later, when a coup d'état in South Korea brought strongly anti-Communist military officers into power, shootings and jailings occurred, yet no one rose in Congress to propose any punishment for South Korea and little talk of "bloodbaths" arose.[75]

Moreover, while the U.S. press and public opinion were denouncing the Cuban Revolution, it was receiving broad sympathy and solidarity from the rest of Latin America, particularly from those countries that had recently suffered under dictatorial rule. One important example was Venezuela, where the Pérez Jiménez dictatorship had been overthrown exactly one year earlier. Sympathy for Cuba was by no means limited to the political Left but included a much wider public with democratic concerns. In addition, at this early point the Soviet Union and the international Communist movement had barely taken notice of events in Cuba.

This contrast between the United States and Latin America was important in yet another sense. For most Cubans and other Latin Americans, the United States lacked the credibility, the political credentials, to criticize the revolution. The repudiation of U.S. criticisms was not incompatible with an admiration for the U.S. standard of living and other accomplishments of U.S. culture (sports, movies, and so forth). Rather, this repudiation concerned U.S. business and foreign policies. In Cuba, significant elements of the middle and upper classes no doubt were profoundly pro–United States in the political and every other sense, and for them, their northern neighbor could do no wrong. But such was not the case for the vast majority of Cubans.

World War II, to a certain degree, enhanced the U.S. image as the perceived enemy of dictatorship and fascism, but its record of interventions at the time of the 1933 revolution against the Machado dictatorship and during the earlier independence struggle against Spain at the end of the nineteenth century had not been forgotten. On balance, the role of the United States in Cuban history was still seen in a negative light. Washington's support for the military coup against the democratically elected government in Guatemala in 1954[76] and its general support for Latin American military dictatorships in the name of anti-Communism further undermined U.S. moral and political credibility, as of course did U.S. complicity in arming and supplying the Batista regime.[77] It stands to reason that under these circumstances, the United States would encounter much resentment when it began making demands and setting itself up as the judge and jury of acceptable political behavior.

We now return to the question posed at the beginning of this chapter: was a different U.S. policy ever possible? Could the Cuban Revolution have taken a form that would have been acceptable to the United States? The comparative method is helpful in answering this question. I will look at the views and role played by Ambassador Philip Bonsal, the most moderate[78] of the U.S. officials dealing directly with Cuba, and then I will examine the prior example of the 1952 revolution in Bolivia, the only social revolution in Latin America during the Cold War that the United States accepted and supported. How does Bonsal, when compared to more conservative U.S. officials, show the limits of U.S. policy makers' willingness to accommodate revolutionary change? What differences between Bolivia and Cuba help to explain such significantly different treatments by the United States?

The Role of Ambassador Bonsal

A close examination of Bonsal's thinking and actions may indicate the limits of what the United States could have tolerated in Cuba in the late 1950s and early 1960s. Bonsal was a career diplomat appointed to represent the United States in Cuba in February 1959, shortly after Batista's overthrow. Significantly, he had just served as the U.S. ambassador to Bolivia. Bonsal projected a positive image. He was respectful and polite and appeared to treat the Cuban leaders and people as equals. He certainly lacked the proconsular style of the reactionaries who had preceded him while Batista was in power, ambassadors Arthur Gardner and Earl E. T. Smith. At least until the fall of 1959, Bonsal followed a policy of exerting pressure phrased by diplomatically correct means and attempting to co-opt the revolution as much as possible. He tried to open negotiations with the Cuban government, including the necessary concessions involved in any such practice. Implicit in this view was the idea that whatever concessions went to the Cuban government would more than pay for themselves by the institutionalized limitations on the revolutionary process. These negotiations never took place, however. Bonsal was also strongly oriented toward the relatively weak liberal wing of the revolutionary government, which included such figures as Felipe Pazos and Rufo López Fresquet. But the U.S. ambassador also hoped for a break between Fidel Castro and the pro-Soviet and pro–Partido Socialista Popular (old Cuban Communist Party) wing of the 26th of July Movement represented by Raúl Castro and Ernesto "Che" Guevara.[79] Others ranging from independent non-Communist leftists and the 26th of July labor leadership at one end of the Cuban political spectrum to liberals and the upper and middle classes on the other also hoped for this split.

Bonsal's attempts to deal with Fidel Castro were frustrated by Castro's great reluctance to meet with the U.S. ambassador and by the Cuban leader's refusal to turn the other cheek to U.S. criticisms, let alone interference. The newly victorious Cuban leader was far more likely to make anti-imperialist pronouncements than he had been while serving as the head of the broadly based anti-Batista coalition, which tried to avoid conflicts with the United States. As Bonsal became increasingly disillusioned with Castro, particularly after May 1959, the ambassador's policy increasingly became one of maintaining strong pressure on the Cuban government while arguing within U.S. government circles against precipitate U.S. action. Bonsal sought to buy time to allow for the development of an internal Cuban opposition, which he hoped would at a minimum significantly curb the actions of the Castro leadership. The ambassador had counted on significant Cuban middle sectors and what he saw as their "democratic preferences, the devotion to the so-called middle-class social and economic values," as well as on the individualism and conservatism of the dominant elements in Cuban society. Years later, Bonsal came to see the failure of this perspective as one of his most important errors of judgment.[80]

This approach of buying time shaped and informed Bonsal's moderate politics even before he had totally given up on Fidel Castro. Thus on May 6, 1959, Bonsal reported to the State Department that he had received news from varied sources, including some well connected with the government of Cuba, that Castro was increasingly disturbed about Communist activities and that tensions were developing between him and his brother, Raúl, regarding a number of issues. The ambassador also reported that more and more Cubans, both in and out of government, were taking outspoken stands against Communism. Bonsal complained that exaggerated stories from the United States regarding the influence and strength of Communism within the Cuban government, such as Stuart Novins's May 3 CBS broadcast, were not helpful in the highly nationalistic atmosphere prevailing in Cuba. Significantly, Bonsal concluded, it would be "much better that initiative for correction come from within Cuba and I am hopeful it will."[81]

On March 26, 1959, the National Security Council seriously considered the rather extreme action of denying a visa to Fidel Castro for his April visit to the United States at the invitation of the American Society of Newspaper Editors.[82] Bonsal, however, sent a telegram to the State Department on April 14, 1959, insisting—in what was to become his perennial warning—that if Castro were to fail, that failure must not be attributed to the actions of the U.S. government. Furthermore, Bonsal optimistically (and paternalistically) predicted that if Castro remained in power,

> we will have many opportunities of discreetly influencing choices
> of courses of actions and of bringing him to a closer understanding
> of political and economic conditions to which he is subjected. I
> respectfully submit that some slight progress has already been made
> and am convinced that Castro can recognize and be guided by facts,
> although his temperament and sensitivity to criticism will probably
> lead to further unfortunate utterances. . . . Condemnation of
> Castro for these utterances alone will be taken as U.S. opposition to
> Cuban revolution which still has very considerable support and was
> justified on many counts.[83]

Even in late September 1959, when relations between the United States and Cuba had already begun to seriously deteriorate, Bonsal wrote a memorandum to Rubottom strongly objecting to cuts in the U.S. quota for Cuban sugar, which "would prove disastrous not only to our relations with Cuba but also to our relations with other Latin American countries. In effect, we would be permanently diminishing the resources of the entire Cuban people and would open a wound which would be a long time in healing."[84]

A decade after Bonsal left Cuba as the last U.S. ambassador to that country, he reflected on other concessions that his country could have made and for which he had hoped early in his stay in Cuba. He had privately wanted a change in the status of the Guantánamo Naval Base that would allow Cuban participation in its operation, similar to the rights enjoyed by North Atlantic Treaty Organization allies on the U.S. bases in their countries. He would also have liked to see a modification of the tariff arrangements between Cuba and the United States that would have allowed the island greater industrialization and agricultural diversification. According to Bonsal, the sale of sugar to the United States should have been placed on a contractual basis between the two countries, as opposed to the current practice of Congress periodically and unilaterally determining how much Cuban sugar could be allowed into the United States. Bonsal also allowed for the possibility or even desirability of transferring from foreign to national ownership some U.S. properties in Cuba. He specifically mentioned the extensive cane lands held by the United Fruit Company and the U.S.-owned public utilities, with a negotiation through "quiet diplomacy" of adequate and prompt compensation that would be "equitable" and would not interrupt "the flow into Cuba of private capital for many much-needed purposes."[85]

Bonsal's willingness to allow for Cuban reforms clearly assumed that the island would remain not only a capitalist country but also a member of the Western political alliance; in the specific case of Latin America, this meant a continued adherence to "the Rio Treaty [against Communist penetration of the Americas], the Charter of the Organization of American States, and the other agreements that defined the rights and duties of the inter-American community."[86] This precluded not only an allegiance to the Communist bloc but also any neutralist or independent stance in international affairs.

Bonsal also approved of the critical arms embargo that Washington maintained against Havana, which included successful pressures on the British and some other European governments not to sell weapons to the Cuban government when Fidel Castro attempted to replace obsolete American weapons with West European military hardware. The arms embargo had originally been declared in March 1958, when the Batista regime entered into a political crisis from which it never recovered. Despite the embargo, the United States permitted certain "exceptional" shipments of military supplies, and the U.S. military mission remained in Cuba to advise the Batista regime until being asked to leave by the newly established revolutionary government in January 1959.[87] The United States continued its arms embargo after Castro came to power, arguing that the weapons might be used against its Caribbean neighbors, particularly the Dominican Republic, ruled by longtime dictator Rafael Trujillo. Although Castro's Cuban government had supported military incursions against the Dominican dictator, Trujillo had also attempted to intervene in Cuba. Most important, at this time Trujillo's military and in particular his air force was superior to Cuba's. Still, according to Bonsal, "there had been no reason to change United States [arms] policy after the fall of Batista, once it had become clear that Castro's policies toward his neighbors were inimical to peace in the area."[88] As for the successful U.S. effort to prevent Britain from selling planes to Cuba, Bonsal rejected the Cuban argument that the planes were essential to the defense of the island.[89]

Bonsal's moderation was even less in evidence when it came to fundamental capitalist principles. He was always unambiguous in his insistence that any expropriation of U.S. properties must be compensated by the Cuban government. After Bonsal had an encouraging meeting with Cuban Foreign Minister Raúl Roa, however, the U.S. ambassador wrote to the State Department on July 31, 1959, recommending a compromise, in the context of possible "unpublicized" negotiations with the Cuban government, between the U.S. demand for immediate cash payment and the Cuban proposal of twenty-year bonds based on municipal tax registrations.[90] Significantly, Acting Secretary of State Dillon responded the next day by authorizing Bonsal to enter into negotiations with the Cuban government but said nothing about the proposed compromise.[91] Thus, while the U.S. ambassador to Havana was willing to make concessions to the Cuban government, the capitalist contractual principle of compensation was untouchable as far as he was concerned.

Along similar lines and notwithstanding his later claim that he had favored revising tariff agreements to support agricultural diversification in Cuba, Bonsal officially complained to the Cuban government about restrictions on the importation of wheat, flour, and rice in spite of a severe lack of dollar reserves in the Cuban treasury. In this context, Bonsal invoked "certain rights which the United States enjoyed under international agreements."[92] The Batista regime had looted the treasury and left Cuba in a financial mess. Consequently, the country was confronting a situation where foreign-exchange reserves had reached a dangerously low point and the balance of payments was precarious, and a budget deficit existed. Conversations between the International Monetary Fund (IMF) and the Cuban government had led nowhere. A memo from the State Department's Bureau of Inter-American Affairs at the time of Castro's visit to the United States in April 1959 addressed the issue of balance-of-payments loans with the business-as-usual recommendation that these loans should be granted only after Cuba had made commitments to the IMF on the basis of its technical and professional advice. The State Department stated that it would be willing to study economic development loans "on a case by case basis taking into account the availability of private capital for these projects."[93] The Cuban government's strategy for dealing with the difficult financial situation relied heavily on steep excise taxes to curtail certain imports as well as on the introduction of foreign-exchange controls on capital and other transactions by local business-people. Not surprisingly, the IMF disapproved of such measures limiting free trade and wanted instead to address the issues of budget and credit prospects. Argentina's recent experience with a similar IMF-approved loan had been accompanied by lowered wages, price increases, and social-welfare budget cuts, measures that were totally incompatible with a popular revolution committed to raising the standard of living of Cuba's laboring classes. In addition, a Treasury Department background briefing paper prepared for Castro's April visit insisted that the satisfaction of any Cuban request for economic aid be made contingent on acceptance of an IMF stabilization loan or concrete assurances regarding the future role of foreign capital in the nationalist development program.[94] Bonsal did not register any "moderate" objections to any of these policies; only later, in 1971, did he suggest, while professing naïveté, that the conversations between the IMF and the Cuban government were inconclusive "in spite of the goodwill shown by all concerned at the Washington end."[95]

In the end, even though Bonsal had given up any hope of influencing or winning over Castro's government by November 1959, the Eisenhower administration completely bypassed the ambassador, failing even to consult him when adopting harsh economic, political, and military measures against Cuba in 1960.[96] He made a last-minute proposal to prevent a ban on Cuban sugar imports by establishing a joint claims commission, including arbitration, to which the Cuban government would make available on an annual basis a negotiated sum of money for the payment of adjudicated claims; the United States would establish a negotiated sugar quota from which, in part at least, the Cuban government could obtain the necessary resources to pay for the settlement of U.S. claims. However, Bonsal recognized that his proposal had "in the Washington mood of those days . . . only the faintest chance of being considered at all."[97] Until he finally returned to Washington, Bonsal continued to insist that the

United States should not place itself in the position of being blamed for things going wrong in Cuba because of the effects this situation would have in both Cuba and the rest of Latin America. He also did not give up on the strategy of buying time. Bonsal specifically argued, in fact, that harsh U.S. measures would have been more appropriate in an atmosphere of declining rather than rising revolutionary fervor.[98]

In sum, Bonsal had the outlook of an intelligent and above all patient reformist conservative. He was willing to support and tolerate some reforms but nevertheless was conservative because his overall goal was preserving the U.S. empire in Latin America, although he sought to do so in a more enlightened manner than his superiors in Washington and the corporate world were willing to contemplate. Again, one is struck by the constitutional inability of both Bonsal and the system he intelligently represented even to understand the nature of radical change.

Why Did the United States Support the Bolivian Revolution but Not the Cuban Revolution?

In 1952, less than seven years before the triumph of the Cuban Revolution, a social revolution began in Bolivia. Led by the Movimiento Nacionalista Revolucionario (MNR, Nationalist Revolutionary Movement) and by the Mine Workers Federation, the organization of the Bolivian tin miners allied with the MNR, a bloody but successful uprising took place both in the cities and in mining areas. The largest mines were nationalized; universal suffrage was established, thereby enfranchising the illiterate Indian population; a substantial agrarian reform law was approved; and the old professional army was downgraded. Nothing like this had happened in Latin America since the Mexican Revolution.[99]

Unlike Cuba, which was among the top four Latin American countries in terms of economic development during the 1950s, landlocked Bolivia was one of the two poorest countries in the Western Hemisphere (the other was Haiti). The United States had a major presence in Cuba, particularly in regard to investments in sugar and other industries, as well as a major U.S. naval base in Guantánamo and substantial political influence in the affairs of the island republic. In contrast, the U.S. involvement in faraway Bolivia was relatively minor by any of these criteria. U.S. capital investment played only a small role in tin mining and was virtually absent among the landowners expropriated under the land reform.

In Bolivia, the ruling MNR had also led the revolution. In Cuba, in contrast, the ruling Communist Party was established only through a merger of the 26th of July Movement, the old pro-Moscow Communists, and the Directorio Revolucionario (Revolutionary Directorate) in the mid-1960s, after the major revolutionary changes had already been carried out. In 1952, the Bolivian Communists split into two small parties, neither of which had much influence, unlike the prerevolutionary Cuban Communist Party.

The MNR was a middle-class nationalist movement. Historically, it had advocated only fairly moderate reforms while calling for support from workers and peasants.[100] The MNR considered the masses too underdeveloped to struggle and took a consciously conspiratorial and elitist orientation. This led the party to support a 1943 coup that provided it with its first brief experience in helping to run the nation. However, after this government was ousted by a 1946 coup, the MNR turned to the rising revolutionary labor movement. To cement this alliance, the party committed itself for the first time to a program including universal suffrage, agrarian reform, and nationalization of the mines.[101]

The Bolivian labor movement, rooted in the militant miners' union, was explicitly socialist and had a revolutionary orientation significantly influenced by Trotskyism. Many union leaders had joined the MNR in the late 1940s, forming a left wing, led by Juan Lechín, head of the miners.[102] But the MNR remained dominated by its reformist middle-class leadership. Once in power, many of these elements became the right wing of the party under the leadership of Hernán Siles Zuazo, who served as president of Bolivia from 1956 to 1960. Unlike the MNR's Left, the Right did not want to draw the peasantry into revolutionary activities. The rightists feared peasant uprisings, perhaps because many of the rightist leaders were small and medium-sized landlords and because their Spanish-oriented culture caused them to fear the Indian peasant masses. However, in the late fall of 1952 and early winter of 1953, a second revolutionary wave of widespread peasant protest led to the adoption of an agrarian reform law that completely transformed the country.[103] After the revolutionary regime sanctioned land distribution, the MNR's rightists found support among many of the peasant caciques who emerged during the postrevolutionary period. President Hernán Siles Zuazo, a leading rightist, used peasant militias to break unauthorized strikes and generally encouraged a growing split between the organized labor movement and the peasantry. Finally, the center constituted the party's smallest and weakest group. That faction was led by Víctor Paz Estenssoro, president from 1952 until 1956 and again from 1960 until his overthrow by a military coup in 1964. Pragmatic nationalists unlike the rightists, the centrists had a vision of a developed and modernized Bolivia and sought the rapid creation of a modern, developed nation-state. They were flexible, even to the point of making at least temporary accommodations to the labor Left if necessary.[104]

Nationalization, Compensation, and Private Property

The Cuban revolutionaries nationalized most of the economy within the first two years of taking power and made short shrift of the issue of compensation. Most of the leaders of the Bolivian MNR, however, insisted on compensation despite the opposition of the labor movement and the MNR Left, which generally though not always consistently or at the most critical moments supported the principle of nationalization without indemnification. This position was a prerequisite for the political support and subsequent economic aid that Bolivia received from the U.S. government,[105] which always insisted on the legal principle of compensation for expropriated property despite the fact that relatively little U.S. investment was at stake in Bolivia.

Bolivia's revolutionary government initially declared a state monopoly on the export and sale of all minerals, including tin, the country's principal product, and moved to protect small private mine operators. After several months, the need to weaken the tin barons led to the October 1952 nationalization of the big three companies owned by the Patiño, Aramayo, and Hochschild families. A state corporation, the Corporación Minera de Bolivia (Comibol), was established to administer these nationalized mines.[106]

The law nationalizing the mines clearly represented a compromise intended to mollify the various factions of the MNR as well as the United States. It did not affect small and medium-sized mining companies, including those owned by foreigners such as the U.S.-based Grace and Company, and it established that the owners of the nationalized companies would be indemnified. In general, the nationalization had only a relatively minor impact on U.S. interests. About 20 percent of the shareholders in the Patiño family's tin company were U.S. citizens, although the share of U.S. investments in tin mining amounted to just 10 percent of the total nationalized capital.[107]

U.S. Policy toward the Bolivian Revolution

When the Bolivian Revolution erupted in April 1952, the U.S. course of action was far from obvious. The MNR leaders were the same people Washington had forced out of the Villaroel administration in the mid-1940s as Nazi sympathizers. The MNR's ideological influences during the 1930s had included fascism. Then, after World War II, MNR leaders came to be suspected of Communist links, a suspicion encouraged by the Marxist elements of their program and by support from Bolivian Communists in the 1951 elections. The MNR's proposal to nationalize the tin mines did not exactly endear the party to U.S. officials under the prevailing McCarthyite climate. However, aside from its demand for nationalization and its leftist rhetoric, the MNR program was rather vague and did not contain a specific plan of governmental action, probably because of the party's political heterogeneity.[108]

Washington's immediate reaction to the 1952 revolution was to withhold recognition. Implied in this hostile gesture was a serious threat that the United States would not negotiate tin purchases with the Bolivian revolutionary government. This clearly provided Washington with a great deal of bargaining power. Faced with similar hostile acts, Fidel Castro's revolutionary government, which had received recognition soon after taking power, frequently and from the beginning responded with loud protests and mass demonstrations denouncing U.S. imperialist policies. The MNR, however, kept a low profile and dedicated itself to calming U.S. fears. The Bolivian party insisted that its administration would be peaceful and would respect international agreements and private property. It pledged that the nationalization of the mines would not be rushed and insisted that the new Bolivian government wanted to reach an agreement with the mine owners. In early May 1952, provisional president Siles Zuazo asserted that the MNR opposed Communism and was independent of Moscow, Washington, and Perón's Argentina.[109] Finally, the United States formally recognized the revolutionary regime on June 2, 1952, a little less than two months after the April revolution. By then, Washington had been reassured that compensation would be paid for expropriated mining properties.[110]

In addition to diplomatic recognition, the United States provided an aid program to Bolivia after Milton Eisenhower, the president's brother, visited the country in mid-1953. Eisenhower was impressed by the MNR leaders and became convinced that they were not Communists. U.S. aid was multifaceted and even included an unusual element: budget support to help cover substantial governmental deficits. An important byproduct of this aid program was the development of close personal and political ties between U.S. diplomats and technicians and their Bolivian counterparts as well as the MNR leadership.[111] These links would be greatly strengthened when John F. Kennedy assumed office in early 1961: Bolivian President Víctor Paz Estenssoro became a favorite of the Kennedy White House. Here was a democratically elected president whose moderate but generally progressive policies could be held up as an example of Kennedy's Alliance for Progress in its Latin American propaganda struggle against the Cuban Revolution.

By the early 1960s, however, the Bolivian Revolution was well on its way to becoming domesticated and subject to U.S. control. An important step in this process was the stabilization plan that Bolivia was forced to adopt in 1957 to bring to an end a hyperinflation crisis. To assist in implementing this plan, the United States sent a June 1956 financial mission headed by George Jackson Eder, a lawyer formerly with the Commerce Department and International Telephone and Telegraph. Eder, a stalwart defender of the free market and an opponent of Keynesian economics, worked closely with President Siles Zuazo. Leftist leaders, headed by Juan Lechín, the leader of the tin miners, and Nuflo Chávez, the vice president, opposed the stabilization program on the grounds that it would not promote economic development, would benefit private interests at the expense of public welfare, and would extract more sacrifices from the poor than from the rich. But Eder threatened to cut off U.S. aid if the plan was not thoroughly implemented. This threat was subsequently used several times to force Bolivia to comply with U.S. wishes. For example, Washington threatened to suspend aid if Lechín, who served as Paz's vice president from 1960 to 1964, became the MNR presidential candidate in 1964, as had been the general understanding among MNR leaders at the time of the 1960 elections. By this time, the Bolivian military had regained sufficient strength to demand and win the replacement of the civilian who was to be Paz's running mate by General René Barrientos.[112] Similarly, after Lyndon Johnson suspended an economic agreement with Bolivia, Paz was forced to sever diplomatic relations with Cuba to have the agreement reinstated.[113] Although the stabilization program eventually checked inflation, it did so at the cost of significantly limiting Bolivia's national independence and shifting the country in the direction of a free-market capitalist model.[114] In short, Eder's program substantially influenced the Bolivian revolutionary process in a conservative direction.

Another major step on Bolivia's road to becoming more conservative was the restructuring of the tin industry. The Triangular Plan, jointly funded by the U.S. and West German governments and by the Inter-American Bank, was implemented shortly after Paz became Bolivia's president in 1960. To take care of the heavy debts incurred by Comibol, the plan's financial sponsors granted loans with generous interest and repayment terms. In exchange, however, Comibol had to dismiss more than a fifth of its labor force and close an unspecified number of mines. Enterprises that restructured received new investments or subsidies.[115] The closeness between the Kennedy and Paz administrations resulted in a great expansion of U.S. aid to Bolivia, which rose by more than 600 percent between 1960 and 1964. Paz felt increasingly confident and pressed ahead with the Triangular Plan, a decision that resulted in conflict in the mines, including strikes, lockouts, and the jailing of labor leaders. Paz had earlier rejected, under U.S. pressure, a Soviet offer to give credits to Bolivia for the construction of a badly needed tin smelter as well as for a variety of transportation, public works, and economic projects.[116] The conflicts provoked by the Triangular Plan reached a high point in 1963. On August 3, Paz decreed the abolition of *control obrero* (workers' control) in the nationalized tin mines. On August 23, he implemented an agreement with Washington whereby Bolivia would receive increased economic aid in exchange for purchasing practically all manufactured products from the United States.[117]

The Bolivian Army, the Revolutionary Militias, and U.S. Policy

A very important feature of the Bolivian Revolution, marking it as one of the few authentic social revolutions in twentieth-century Latin America, was the role played by the miners' and peasants' militias. These groups were far more autonomous than the Cuban militias created in late 1959. Contrary to the myths propagated by supporters of the Castro regime abroad, the Cuban militias were created and always remained under the firm control and management of the representatives of the central state.

The left wing of the MNR and other revolutionary forces, such as the

Trotskyists, a small but significant current with considerable influence among the tin miners, wanted to eliminate the traditional army. The rightists opposed any move in that direction. Under a compromise, the officer corps was thoroughly purged by a military tribunal, not a revolutionary court, and the army was greatly reduced in size. An estimated 80 percent of the armed forces were demobilized within a matter of days, and the proportion of the central government budget allocated to the military declined from 23.0 percent in 1952 to 6.7 percent in 1957. The old military academy was closed. Shortly thereafter, a new air force academy was inaugurated, and the military academy was reopened with a new name and approach, including the recruitment of officers from humble social backgrounds—lower-class mestizos and educated Indians. For several years, the reorganized military was forced to maintain a very low political profile, leading some observers to think that the army had been entirely eliminated from Bolivian social and political life.[118]

This situation did not last very long. As the MNR became more conservative, the militias' role declined and the traditional army's power grew, although not without a great deal of friction and conflict. The clash between President Siles and the leaders of the miners' and peasants' movements over the economic stabilization program led the government to begin rebuilding the armed forces. The militias declined, counting no more than sixteen thousand men in 1963, a sharp drop from their 1956 peak between fifty thousand and seventy thousand. Military appropriations rose to more than double their lowest point, reaching 13.9 percent of the budget in 1964.[119]

Washington played an important role in remilitarizing Bolivian society, exerting extensive pressure on the government to rebuild and strengthen the traditional armed forces.[120] In 1956, the two countries renewed agreements permitting the stationing of U.S. military officers in the capital city, La Paz, and the U.S. economic mission began to provide technical advice to Bolivian law enforcement agencies. By early 1964, twenty of twenty-three senior Bolivian army officers had either attended the School of the Americas in Panama or had visited the United States. Many of these officers would occupy major government positions in the military regimes that succeeded the 1964 overthrow of the MNR government.[121]

In sum, the contrasts between the Bolivian and Cuban revolutions and the U.S. responses to them are clear and important. First and most obvious, the Bolivian Revolution lacked a figure comparable to Fidel Castro, an apparently unchallengeable leader who could by virtue of personal authority, prestige, and power prevail over the conflicting ideological currents within and outside the revolutionary camp. By withholding an early and clear commitment to a specific political organization and program, Fidel Castro retained a freedom of action that immensely enhanced his ability to dispose of his social and political enemies one at a time, thereby preventing the formation of an early and strong opposition coalition. Such a situation clearly did not exist in Bolivia.

In addition, the thirty-two-year-old Castro and the other young revolutionary leaders, all inexperienced in governmental matters, had the support of the experienced leadership cadre of the pro-Moscow Cuban Communists in the crucial early years of revolutionary consolidation, even though the power of these older leaders declined in the following years. The influence exercised by the Communists and their friends in the pro-Soviet wing of the 26th of July Movement was, of course, anathema to Washington. By the same token, the weakness of the Bolivian Communists reassured Washington and facilitated U.S. recognition of and aid to that country.

The right wing in the Bolivian revolutionary camp was much stronger than its equivalent in the early revolutionary government of Cuba, both in terms of relative size and, more important, in terms of organized power. The right wing of the Cuban revolutionary government in 1959 was weak most of all because it was fundamentally subordinate to Castro and was thus in no position to bargain independently for its views on social and economic policies or to recruit openly among the population at large. Ironically, the potential middle-class constituency for the Cuban government's right wing was far larger than the middle-class supporters of the MNR Right. In contrast, the MNR Right was a major player in the policy bargaining that took place within the Bolivian revolutionary coalition. As a result, the right wing seriously limited the radicalism of the revolutionary process and, probably more critical, became an important U.S. ally. It is thus no wonder that Ambassador Bonsal, with his ample experience in Bolivia, tried to implement the same orientation toward the right wing of the Cuban government; however, as we saw earlier, he did so without success.

CHAPTER FOUR

The Driving Force of the Cuban Revolution

From Above or From Below?

THE INTERNAL SITUATION IN CUBA

What was the nature of Cuba's internal situation as the country's relationship with the United States was rapidly changing in the late 1950s and early 1960s? How was the transition from an antidictatorial political movement to a far more radical project possible, and why did it occur at that particular point in time?

In contrast to those analyses that portray the Cuban leaders as merely reacting to U.S. policies and actions, I maintain that these leaders were actors greatly influenced by their own political predispositions and ideological inclinations. The minds of the Cuban leaders were made up not primarily as a result of U.S. Cuban policies in the late 1950s and beginning of the 1960s but rather as a reaction to earlier U.S. policies in Cuba and elsewhere. The events leading up to the U.S.-supported military takeover in Guatemala in 1954 had a big impact; even more important was, of course, U.S. foreign policy related to Cuba in the late nineteenth and early twentieth century. This is not to deny that U.S. policy at the time of the revolution played a significant role, but these actions must be placed in their appropriate political and historical context. Thus, it may well be that U.S. policy in this period was not very important in forming the mind-set of the more radical elements of the Cuban leadership, whether pro-Soviet or not. Instead, U.S. policy may have provided further evidence confirming what these radicals already knew or expected about the United States. Many revolutionary leaders were aware of the systemic policy limitations and constraints imposed by imperial capitalism. That does not mean that the revolutionary leaders may not have misunderstood or miscalculated the extent of U.S. power—for example, assuming that the United States could not easily dispense with the purchase of Cuban sugar. Perhaps the most important effect of U.S. Cuban policy was to undermine and diminish the influence of the significant although not decisive pro-U.S. liberal elements in the Cuban revolutionary government in 1959 and to radicalize the great majority of the population.

The transition from political to social revolution that began with Fulgencio Batista's overthrow on January 1, 1959, brought about a social and political project that was fundamentally incompatible with the interests of the United States and of Cuba's propertied classes. It is thus not surprising that a radicalizing process of measures and countermeasures between the United States and Cuba came into play. However, this process should not be assumed to be identical to the related but different idea that the objective obstacles encountered by the revolutionary leaders rather than their politics constituted the primary factors in the radicalization of the Cuban Revolution. Morris H. Morley communicated this idea in his study of U.S.-Cuban relations, arguing that "any attempt at economic transformation when U.S. companies dominated Cuba was bound to engender conflict, and it was the incapacity of political revolutionaries to institute partial changes in the face of internal and external opposition that led to a major confrontation with the United States and eventual nationalization of all alien enterprises."[1] But Morley seems to ignore the fact that when confronted with the undoubtedly great costs and pressures of pursuing a radical revolutionary course, the leadership might have stepped back and retreated, a phenomenon historically more common than revolutionaries staying the course. Admitting that such a choice might have been possible is independent of whether one approves of a particular course of action. Most important, Morley ignores the issue of whether the leaders' unwillingness far more than their incapacity to step back from a radical program led to the revolution's eventual outcome.

To be sure, costs accrued no matter which road the revolutionary leadership chose. One obvious cost of taking a more reformist route would have been a significantly reduced scope for the revolutionary process and the obvious danger of Cuba suffering a fate similar to that of the Bolivian Revolution. Another cost might have been a split among the leaders had Fidel Castro called for a retreat, although it is fairly certain that he would have emerged victorious had any such split taken place. Some observers have claimed that mass pressures from below played a critical role in determining the course eventually followed by the revolutionary leadership. This is an ambiguous contention, however. It is one thing if the concept of pressure is taken to refer to the strongly rising expectations of a higher standard of living among the Cuban people in 1959 and 1960, but it is quite a different matter to talk about pressure to suggest that the great majority of the Cuban people were pressuring the government from the left—that is, that popular impatience, distrust, or discontent arose with the government's pace of reform. In this sense, the claim that mass pressures from below, particularly during 1959 and early 1960, left Castro no other option but to stay the radical revolutionary course is not credible.[2] At that time, the government's redistribution policies and other widely popular measures that fell far short of Communism had created a great deal of credibility and huge political capital for the revolutionary government, aside from the fact that the great majority of the population had not yet experienced the impact of shortages and rationing. By any comparative standard—the Cuban Revolution of 1933 or the Mexican, Russian, or Chinese Revolutions—remarkably little rural or urban turmoil occurred in Cuba in 1959–60.

These sorts of splits among revolutionary leaders have been a common phenomenon in revolutionary regimes in the Third World (e.g., Algeria and Kenya). In fact, as we saw in chapter 2, evidence suggests strains within the Cuban revolutionary leadership—specifically, between Fidel Castro on one side and Raúl Castro and Ernesto "Che" Guevara on the other—in the spring and early summer of 1959.[3] This finding points to an understudied aspect of the Cuban revolutionary process: the existence of a number of political currents within the revolutionary regime, at least during its first years in power. In addition to the aforementioned liberals, who were out of the Cuban revolutionary government by the end of 1959, a number of independent and non-Communist radicals existed (David Salvador, Marcelo Fernández, Faustino Pérez, Carlos Franqui, and Enrique Oltuski).[4] A powerful pro-Communist and pro-Soviet wing also existed (Raúl Castro, Che Guevara) and was organizationally independent of the Partido Socialista Popular (PSP, the old pro-Soviet Cuban Communist Party).

The existence of these ideological tendencies within the revolutionary government reinforces the proposition that the revolutionary leaders were not merely reacting to U.S. policies but had social and political ideas that they were determined to carry out in practice. As previously suggested, the masses of revolutionary followers were more affected and radicalized by the U.S. opposition to the policies of the revolution. By the time they came to power, the principal revolutionary leaders (except for the liberals, who had relatively little influence and power) were already ideologically committed to something more than the traditional type of Latin American reform program. Of course, this ideological commitment would not by itself have been sufficient unless these leaders had also found opportunities beyond their greatest expectations. This is exactly what happened: the traditional Cuban army collapsed, taking with it the main support for the Cuban prerevolutionary state structure.

THE IMPORTANCE OF FIDEL CASTRO

Fidel Castro's leadership made a major difference in the triumph of the Cuban Revolution. The Batista dictatorship, already in an advanced state of decomposition, would have collapsed sooner or later, even if Castro had died in battle in, say, late 1958. But Castro's skillful political intervention helped to prevent a military coup that might have at least delayed the disintegration of Batista's army. Castro's political leadership made an even greater difference in determining the course taken by the Cuban Revolution after it came to power.

Castro's role was made possible by the particular social context of the Cuba of the late 1950s. As we saw in chapter 1, prior to the revolution, Cuba was among Latin America's most economically advanced countries, with significant capitalist, middle, and working classes. Yet these classes became politically weaker after the Revolution of 1933, from which the Cuban capitalist class emerged with a significantly diminished hegemony, at least in a political sense.[5] A group of mutinous sergeants replaced the traditional officer class rooted in the higher circles of Cuban society, thereby considerably weakening the organic tie between the armed forces and the upper classes, while the latter continued to view the U.S. government as their political guarantor of last resort. The substantial working class was highly organized in trade unions that, by the 1950s, had become highly bureaucratic and corrupt, thereby making it very difficult for this class to play the significant role in the struggle against Batista that it had played in the struggle against the Machado dictatorship. Also, by the mid-to late 1950s, the weak political parties, including the reform Ortodoxos, that had existed prior to Batista's seizure of power had fallen apart, reflecting the political weaknesses of all of Cuba's social classes. In this context, the Movimiento de Resistencia Civica (Movement of Civic Resistance), the anti-Batista organization formed by professional and other primarily middle-class elements, dissolved itself into the 26th of July Movement in February 1959, a symptom of its political subordination to Fidel Castro's leadership.

This situation was even more conducive to the thriving of Bonapartism in Cuba than was the pre-Batista period. Marx, Engels, and subsequent Marxists developed the concept of Bonapartism to explain the ability of individual political leaders to acquire a considerable degree of power and freedom of action in relation to the ruling and subordinate classes. The ruling classes' inability to govern on behalf of their interests facilitated the rise of Bonapartism for a number of reasons, including a deadlock among the various social classes.[6] The other side of this coin was a revolutionary political leadership that rather than being radical petty bourgeois, as the Cuban Communists claimed at the time, was declassed in the sense that it had no strong organizational or institutional ties either to the petty bourgeoisie or to any of the country's other major social classes. Other factors also helped to bring about a social revolutionary situation in Cuba: the stagnant economy; the great sense of frustration, failure, and demoralization left by the uncompleted revolution of 1933;[7] the betrayals and disappointments produced by the degeneration of most of the revolutionaries of that era into practitioners of a thoroughly corrupt *politiquería* if not outright gangsterism; the compromise of national sovereignty by the neocolonial relationship with the United States; and the geopolitical fatalism of most traditional Cuban politicians as expressed by the notion that nothing could occur in Cuba without U.S. approval.

FIDEL CASTRO AND THE 26TH OF JULY MOVEMENT ACHIEVE SUPREMACY

By the end of 1958, the rapid development of the armed struggle against the Batista dictatorship had brought about startling results that surprised even the revolutionary leaders. Celia Sánchez, Castro's confidant and chief of staff, explained that the rebels never expected that they "would be so strong and popular. We thought we would have to form a government with [other opposition parties such as the] Auténticos, Ortodoxos, and so forth. Instead we found that we could be the masters of Cuba."[8] Along the same lines, seventeen months earlier, in August 1957, Armando Hart and Faustino Pérez, national leaders of Castro's 26th of July Movement, contemplated three possible scenarios after the fall of Batista. As they saw it, the two most likely scenarios were that the movement would either reject or be unable to formally support the new post-Batista government, while the third and least likely scenario was that their movement would be included in the new government. They did not even consider the possibility that a government headed by the 26th of July Movement would come to power.[9]

In 1957, Fidel Castro and the 26th of July Movement began to predominate over the various opposition groups and forces that had taken up arms to overthrow Batista's government. Castro's eventual success depended in part on the defeats suffered by the other opposition movements. In mid-1956, a coup planned by anti-Batista military officers was uncovered and its leaders sent to prison. In September 1957, a navy rebellion supported by the 26th of July Movement was crushed in the port of Cienfuegos in central Cuba. Those two events almost eliminated the traditional military as a source of rebellion, at least in the near future. The student-based Directorio Revolucionario (Revolutionary Directorate) suffered a severe blow when it failed in its attempt to assassinate Batista when it attacked the Presidential Palace in March 1957. The Auténticos, a traditional political group that had taken up arms against Batista, also suffered irreversible defeats. The army assassinated most of the fighters belonging to former president Carlos Prío's Organización Auténtica shortly after their boat *Corinthia* landed on the northern coast of Oriente Province in May 1957.

While these other groups suffered serious if not fatal defeats, Castro's movement had many more successes than failures. First, the fact that Castro had fulfilled his promise to return, illegally landing in Cuba in 1956, constituted an initial but major step in the process of building his mystique among the Cuban opposition and people at large. As the other groups were suffering serious setbacks, Castro eventually defeated the army in a number of skirmishes and ambushes, some of them at small rural outposts. He thus built a base in the Sierra Maestra to which he successfully recruited several hundred armed men in 1957. Before these successful military encounters, however, the 26th of July Movement had suffered some serious but not crippling defeats, including the failure of the November 30, 1956, Santiago de Cuba uprising and the wiping out of most of the eighty-one men who accompanied Fidel Castro on a landing on the southern coast of Oriente Province in early December 1956. However, the Sierra Maestra stronghold in Oriente Province continued to prosper militarily and even more politically as it emerged as an opposition to the Batista dictatorship. Its political attraction was greatly enhanced with the February 1958 establishment of Radio Rebelde. By telling the truth about rebel victories and defeats, the radio station obtained a reputation for veracity sharply at odds with the fantastic claims made by spokesmen for Batista's army.

The successes attained by the 26th of July Movement and its Sierra Maestra stronghold enabled the movement to survive its greatest defeat, the long-planned national general strike called with little notice in April 1958. Batista's repressive apparatus quickly crushed the action, yet the relative stability that the rebels had already created in the Sierra Maestra allowed them to recover from this serious defeat. The rebels soon branched out with the establishment of two other fronts in other mountainous areas in Oriente Province: one front, led by Raúl Castro, was established in the Sierra Cristal in northeastern Oriente Province; the other, led by Juan Almeida, was opened at the other end of the Sierra Maestra, east of the provincial capital of Santiago de Cuba.[10]

The cumulative effect of the growth of the guerrillas resulted in the ascending hegemony of Fidel Castro and his 26th of July Movement. The strike's defeat led to a consolidation of Castro's internal control of the movement and concomitantly to a far greater political and military role for the Sierra's mountain guerrillas at the expense of the movement's urban struggle, which, contrary to myth, accounted for the great majority of the membership and most dangerous activities of the 26th of July Movement.

Castro's ascending influence became almost invulnerable to challenge after the 26th of July guerrillas defeated a major offensive by Batista's army in the summer of 1958. By the end of July, the rebel army had beat back Batista's offensive, winning thirty battles that were more substantial than the skirmishes typical of the 1957 encounters. Radio Rebelde disseminated the news of these victories to Cubans on the island and abroad. By mid-August, Batista's troops had completely cleared out of the Sierra Maestra.[11] The government retreat removed a major obstacle to the rebel army's eventual conquest of the island. With this, the 26th of July Movement fundamentally succeeded in its long-sought-after goal of obtaining unchallenged hegemony within the opposition to Batista. Although other armed guerrilla groups fought the Batista government, particularly in central Cuba, they were much less significant than Castro's movement in military as well as political terms.

THE COLLAPSE OF THE TRADITIONAL ARMY

Two key events took place in the second half of 1958 and beginning of 1959 that made possible the particular kind of social revolution that developed after January 1, 1959. One was the hegemony of Castro's movement among the opposition to Batista. The other was the total collapse of the Cuban army, the bulwark of the Cuban state. Since the 1933 revolution, the army had severed its organic connection with the Cuban upper classes, becoming a fundamentally mercenary and corrupt institution with no solid social base or ideological and political motivation. When forced to engage in real combat against the rebels, the army fell apart, plagued by desertions and corruption. While the rebel leadership worked hard to prevent a military coup d'état supported by the U.S. embassy when Batista fled the country, the causes of the collapse of the army were rooted in these long-term trends.[12] Thus, the defeat of the army was far more a result of its own weaknesses than of the military prowess of the rebel army.

The collapse of the traditional army dramatically altered the relationship of social and political forces in Cuban society and completely removed from the scene a major source of support for opposition to the revolutionary regime from either the imperial United States or the Cuban upper classes at home. A radical transformation if not elimination of the traditional armed forces has been a necessary condition for the development of social revolution in Latin America.

CASTRO'S POLITICAL INITIATIVE
AND CONTROL

While the collapse of the traditional army removed an important obstacle to revolutionary change, the control achieved by Fidel Castro became a critical element in the development of a revolutionary process in which the revolutionary leadership always retained political initiative and control. Even though the mass of the Cuban population became politicized and radicalized after January 1, 1959, the revolutionary political leadership always stayed ahead in implementing radical policies. They did not do so because popular pressures left the leaders no alternative, as some have argued, but because of the political weakness of the domestic opposition and the leadership's political purposes and ideas.

A strategic and tactical continuity existed in Fidel Castro's leadership of the revolutionary movement both before and after Batista's overthrow. On the one hand, he maintained the political initiative, remaining ahead—but not too far ahead—of mass sentiment; on the other hand, he made temporary ideological and political accommodations to supporters and allies without surrendering the slightest amount of political control. Castro's many accommodations were never disrupted by pressures, eruptions, or demands from below. Thus, for example, in October 1958, Castro signed a moderate agrarian reform law in the Sierra Maestra mountains. No records indicate that any groups or individuals objected that this was an insufficiently radical measure. Yet although this reform involved political and ideological accommodations to Cuba's capitalist and upper-middle classes, Castro stood firm with respect to issues of political control. A revealing incident took place in November 1957, when representatives of all opposition forces, including the 26th of July Movement (whom Castro would later claim were unauthorized by him to do so) met in Miami and signed a "Document of Unity of the Cuban Opposition to the Batista Dictatorship." The Miami Pact included the establishment of a provisional government with the understanding that prominent Cuban economist Felipe Pazos would become the provisional president. Pazos supported Castro and in July 1957 had signed an earlier historic manifesto with Castro and Raúl Chibás (brother of deceased political leader Eduardo Chibás). However, in Miami, Pazos acted as an essentially free political agent: he had not obtained Castro's approval before accepting the Miami conclave's designation. In an open letter addressed to the signers of the Miami document, Castro promptly repudiated it.[13] In this letter, Castro criticized serious omissions in the Miami document, such as the absence of an explicit rejection of foreign intervention in Cuba and of a military junta as a replacement for Batista. But, most importantly, Castro demanded and won the sole authority to nominate the future president and to keep "public order" after Batista's overthrow.[14]

Shortly after the revolutionary triumph, a number of major critical issues came up in a wide variety of areas, including agrarian reform, housing legislation, and the control of trade union and party organizations. The resolution of these issues allowed Castro and his close associates to establish the bases for a social revolution and a class struggle that has all along been closely managed and controlled from the top.[15] This management and control allowed the leaders to maneuver aggressively or with caution without risking a challenge to their control. In February 1959, an important episode took place that clearly revealed these strategic and tactical conceptions. At a time when the PSP's support for and alliance with Castro were tentative and uncertain and the PSP remained to Castro's left on social and economic questions, elements of this party encouraged several instances of "spontaneous" land seizures. While the Cuban Communists were in no position to seriously challenge Castro, their initiative irritated and provoked him into making some of his strongest anti-Communist remarks of the 1959 period. Castro unambiguously stated his position on the question of land distribution in a televised February 16, 1959, interview: "We are opposed to anarchic land distribution. We have drafted a law that stipulates that [persons involved in] any land distribution that is made without waiting for the new agrarian law will lose their rights to benefits from the new agrarian reform. Those who have appropriated lands from January 1 to the present date have no right to those lands. Any provocation to distribution of lands disregarding the revolutionaries and the agrarian law is criminal."[16]

The Communist Party cautiously backtracked on what may have been a political experiment on its part, and a few days after Castro's speech the party endorsed Castro's land distribution policy. Thereafter, no significant Cuban political group encouraged spontaneous takeovers or seizures of any kind. Those types of outbreaks characterized virtually all twentieth-century social revolutions; however, in Cuba, particularly after the enactment of the May 1959 agrarian reform law, the government seized land through Instituto Nacional de Reforma Agraria (National Institute of Agrarian Reform) functionaries and/or rebel army officers. On many occasions, these seizures occurred in response to peasant complaints and requests.

As another means of maintaining personal control of political developments, Fidel Castro discouraged any effort to make the 26th of July Movement into a regular party with an ideology, program, and organization. An independent non-Communist radical, Marcelo Fernández, the national organization coordinator of the 26th of July Movement, proposed precisely such a change in a February 16, 1959, editorial in the movement's daily, *Revolución*.[17] However, the movement never developed as a serious organized force. Fidel Castro allowed the 26th of July Movement to deteriorate organizationally until it was merged into what eventually became a new and reconstituted Communist Party in the mid-1960s, after virtually all of the fundamental socioeconomic and political changes in Cuba had already been carried out.

What is perhaps uniquely striking about Fidel Castro's adoption of this mechanism of control from above is that he insisted on it even when he could have obtained his immediate political objectives through the use of democratic means. One instance was the important trade union movement. In November 1959, shortly after Fidel Castro began to make a clear turn toward the Communist countries abroad and the Cuban Communists at home, the first postrevolutionary trade union congress took place. At this congress, the Cuban leader virtually imposed a leadership with a much greater Communist representation than was warranted by the 10 percent of delegates who were members of that party. After the congress concluded, the Labor Ministry, which was of course under Castro's control, launched a purge of large numbers of trade union leaders who had resisted Communist influence. The purge took place by means of purge commissions and carefully staged and controlled union meetings rather than through elections. About 50 percent of the labor leaders, most of whom belonged to the 26th of July Movement and had been freely elected in the April and May 1959 local and national union elections, were removed, while veteran PSP cadres and their union collaborators took over these leadership positions. Yet as Marifeli Pérez-Stable has pointed out, Castro and his revolutionary government enjoyed such great support in 1960 that the objectionable labor leaders could have easily been removed from office by holding new elections; any slate of candidates supported by Castro and his government would undoubtedly have won.[18] However, from the standpoint of the Cuban leader's long-term perspectives, new elections would have allowed the unions to retain their autonomy instead of becoming mere policy tools in the hands of a government leadership that at this point had begun to move in a political direction toward the Soviet Union and the Cuban Communists.

Yet even during these very decisive fall 1959 days, Castro could be tactically cautious as well. In November 1959, as we shall see in chapter 5, the Soviet government and its informal envoy to Cuba expressed their impatience with Castro's delays of Soviet leader Anastas Mikoyan's visit to Cuba. The Cuban leader was especially apprehensive about the forthcoming two-day National Catholic Congress in Havana. On November 28, more than a million Cubans gathered to hear Pope John XXIII address the Cuban people over Vatican radio at the opening of the Congress. At that Congress, several priests denounced the Communist threat to Cuba. This open display of Catholic strength restrained Castro and delayed his movement toward the Communist world. Mikoyan's visit to Havana did not take place until February 4, 1960.[19]

THE RESULTS OF CASTRO'S POLITICAL STRENGTH AND METHODS

The supremacy that Fidel Castro and his 26th of July Movement had achieved by mid-1958 greatly facilitated Castro's defeat of his actual or potential domestic political opponents after he came to power, most strikingly in the case of the substantial Cuban bourgeoisie and middle classes, which were important for their number as well as for their economic and cultural weight. Cubans of those backgrounds had played important roles in the struggle against Batista: Cuban capitalists had contributed substantial amounts of money to Castro's 26th of July Movement.[20] Middle-class professionals and small businessmen also contributed financially to the movement and participated in revolutionary activities in a number of organizations, including the 26th of July Movement and its allied Movimiento de Resistencia Cívica.

The first formal government apparatus established in January 1959 and headed by former provincial judge Manuel Urrutia included important liberal figures from these milieus and collectively constituted the largest group among the cabinet ministers. In a sense, however, these ministers were caught in a bind. They had no real power, which always remained in Castro's hands. Although personal ambition may have played a role in their assuming their ministerial positions, these liberals were also politically motivated by the idea that they could play a role in moderating the rebel leaders' radicalism. In fact, however, membership in the cabinet restrained these liberals from openly criticizing the radical measures that Castro, who had officially become prime minister in February 1959, was beginning to put into effect—most notably, the May 1959 agrarian reform law, promulgated while almost all of the liberal ministers remained in office. One of the more conservative of these liberals, Minister of Agriculture Humberto Sorí Marín, had authored the moderate agrarian reform act that had been approved in October 1958. His views were ignored in the drafting of the subsequent agrarian reform law, and he later joined the opposition and was eventually executed.

The cabinet liberals' inability to publicly criticize the government also meant the loss of whatever political ability they might still retain to mobilize and organize their substantial middle-class base. The lack of middle-class political representation had been considerably aggravated by the collapse of the traditional reform parties—first the Auténticos and then the Ortodoxos—in the late 1940s and early 1950s. As discussed in chapter 3, this represented a major difference between Cuba and Bolivia, where the right wing of the Movimiento Nacionalista Revolucionario amply and successfully represented the perspectives of the middle-class sectors of the population. One important consequence of Castro's supremacy was that it aggravated the absence of channels for the political expression and representation of the Cuban middle classes. By the end of 1959, virtually no liberals remained in the Cuban cabinet—all had been replaced or had left of their own accord. However, this process occurred gradually, rather than as the result of one single blow by Fidel Castro, in itself evidence of Castro's shrewd use of "salami tactics," of taking on and defeating one enemy at a time.

The cabinet liberals, potential articulators of the views and interests of major class forces such as the Cuban bourgeoisie and middle classes, were not the only people captured by the political tentacles of Castro's supremacy. This was also true of a number of other political groups and currents. Such was the case, for example, of the Directorio Revolucionario, a significant student-based group that in 1958 had had a guerrilla movement in central Cuba. After Batista's overthrow, this group attempted, in an awkward and politically unsophisticated manner, to obtain a slice of power. In early January 1959, group members occupied the Presidential Palace (where they had staged a daring but unsuccessful attack against Batista in March 1957) and stole some weapons from one of the military headquarters. These actions played right into Castro's hands: he raised the then popular slogan "Weapons for What?" and evoked the specter of the political gangsterism that had plagued Cuba during the 1940s, thus quickly marginalizing the Directorio Revolucionario. The group's remnants—that is, those who had not broken with the government— eventually merged into the newly formed Communist Party in the mid-1960s. They had neither an organizational nor a political perspective to counterpose to the Maximum Leader.

The primarily middle-class Movimiento de Resistencia Cívica, which played important active and support roles in the urban underground and represented the closest organizational embodiment of what today would be called civil society, dissolved itself and merged into the 26th of July Movement in late February 1959. This development was not surprising because the Movimiento de Resistencia Cívica had a more affluent and educated social base than the 26th of July Movement but had always functioned as an auxiliary arm of Castro's movement. The independent revolutionaries within the weakly organized 26th of July Movement (Salvador, Pérez, Oltuski, Fernández, and Franqui), who, in the words of Paco Ignacio Taibo II, constituted a left-wing sector that combined "anti-imperialism with a strong critique of the Communists, who [were] considered to be conservative and sectarian,"[21] did not constitute an organized group. At best, they constituted an incipient political current that was also limited by its dependence on Fidel Castro because its members were not well known and were not established political figures in their own right. However, they did for a while enjoy more political influence than the liberals, perhaps because the politics of these independent radicals overlapped with Castro's political stance early in the revolution and in particular with Castro's early maintenance of a political distance from the PSP. Franqui served as the editor of *Revolución*, the official newspaper of the 26th of July Movement and a paper that openly polemicized with the Communists until September 1959. *Revolución* also sponsored one of the most interesting and independent left-wing literary supplements in Latin America, the weekly *Lunes de Revolución*, which the government suppressed in 1961. As head of the Cuban trade unions, David Salvador had fought the Communists for control of the union movement. He also attracted public attention in the United States and Latin America in March 1959, when he publicly interrupted a speech by liberal Costa Rican leader José Figueres and strongly criticized his pro-U.S. Cold War stand. Yet as a trade union leader, Salvador was, more than anything else, Castro's man, and he ultimately depended on the Cuban leader's popularity among workers. (At times, this dependence on Castro opened Salvador to justified Communist criticism—for example, when Salvador defended the government-inspired no-strike pledge.) This incipient non-Communist radical current lasted only a short time. Former top officials such as Fernández, Oltuski, and Pérez abandoned their earlier independent radicalism and remained in the government, although for the most part in somewhat less prominent positions. Franqui went into exile in the late 1960s, and Salvador was deposed as trade union leader in 1960 and arrested as he was illegally trying to leave the country. The group of "humanist" trade union leaders who had collaborated with Salvador against the Communist attempt to take over the unions did not survive the purges that followed the November 1959 trade union congress.

Finally, neither the pro-Communist wing of the 26th of July Movement led by Raúl Castro and Guevara nor the PSP was immune to Fidel Castro's all-encompassing power. Had Fidel turned in a different political direction, Guevara and Raúl might have split with him and attempted to create their own political organization, perhaps in alliance with the old Communists. But it is doubtful that they could have made major political inroads in challenging Fidel Castro. Guevara was not even Cuban-born, a fact that would have surely become a political issue if he had publicly broken with Fidel in 1959 or 1960, at the very height of Castro's popularity. Raúl Castro was and continues to be, almost fifty years after the revolution, far less popular than his older brother. For their part, the old Cuban Communists had a very compromised political history and questionable revolutionary legitimacy because they physically joined the guerrilla camp only in 1958, a few months before victory. Given their close ties and subordination to Moscow, they also had at best doubtful credentials as Cuban nationalists and a proclivity to organizational sectarianism that seriously damaged many of their leaders even when their party came around to supporting Castro's regime. This sectarianism led to a serious confrontation with Fidel Castro in 1962 and a less serious one in 1968, the so-called microfaction dispute.[22] The more sectarian members of the PSP, led by

Aníbal Escalante, predictably lost to Castro's new Communists in both instances.

Castro's hegemony and mechanisms of political control had remarkable success in enabling him to quickly consolidate political and social power at home. This rapid victory was also facilitated by the Cuban refugee policy adopted by the United States shortly after the Cuban revolutionaries' victory. By facilitating Cuban emigration to the United States, the U.S. government unwittingly provided a safety valve for the Cuban government, which would otherwise have confronted a far larger opposition constituency at home. However, the Cuban revolutionary government had much less success in dealing with U.S. opposition than with its Cuban domestic counterpart. Castro's political dissimulation of his anti-imperialist politics significantly helped to delay U.S. hostility toward his movement while it was in opposition and, to a degree, after it came to power. The U.S. government quickly recognized the revolutionary government and refrained from open and total hostility during the first five months of 1959. But while the politically unorganized Cuban domestic opposition succumbed to Fidel Castro's salami tactics, such was hardly the case with the U.S. government. In this context, it is useful to compare the reaction of the U.S. oil companies with the reaction of the U.S. government to the Cuban demand that the companies refine Russian oil. As we saw in the previous chapter, the oil companies were willing, to a certain extent, to play ball with the Cuban government, thus allowing themselves to be part of Fidel Castro's divide-and-conquer methodology. In this context, the existence of a strong, centralized, and determined opponent of Fidel Castro in the form of the executive wing of the U.S. government made those tactics inoperable.

Castro's political mode of functioning, particularly in regard to his tactics, shows him as a clever revolutionary politician cast in a very different mold from the PSP leaders. By the time of the revolution, these older leaders already had very long and compromised political careers—they had supported Batista from 1938 to 1944. Yet in spite of their considerable political skills and opportunism, these leaders were nevertheless compelled to operate within the limits of their Stalinist ideology and their organizational and international political commitments to the Soviet bloc. As we saw in greater detail in chapter 2, such was certainly not the case with Fidel Castro.

If the revolutionary process was at all times firmly controlled from above, is it correct to conclude, as many Cuban liberals and conservatives have, that the revolutionary process was artificially imposed on a Cuban reality that did not need a social revolution? Prior to January 1, 1959, certain political factors had led to the predominance of a revolutionary political perspective and the absence of a socially revolutionary approach. This contributed to the mistaken impression that the country was not, objectively speaking, in need of a social revolution.

The prevailing popular consciousness among Cubans of all social classes during the struggle against Batista was not one of class struggle, social revolution, or anti-imperialism. Between 1952 and 1958, a growing and widespread consciousness supported a political revolution to reestablish the rule of the democratic and progressive pro–welfare state constitution of 1940. There was also a wish to abolish *politiquería*.

The political consciousness that prevailed in the 1950s differed from the one that prevailed during the 1933 revolution, which had an explicit social component.[23] During the 1950s, serious poverty and the chronic problems of substantial unemployment resulting primarily from the cyclical nature of the sugar industry plagued Cuba's economy and society. However, at least in the urban areas, no major depression occurred, bringing with it desperation and extreme poverty, as had been the case during the 1930s. By the 1950s, the apparently strong unions, which had organized close to half of the labor force, had become highly bureaucratic and corrupt and had agreed to support the Batista dictatorship in exchange for the general preservation of the collective bargaining status quo. This meant that no frontal attack or major state/employer offensive occurred against the unions; instead, their previous gains were gradually eroded. The central union leadership forcefully suppressed dissident forces whose activity could threaten this agreement. The organized working class thus suffered under a double dictatorship: that of Eusebio Mujal's trade union leadership and that of Fulgencio Batista. Without autonomous organizations, the Cuban workers became atomized. One major result was that as the workers increasingly turned against the Batista dictatorship, they did so as individual citizens rather than as members of working-class collective organizations.[24] In contrast, the struggle against Gerardo Machado's dictatorship coincided with early militant efforts to organize the working class into unions; consequently, a radical working-class consciousness played a much more significant role in that process.

In the 1930s, when the Platt Amendment was still in force and the U.S. government openly interfered in Cuban political affairs, the popular movement against the Machado dictatorship had been imbued with an open and explicit anti-imperialist sentiment. Such was no longer the case by the 1940s and 1950s, when although most Cubans criticized the U.S. foreign policy of supporting Latin American dictatorships, these criticisms were framed in the liberal populist terms of the "errors" and "mistakes" of U.S. foreign policy and did not constitute part of a critique of U.S. foreign policy as a systemic imperialist expression of capitalist and Cold War interests. Even the term "imperialism" had disappeared from the Cuban political vocabulary except among Communists and a handful of others. Fidel Castro has commented on this development on several occasions, most recently on a September 4, 1995, visit to the University of Havana that commemorated the fiftieth anniversary of his enrollment in the School of Law. Castro pointed out that in 1945, "the anti-imperialist sentiment had grown much weaker, including in our university, which had been the bastion of anti-imperialism. . . . I was a witness to all this. I talked with all kinds of people, law students, people in every faculty, and almost never heard anyone say anything anti-imperialist."[25] Communist leader Carlos Rafael Rodríguez expressed a similar view about the situation prevailing eight years later. On the first postrevolutionary anniversary of Fidel Castro's July 26, 1953, attack on the Moncada barracks, Rodríguez recalled,

> Anti-imperialism was then a proscribed word, a set of ideas that
> the majority of our *compañeros* considered to be deadly. For saying
> that anti-imperialism was the present Cuban form of patriotism,
> those who thought in that fashion were considered to be agents of
> a foreign power. I am not referring here to the professional servants
> of imperialism or to the anti-revolutionaries who have always
> existed. . . . Young people whom we knew to be honest, stung as
> we were by the suffering of our fatherland, lived convinced that
> Cuba's independence was a Yankee gift and that our denunciations
> of national oppression were simply ways of serving an idea that
> they considered anti-Cuban.[26]

A number of reasons accounted for this important ideological and political change. The Platt Amendment had been abolished in 1934, bringing about a more indirect, less visible role for U.S. influence and pressure on Cuban politics. The nationalist legislation and the political and cultural climate that emerged from the 1933 revolution had brought about a certain degree of Cubanization of the lower and middle managerial personnel in U.S.-owned businesses in Cuba, reducing the likelihood that Cuban workers and peasants received direct orders from North American supervisors. Franklin D. Roosevelt's New Deal and Good Neighbor Policy were received sympathetically in Cuba, and widespread anti-Franco and antifascist popular sentiment channeled into support for the United States and the allies in World War II. This pro-West political climate developed with considerable help from the Cuban Communists and was furthered by the island's postwar economic boom caused by higher world consumption of sugar and the war damage suffered by many of Cuba's sugar-producing competitors. Much of this political climate later became incorporated into Cuban support for the United States and its allies during the Cold War, to the obvious detriment of the Cuban Communists, who had encouraged the earlier support for the Allied powers. Finally, the term "left" had disappeared from the political vocabulary except, again, among Communists and a few others. The term rarely, if ever, appeared in any of the documents and manifestoes drafted by the 26th of July Movement, at least at the national level.

In the years following the depression, Cuba became more modernized, particularly in the urban areas, which were home to 57 percent of the population according to the 1953 census. As we saw in greater detail in chapter 1, Cuba had relatively developed means of communication and was among the first countries to have commercial television. Contrary to the expectations of African American singer and poet Gil Scott Heron, the revolution was televised, at least in the case of Cuba. Commercial radio enveloped the country and had been culturally influential since the late 1920s, and the same held true for the mass consumption of movies, particularly in the cities. All of these processes led to a considerable diffusion of U.S. cultural artifacts, a phenomenon that historian Louis A. Pérez has explained in illuminating detail.[27] This may help to explain why post-1959 Cuban nationalism and anti-imperialism was and continues to be more political and less cultural, at least in Third World comparative terms. Cuba has proven itself willing to accept modernity in spite of its real and imagined connection with the United States. However, the pervasive U.S. cultural influence was nevertheless more marked among the middle and upper classes and, as suggested earlier, in urban areas. In Cuba, U.S. cultural influence competed with the substantial weight of Spanish and Latin American culture. Postcolonial twentieth-century Cuba experienced extensive Spanish immigration, and popular identification with the rest of Latin America was strong, deeply rooted, and greatly encouraged by such important phenomena as the Mexican cinema, especially during its golden age of the 1940s and 1950s.

None of these factors that militated against anti-imperialist politics precluded the existence and even strengthening of a certain kind of nationalism of what could be called the "Cuba is beautiful" variety, referring to a multiclass cultural nationalism almost universally shared by the Cuban population. Largely devoid of a specific social and political content, it expresses pride in the cultural distinctiveness of Cuban society and its particular contributions to world culture, such as its music. It is also a "flag and national anthem" nationalism that affirms the blind devotion to one's native land and defense against those who might defame it or diminish its importance. In this sense, right-wing Cuban exiles in South Florida are nationalist even though quite paradoxically they may also be Plattistas (after the 1901 Platt Amendment), fully supporting the reestablishment of U.S. economic and political control of the island. A few of these exiles, such as writer Carlos Alberto Montaner,[28] have openly supported Cuba's annexation to the United States while remaining nationalists in the cultural sense.

By the 1950s, the radicalism of the 1930s, including the radicalism of the working class, had been largely submerged and replaced by a sort of militant but yet somewhat classless democratic populism that for the most part represented a response to the profound popular disappointment with the failures and corruption of the revolutionaries of the 1930s who held power from 1944 to 1952. After this traumatic political failure, cynicism, disappointment, and fatalism pervaded the Cuban body politic. In this context, a political phenomenon such as Chibasismo (after Eduardo Chibás, the former Auténtico leader who in the late 1940s founded the Ortodoxo Party) developed as a political revival movement with a strong emphasis on public morality. This phenomenon should not be confused, however, with the North American ideology of puritanism, with its strong emphasis on individual, private morality—for example, the North American political obsession (right, left, and center) with the institution of the family and the sometimes implicit and sometimes explicit premise that no important differences exist between the public and private realms.[29] This emphasis on public morality was critical to the revival of Cuban political life in the late 1940s and 1950s but did not constitute a strong class- and socially rooted set of politics. Although this view strongly dominated among the population at large, a number of militant political groups took a socially radical perspective, typically expressing it in a rather vague, nonspecific fashion. Thus, for example, the Directorio Revolucionario's February 25, 1958, Declaration of Escambray insisted that a successful revolution should, beyond the immediate task of restoring the rights and social gains suppressed by the Batista dictatorship, bring about education, administrative honesty, agrarian reform, and industrialization, but the declaration did not even hint at how those worthy goals could or should be brought to fruition.[30] Even the Workers' Bureau of the reputedly more left-wing Second Front led by Raúl Castro in Oriente Province declared itself in favor of agrarian reform but did not specify what such reform would mean in concrete policy terms. The bureau's pronouncement in favor of the elimination of latifundia was cast in very general terms (e.g., it entirely avoided the issue of compensation for land seized by the state) and was therefore unlikely to provoke disagreement within the broad coalition opposing the Batista dictatorship.[31] In any case, whatever social-radical perspectives existed within the rebel forces had no major political effect before January 1, 1959. The changes that took place in the 26th of July Movement, by far the most important of the opposition groups, are instructive in this regard. Although Castro's group originally maintained socially radical positions, its orientation changed after 1955, when, as we saw in chapter 2, Fidel Castro decided to adapt himself to the prevailing political consciousness and put forward a program of militant political revolution.

Instead of challenging the prevailing ideology pertaining to social questions, Castro opted to obtain organizational control as the way to maximize his future political options when the relation of social and political forces changed in his favor. This organizational control became possible for two reasons: the failures and collapse of alternative opposition organizations, and the monopoly of power he obtained within the 26th of July Movement after the deaths of Frank País and other leaders and the failure of the April 1958 strike. Castro's strategy constituted a manipulative response to the major gap that prevailed in the late 1950s between what the top revolutionary leaders perceived as the objective possibilities for a social revolution in Cuba and the lack of subjective readiness for it among the overwhelming majority of the population. After Batista's overthrow and having achieved hegemony in the country, Castro could close the gap by choosing the time and manner in which to adopt radical measures, taking into account only the strength of the propertied classes' opposition. He knew or could anticipate that he could more or less take mass support for granted, since his radical measures would find support among those deriving material benefit from them. Thus, these masses would support and participate in what would come to be known as the mass organizations but would not truly and democratically control these organizations, let alone their own destiny. The mass rally, in which leaders control the podium and speak and spell out policies while the masses applaud, not daring to amend or object, became emblematic of the regime.

Such manipulative methods, together with the spying functions of the Committees for the Defense of the Revolution, the activities of the newly established state security apparatus, the purging of many individuals and groups, and the elimination of all opposition and independent newspapers (which occurred during the summer of 1960, when most of the printed and visual media supported the regime and the government faced no clear and present danger), completed the tripod on which Castro consolidated his power: popular support, manipulation of that support, and repression. When the first two could not be trusted to secure the government's power, the third took over.

PARTICIPATION WITHOUT CONTROL

Fidel Castro's political hegemony and the complete collapse of Cuba's traditional army opened ample opportunities for the revolutionary transformations necessitated by the serious problems and distortions of Cuba's economy and society. Although the social revolution and class struggle were always controlled from above, they were accompanied by mass radicalization and participation. During the earliest stages of the revolution, most Cubans were in a true state of euphoria while all sorts of long-suppressed popular demands, complaints, and requests emerged into the public limelight, often with the support of strikes. Castro and the revolutionary government quickly became concerned about the frequency of such strikes and virtually eliminated them while preventing the development of any sense of frustration, let alone betrayal, among Cuban workers. Castro skillfully utilized this situation to educate the working class to subordinate its immediate material demands to what Castro considered to be the revolution's political needs. At the same time, he kept the Communists at bay by holding over their heads the threat that they could be blamed for inspiring strikes or other actions called independently of his government. In this manner, Castro killed two birds with one stone: he served notice to the Communists that he was in charge and that they had better toe the line, and he ingratiated himself with those concerned with the rise of Communist influence.

The Castro-led forces came to power with a great deal of popular support, prestige, and credibility. Fidel Castro's political dexterity and tactical skills allowed him to preserve and build on this political capital. The execution of several hundred Batistiano war criminals under widely varying conditions of fairness—those executed in Santiago de Cuba under the supervision of Raúl Castro came closest to legal lynchings—in the very early stages of the revolutionary process served important political purposes that have not yet been fully appreciated. Those shootings constituted key instruments in shaking up the political cynicism that had gripped the Cuban political psyche for the previous twenty-five to thirty years. With these executions, the revolutionary government signaled that 1959 was not 1933 and that the new revolution meant business. Similarly, the honest and disciplined behavior of the rebel soldiers and authorities in the early stages of the revolution reinforced the message that the people's trust would not again be betrayed. The announcement early in the Castro regime that serious cases of misappropriation of funds by public officials might be punished with the death penalty might have sounded harsh to foreign observers, but it was music to the ears of most Cubans, who had despaired of and become cynical about the possibility of public officials ever being honest. Cubans of all classes, particularly the working class and the poor, were pleased by the brand-new revolutionary police force's lack of abusive behavior. Many of these new police officers were politically aware revolutionaries and had had no time to develop the deformation of character common to members of all professional repressive institutions. Other early measures—for example, the opening of all beaches to the public early in 1959—met with widespread approval among workers and the poor, especially the black population, which had been the principal victim of the private appropriation of public facilities such as beaches and, in some provincial towns, parks. So, without explicitly appealing to specific class-warfare themes early in his regime, Castro obtained and consolidated an overwhelming amount of popular support.[32]

Months later, however, Castro started to take measures that had sharper teeth and shattered the multiclass coalition of the 1956–58 period. Thus, for example, the drastic reduction of rents by as much as 50 percent in March 1959 shook up Cuban society. While this action alienated some sections of the upper and upper-middle classes, it cemented popular support and definitively established that the revolution was dedicated to the material improvement of the working class and the poor. The May 1959 agrarian reform law eliminated whatever doubt might have remained on this score. By this time, the revolutionary regime was clearly enjoying huge popular support materially based on the substantial redistribution of income that took place during its first year in power.[33]

Although an undeniable radicalization of the Cuban masses occurred early in the revolution, that shift moved from the leaders to the masses rather than the other way around. The various forms of the leaders' radicalism had filtered in various ways down to the masses, who continued to support the various measures Castro periodically and unexpectedly produced after long sessions with his close associates. Thus, very few Cubans had any idea about the nature and degree of radicalism of the May 1959 agrarian reform law prior to Castro's announcement of the measure, and the government followed this procedure with virtually all important social legislation during this and subsequent periods. While prosperity and popular policies of redistribution continued at least until the first shortages began to be seriously felt in 1961, the leadership garnered great success in selling its revolutionary fait accompli to most Cubans.[34]

As indicated in the preceding chapter, the May 1959 agrarian reform law had the critical effect of raising U.S. hostility to the Cuban regime to a new level. The U.S. press and government's animosity to the January 1959 executions had already began to resurrect a mass anti-imperialist sentiment that had not existed since the 1930s. The multifaceted U.S. opposition to the Cuban government that developed after May 1959 raised popular anti-imperialism to a level that surpassed that of 1933. The contrast with the Bolivian Revolution, also discussed in chapter 3, is also relevant here. The leaders of the right wing of the Bolivian Movimiento

Nacionalista Revolucionario typically disavowed an intransigent opposition to imperial capitalism, hoping to come to the earliest possible agreement with Washington and U.S. capital. The opposite happened in Cuba: instead of quieting down popular anti-imperialism, Cuban leaders typically raised the ante and encouraged its development, often at massive demonstrations. Unlike the Bolivian leaders, the Cubans were in no hurry to enter into negotiations with the United States, as demonstrated by Fidel Castro's avoidance of and repeated delays in meeting with U.S. Ambassador Philip Bonsal. More than anything else, Castro seems to have wanted to have the process of mass radicalization run its course rather than to bring it to a halt by an early agreement with the United States. This behavior expressed a combative and aggressive attitude toward imperial capitalism rather than a defensive and measured response to U.S. acts against Cuba.

It is therefore not difficult to understand the reaction of people who opposed the radicalization of the revolution and who still had fresh memories of the revolution's pre-1959, socially moderate stage. These people might have perceived the sudden radicalization, whether in anti-imperialist or in domestic terms, as merely representing the outcome of sinister maneuvers by Castro and his close associates. Whether or not Fidel Castro fabricated some accusations to exacerbate mass anti-imperialist sentiment,[35] the rebirth of mass anti-imperialism in Cuba cannot simply be attributed to Castro's manipulation. Castro did not need to invent a popular reaction among a people becoming more conscious of their subordination to U.S. imperial power, the reality of which was constantly being proven by the actions of the U.S. power structure itself. This deepened anti-imperialist consciousness was accompanied by a growing sentiment of solidarity with Latin America, particularly with those countries such as the Dominican Republic and Nicaragua that remained under corrupt dictatorships endorsed and supported by the United States.

CHAPTER FIVE

The Role of the Soviet Union and the Cuban Communists

By 1959, the Soviet Union, a relatively new imperial state, was involved in a serious conflict with the United States, the most powerful of all the imperial states. Beyond the geopolitical elements underlying the clash between the two major powers, a major conflict existed between two competing modes of production: the traditional capitalist system represented by the United States versus a new class system based on a nationalized economy administered by a Communist Party–dominated bureaucracy. Unlike the Partido Socialista Popular (PSP, the Cuban Communist Party), which for obvious reasons was primarily concerned with Cuba, the Soviet Union had to fit its interest in Cuba and Latin America into a much broader set of interests encompassing the capitalist, Communist, and Third Worlds and particularly its often tense and delicate Cold War relations with Washington. A downturn in Soviet relations with Washington in the spring and summer of 1960, when it was generally thought that Soviet power was rising relative to that of the United States, facilitated the Soviet Union's support for the radicalization of the Cuban process.

The Soviet Union and the Cuban Communists shared a bureaucratic approach to revolution that differed from both the classical Marxist approach and that of Fidel Castro when the latter was a rising, not yet fully established revolutionary leader. Classical Marxism posited a rising autonomous workers' movement struggling for its self-emancipation and that of its class allies. At the center of this theory lay a peculiar tension between objective factors (primarily existing economic conditions) and subjective factors (the existing state of working-class consciousness). "Ripe" economic conditions would not by themselves bring about a revolution. At most, these conditions could create a favorable setting that could be used to advantage by the active, conscious efforts of the revolutionary subject, without which the revolutionary project could not be realized.

For his part, Fidel Castro paid little attention to objective factors but placed a great deal of emphasis on subjective factors. In fact, he was a tactical master at detecting the readiness of public opinion for whatever political steps he was contemplating. As discussed in chapters 2 and 4, this was an intrinsic part of the manipulative approach of a revolutionary caudillo rather than that of a democratic leader of a self-emancipatory movement. At the same time, however, early in the revolution Castro was not a bureaucratic leader in the manner of the PSP. He led a fundamentally declassed group of revolutionaries that as yet had no organizational machine to protect. The 26th of July Movement was an amorphous entity that Fidel Castro had no interest in protecting. Moreover, the movement's social and ideological heterogeneity and potential factionalism made it an obstacle that, from Castro's perspective, deserved liquidation. The Cuban PSP was a small but significant political force that, although substantially diminished by the Cold War, had, unlike Fidel Castro and his associates, a long institutional past in Cuban union and national politics. That long past, full of electoral and politicking deals, had created organizational machine interests that the PSP leaders had trained themselves and their members to defend. Most important, the PSP leaders had a corporate historical perspective about the destiny and interests of their organization, transcending the fate of any of its individual leaders. On the whole, this perspective was absent among the Fidelista leadership.

When it came to the question of taking risks, the PSP's behavior, like that of the Soviet leaders, resembled that of a capitalist business firm. Risks had to be taken, but only if there was a reasonable expectation of a fair rate of return in terms of political gain. This approach differed greatly from Castro's mind-set. While he could be tactically cautious, he was a strategic risk taker, as befits a revolutionary, whether authoritarian or democratic. Although all political actors must be somewhat judicious in taking risks and in using their political assets, a revolutionary must be willing to take undue organizational risks, not for the sake of adventure but because of a willingness to subordinate narrow organizational interests to a larger political project. One must wonder whether Cuban

Communism would have come about if Fidel Castro had been less bold and had followed instead the more strategically and tactically cautious approaches followed by the Soviet Union and the PSP.

THE SOVIET UNION AND THE THIRD WORLD

After Joseph Stalin's death in 1953, the Soviet Union inaugurated a large-scale, systematic policy of engagement with what had now come to be known as the Third World that contrasted with earlier Soviet episodic relations with those countries. In the early 1920s, Lenin's Russia had established relations with some less developed countries bordering on the Soviet Union, such as Mustafa Kemal Atatürk's Turkey. Stalin's "socialism in one country" policy later led him to cultivate relations with governments outside Europe in the expectation that these relations would strengthen the position of the Soviet state even if doing so meant sacrificing the prospect of Communist revolutions abroad. This policy translated into an alliance with Chiang Kai-shek that played an important role in the defeat of the Chinese Revolution in 1927.[1] This defeat in turn contributed to a Stalinist isolationist trend and, after Hitler's rise in 1933, to a preoccupation with Europe that lasted at least until the end of World War II.[2]

After the war, Stalin controlled Eastern Europe and attempted to expand his military power to those parts of the old colonial world that were contiguous with the Soviet Union. He appropriated some Iranian territory but had to withdraw in the face of strong resistance from the United States. Similar territorial advances and gains in China were later relinquished to the Chinese Communists after they came to power in 1949.[3] The era from 1945 until Stalin's death in 1953 was a transition period with widely varying policies, from friendly to hostile, toward the nationalist leaders and movements coming to power in the collapsing colonial world.[4] On the one hand, Soviet leader Lavrenty Beria complimented Indian foreign policy positions on the anniversary of the Russian Revolution in November 1951;[5] on the other hand, Soviet leaders described Egypt's Gamal Abdel Nasser as a fascist usurper when he first came to power[6] and failed to support Iranian nationalist leader Mohammed Mossadegh.[7]

After Nikita Khrushchev rose to power in the mid-1950s, the Soviet

Union began to orient toward the Third World more consistently and to implement a systematic new policy to support the so-called bourgeois nationalists and their anti-imperialist foreign policy. The Soviet Union politically supported the Afro-Asian conference of nonaligned states that took place in Bandung, Indonesia, in April 1955. That year also marked the beginning of a substantial program of military and economic aid to Egypt[8] and Khrushchev and Nikolay Bulganin's visit to Afghanistan, Burma, and India.[9] For a considerable time thereafter, the Soviet Union provided strong support to such nationalist leaders as Egypt's Nasser, Mali's Modibo Keita, Indonesia's Sukarno, and India's Jawaharlal Nehru.

This new strategy developed in the context of the Cold War received theoretical justification at a number of Communist Party congresses and international conclaves as well as in publications beginning in the second half of the 1950s.[10] Khrushchev and the Communist theorists contended that the bourgeois nationalists could, in addition to being useful allies in pursuit of the goals of Soviet foreign policy, evolve ideologically toward "Marxism-Leninism." At the twentieth congress of the Communist Party of the Soviet Union in February 1956, Khrushchev declared that no single road existed for the transition to socialism. This admission was soon coupled with a revived interest in the idea of a noncapitalist path of development according to which the underdeveloped countries, even in the absence of Communist leadership, could entirely skip the capitalist phase and make the transition to socialism in a relatively short period of time.[11] This was a risky policy based on the dubious proposition that Third World nationalist leaders could somehow resist the pressures of the world market and reject the capitalist model of development.

THE SOVIET UNION AND LATIN AMERICA

While Khrushchev's rise to power in the mid-1950s brought about a Soviet strategic shift toward the Third World, the Soviet Union's foreign policy placed a much higher priority on Asia, Africa, and the Middle East than on Latin America. This region was not only far away from the Soviet Union but, most important, was located in the U.S. backyard and was therefore considered part of the U.S. geopolitical sphere of influence. Prior to the 1959 Cuban Revolution, the Soviet press published relatively few articles on Latin America, and the 1958 May Day slogans did not even mention the region.[12]

Nevertheless, the Soviet Union had not entirely ignored Latin America. The Communist International had sent agents to help organize Latin American Communist parties as early as the 1920s and continued to do so for a long time thereafter. While helping to establish ostensibly revolutionary parties whose supposed object was the overthrow of the native governments and ruling classes, Moscow conducted normal diplomatic relations with those governments in pursuit of Soviet state interests.[13]

For the next several decades, the Latin American Communist parties, including Cuba's, faithfully followed the flip-flops of Moscow's political line. From 1928 to 1935, they collectively adopted the ultraleftist line of the Communist International's "Third Period," promoting reckless and adventurous political actions and denouncing all other leftist groups as counterrevolutionary, with disastrous results. By the end of this period, the Latin American Communist parties had either been destroyed and declared illegal (Mexico, Brazil, Argentina, El Salvador, and Cuba) or had lost most of the political influence they had previously acquired (Uruguay, Chile, and Peru).[14] In the course of the Popular Front stage that followed (1935–45), the Communist parties forged an alliance with many of the leftist and progressive forces they had denounced during the preceding period and with social forces and parties that did not even constitute part of the Left. The U.S. alliance with the Soviet Union during World War II greatly facilitated the functioning of the Latin American Communists, and by the end of the war these parties had reached their greatest strength. They became legal virtually everywhere in the Western Hemisphere, with representatives serving in the legislatures of Cuba, Colombia, Peru, Ecuador, Brazil, Chile, Bolivia, Uruguay, and Costa Rica. Three Communist Party members served in the Chilean cabinet, and two served as ministers in General Fulgencio Batista's Cuban government.[15]

The Cold War between the United States and the Soviet Union that began in the second half of the 1940s brought about the alignment of Latin American governments with the United States and its conservative foreign policy. The previously friendly political climate turned hostile toward the Latin American Communist parties, a development that led to a considerable loss of membership and political influence as the party was declared illegal in country after country. These losses came about even

though Latin American Communism did not return to the ultraleft policies of 1928–35. Latin American Communists strongly attacked the United
States and their own national governments allied with Washington, but
there was no return to the armed uprisings and other extreme tactics of
the Third Period.[16]

The U.S.-supported overthrow of the leftist, anti-imperialist government of Jacobo Arbenz in Guatemala[17] had an impact on Soviet atti-
tudes and policies toward Latin America even though the Soviet Union
had deliberately provided very limited support to Arbenz.[18] His defeat
caused the Soviet Union to lose a certain degree of political interest in
Latin America and reinforced Moscow's long-held belief that the local
Communist parties should not play the role of a revolutionary vanguard
but should limit themselves to supporting the anti-imperialist and anti-
feudal struggles conducted by the national bourgeoisie.[19] The Soviet Union
also sought to promote trade and government-to-government relations
with Latin America.[20] Although Eastern European and Soviet trade with
Latin America increased and surpassed the figures attained around World
War II, the rate of increase remained relatively minor in comparison with
other Third World regions. Between 1953–54 and 1956–57, total Soviet
bloc trade with Africa and the Middle East rose by 189 percent, while
trade with Asia grew by 226 percent; in Latin America, however, the rise
totaled a mere 23 percent.[21]

THE INTERNATIONAL RELATION OF FORCES IN THE LATE 1950S AND EARLY 1960S

To explain the Soviet Union's willingness to make a substantial commitment to the unfolding Cuban Revolution, it is necessary to understand
the causes of the prevailing perception that the international balance of
power was shifting in favor of the Soviet Union in the late 1950s and early
1960s. In 1959 and 1960, more than ever before or since, powerful groups
in the United States and elsewhere thought that the Soviet Union was
catching up and perhaps even surpassing the North American empire.
The test of the first Soviet intercontinental ballistic missile and Sputnik's
launch in 1957 had caused serious apprehension in the United States, and
it was reinforced by the concern that while the U.S. economy was growing at a rate of 2 to 3 percent per year, the Central Intelligence Agency and

other U.S. government agencies had estimated that the Soviet economy was growing approximately three times as fast.[22]

A brief review of Third World events at the time shows a series of developments from which Khrushchev and the Soviet Union derived considerable satisfaction. The Indian Communists won the elections in Kerala in 1957,[23] and a left-wing military coup overthrew the Iraqi monarchy in 1958,[24] although a U.S. invasion of Lebanon followed shortly thereafter. It was also evident by the end of 1960 that Soviet foreign policy had achieved significant success in Laos.[25] Soviet expectations about the radical potential of Third World nationalists seemed to have been vindicated by events in Indonesia and Egypt. Sukarno nationalized Dutch property in 1960 and 1962,[26] and from June 25 to July 23, 1961, Nasser carried out a "third revolution," issuing seventeen laws and decrees that, among other things, limited land holdings to forty-two hectares and nationalized all banks, insurance companies, and transportation as well as fifty companies in heavy industry. By 1964, the majority of Egyptian Communists, many of whom Nasser had previously imprisoned, supported the dissolution of the Egyptian Communist Party and its integration into the framework of Nasser's Arab Socialist Union.[27] In 1962, Ne Win's successful military coup in Burma opened the way for a radical transformation of that country's economy.[28]

Khrushchev's September 1959 trip to the United States took place in the midst of this process of change. Although Soviet leaders had reason to feel optimistic, tension continued over the status of Berlin, an issue that was far from being resolved. Soviet leaders were also beginning to face growing strains with the Chinese Communists.[29]

THE SOVIET UNION AND THE CUBAN REVOLUTION

Was the Soviet Union a conservative force that reluctantly supported the radicalization of the Cuban Revolution only because of the relentless pressure of Fidel Castro and the PSP?

The Soviet Union did not anticipate a "socialist" course for the Cuban Revolution. In his memoirs, Khrushchev unambiguously stated that he had been unhappy with Fidel Castro's official declaration of the revolution's socialist character in April 1961.[30] In stark contrast, when the Cuban revolutionaries came to power at the beginning of 1959, the Soviet Union had pushed for the most radical course, supporting a more anti-imperialist policy toward the United States and a more militant reform policy at home, wanting to move farther and faster than Castro did. Castro's radicalism eventually overtook that of the Soviet Union and the Cuban Communists, although the Soviet Union was usually more cautious than the Cuban Communists. In any case, the Soviet policy toward the Cuban Revolution cannot be explained in the simple terms of having been either radical and aggressive or conservative and defensive. The Soviet Union was guided by tactical considerations influenced by a number of factors, including the existing state of relations with Washington, the Soviet Union's fears of economic and military overcommitment to Cuba, and the gradually emerging pressures from Communist China and its effect on the Soviet Union's standing in the international Communist movement. Tactical disagreements arose at times within the top Soviet leadership. The Soviet Union's course of action was also affected by changes in the domestic situation in Cuba, particularly as the Soviet Union began to perceive radical possibilities (again, short of a full "socialist" course) that it had not initially foreseen. Although Soviet policy toward Cuba remained, on the whole, cautious and prudent, this approach did not preclude a willingness to take advantage of opportunities for sometimes daring political interventions if the Soviet Union believed that such actions would succeed. This policy sometimes required secrecy and dissimulation to prevent U.S. intelligence services from finding out what the Soviet Union was doing.

Before January 1, 1959, the Soviet government and press paid little attention to Cuba, in accordance with the low priority it gave to the island republic and the rest of Latin America. In 1957 and part of 1958, the Soviet press described the struggle against Batista as an "uprising," "rebellion," "insurrection," and "guerrilla war" but not as a revolution.[31] By early August 1958, however, both *Pravda* and *Izvestia* began to define the anti-Batista rebellion as a "national liberation" movement. This new designation may have been based on the rebels' denunciation of Washington's military aid to Batista and on Soviet knowledge of the ongoing negotiations between Castro and the PSP.[32] Despite Moscow's greater appreciation for the Cuban struggle, the Soviet Union had no great expectations when Batista was overthrown. Yuri Pavlov, the former head of the Soviet Foreign Ministry's Latin American Directorate, indicated that the prevailing opinion in the Soviet Union in early 1959 was that Fidel Castro's regime would not go beyond the limits of bourgeois democratic reforms, which led the Soviet Union to take a restrained wait-and-see attitude toward island events.[33] If Castro was engaged in a "conspiracy" to carry out a Communist transformation in Cuba, as some have claimed,[34] Soviet leaders knew nothing about it. In fact, Soviet officials knew little about Cuba, and what they did know was based, for the most part, on periodic reports from the PSP.[35] In his memoirs, Khrushchev recalled that the Soviet leadership "had no idea what political course [Fidel Castro's] regime would follow."[36] According to Khrushchev, he and his associates knew that Raúl Castro was a "good communist" and that Ernesto "Che" Guevara and some other revolutionary leaders were also communists. Nevertheless, as Khrushchev pointed out, "we had no official contacts with any of the new Cuban leaders and therefore nothing to go on but rumors."[37]

The overall low level of contact between the Soviet Union and the Cuban revolutionary leadership did not prevent Soviet authorities from taking advantage of any opportunity to play a role in the Cuban revolutionary process. As previously classified Communist Party of the Soviet Union and Soviet government documents reveal, in December 1958, representatives of a Costa Rican importing company approached the Czech embassy in Mexico to discuss the supply of arms and ammunition for Fidel Castro's rebel detachment. The Czech government requested guidance from Moscow on December 17, and the Soviet government gave its approval ten days later with the proviso that the Czechs would carefully investigate the company making the request, that no document would state the eventual Cuban destination of the weapons, and that no Soviet-made weapons would be included in the shipment.[38] Batista's overthrow a few days later made the Costa Rican company's request moot.

In the first months after the victory of the revolution, PSP emissaries maintained contact with Moscow but did not pretend to speak on behalf of Fidel Castro. They did claim to have "influenced" him, but no PSP leader visiting the Soviet Union claimed that Castro was a Communist or Marxist. Moreover, PSP reports to Moscow subtly hinted at Castro's self-possession and unrestrained energy. Moscow lacked full confidence in the Cuban revolutionary leadership despite having supporters such as Raúl Castro and Guevara. In addition, the PSP was far from being in control of the revolutionary process in spite of its growing influence in certain circles such as the revolutionary army. At this time, Soviet leaders did not respond favorably to Cuban feelers on behalf of an expansion of economic relations or to one of what were to become frequent requests from the Cuban PSP for more Soviet involvement in Cuba—in this case, a request for a Soviet press campaign on behalf of the Cuban Revolution. The editor of *Pravda* felt that such a campaign was premature given that things were going well in Cuba and that there was no need at that point to provide Washington with political ammunition.[39]

The Soviet leaders provided help to their Cuban supporters and friends despite the low profile and somewhat reserved support for the Cuban revolutionary process, thus building a pro-Soviet niche and base of support on the island. This approach explains why Moscow was willing to provide secret assistance to Cuba's armed forces. In March 1959 a PSP representative met with the chief of staff of the Soviet armed forces, Marshal V. Sokolovsky, to discuss future relations between the two armed services.[40] Most important, in April 1959, at about the same time as Fidel Castro visited the United States, Raúl Castro sent Lázaro Peña, a top PSP official, to Moscow to request a few Spanish Communists who had graduated from the Soviet military academy to help the Cuban army with general matters and with organizing intelligence work. Khrushchev's presidium approved Raúl Castro's request on April 23, and two officers of Spanish origin were immediately sent to Cuba, while fifteen others joined them a short time later. The Soviets paid for their salaries and expenses, since the Cuban army had little money and the civilian anti-Communist officers of the Cuban treasury were not to be told, for obvious reasons, about this Soviet operation.[41] At this time, Sokolovsky raised with a PSP representative the possibility of training Cuban pilots and inquired about the party's goals for the armed forces.[42]

The Soviet leadership's overall attitude toward the Cuban process was not frozen or carved in stone and was substantially affected by developments inside the island republic. Just as the U.S. view of Cuba was negatively affected by the radical May 1959 agrarian reform law, the Soviet view was affected in the opposite direction. The Soviets were encouraged not only by the passage of this law but also by the fact that Fidel Castro had not requested economic assistance from Washington during his visit to the United States during the previous month. The Soviet Union also welcomed the forced resignation of anti-Communist President Manuel Urrutia in July 1959.[43] This attitude too was the mirror image of the critical posture that Washington adopted, based in part on U.S. Ambassador

Philip Bonsal's political interest in President Urrutia as an important representative of the liberal wing of the revolutionary government that was being pushed out. Nevertheless, *New Times*, an important Soviet press organ, thought that the Cuban revolutionary process had not advanced enough, believing that the Cubans needed to go beyond agrarian reform and limit the activity of the foreign monopolies and the native comprador bourgeoisie. The journal also hinted at the PSP's inclusion in the government.[44]

Although Soviet leaders were significantly affected by developments inside Cuba, the radicalization of the Cuban revolutionary process also helped to create differences of opinion among the top Soviet Communist chieftains. Thus, for example, on September 23, 1959, the Soviet presidium initially decided not to provide military aid to Cuba for fear of a U.S. reaction. This decision was reversed after Khrushchev returned from his visit to the United States. He accused the Americanists in his foreign policy bureaucracy of timidity and argued that the Cuban Revolution was too important and unusual to deny it assistance. On September 30, the presidium reversed itself and voted secretly to send Warsaw Pact weapons to Cuba. Although Khrushchev's personal views were instrumental in this context, the presidium's sense of the existing international relation of forces clearly allowed for such a change of opinion.[45] As events progressed, several Soviet officials remained more favorably disposed toward the Cuban government than others, as was the case with some intelligence agents and with Soviet leader Anastas Mikoyan after his February 1960 visit to Cuba. One factor at work was the apparently genuine enthusiasm that some Soviet leaders felt for the Castro-led revolution. As Mikoyan told Dean Rusk, "You Americans must realize what Cuba means to us old Bolsheviks. We have been waiting all our lives for a country to go communist without the Red Army. It has happened in Cuba, and it makes us feel like boys again."[46]

ALEKSANDR ALEKSEEV ARRIVES IN CUBA

The October 1, 1959, arrival in Havana of Aleksandr Alekseev, a Soviet intelligence agent posing as a journalist and later as a diplomat, constituted a major development in the relations between Moscow and Havana as the revolutionary process was reaching an important turning point. He soon became the first direct political link between Moscow and the top Cuban leadership. This meant, among other things, that the PSP would no longer be needed as a go-between. Alekseev met with Guevara on October 12 and with Fidel Castro four days later. The substantive issues discussed at the meeting with Castro included the matter of reestablishing diplomatic relations between Cuba and the Soviet Union, which had been severed after Batista's 1952 coup. Castro informed Alekseev that Cuban public opinion was still not ready for an exchange of ambassadors with the Soviet Union. The Cuban leader was also cautious about requesting financial assistance from Moscow.[47] Instead, Castro suggested that the Soviet Union send to Cuba the Soviet cultural and technological exhibition that Moscow had sent abroad earlier in 1959 and that was about to close in Mexico. The Kremlin had sent Mikoyan to inaugurate the exhibition at the various cities it visited, and Castro suggested that Alekseev ask Mikoyan to come to Cuba to open the exhibit. The Soviet Union initially hesitated to send Mikoyan and the exhibition to Cuba, in part because of the rising opposition among Cubans to Fidel Castro's recent alignment with the pro-Communist wing of the 26th of July movement, which led to the public resignation and subsequent arrest of Major Huber Matos, one of the leading figures of the 26th of July Movement in eastern Cuba. However, Castro's caution eventually brought about a postponement of the exhibition's visit to Cuba.

At the end of November 1959, a Catholic Congress took place in Havana, with more than 1 million people gathered to hear Pope John XXIII address the Cuban people over Vatican radio. This massive show of Catholic strength caused Castro to retreat temporarily from anything associated with the Soviet Union or Communism. Mikoyan could not understand Castro's hesitation, probably because he was not familiar with Cuban politics and society.[48] Castro may also have been unsure about Soviet intentions, which may help to explain his willingness to participate, for a short while, in a mediation effort initiated by the U.S. embassy and carried out by Julio A. Amoedo, Argentina's ambassador to Havana, in late January 1960.[49] Mikoyan's visit did not take place until February.

This was not the only occasion when Fidel Castro was more cautious than Alekseev and refused to follow his suggestions. Almost a year later, at the beginning of September 1960, Castro rejected Alekseev and the PSP leadership's recommendation, made without Moscow's endorsement, that he implement a campaign of repression against the regime's domestic enemies. The recommendation had been prompted by rumors about plans to assassinate the Cuban foreign minister, the Soviet ambassador to Cuba, and several other officials.[50]

The Soviet attitude at the end of 1959, after a year of dramatic developments, was most clearly expressed in a book by Konstantin M. Obyden, *Cuba in the Struggle for Freedom and Independence.*[51] Released in late 1959 and covering events through November, the book reflected a strong optimism concerning the revolution's future, although it claimed that the revolution was not headed toward "socialism" and had remained fundamentally bourgeois democratic, anti-imperialist, and agrarian. Obyden was encouraged by the replacement of Batista's army and police as well as by the takeover of the non-Communist trade union organizations by forces friendly to the Communists and loyal to Castro. Obyden and many subsequent Soviet writers claimed that the "geographic fatalism" theory, according to which Latin American countries by virtue of their proximity to the United States could not carry out a struggle for national and social liberation, had been refuted by the Cuban Revolution. In other words, Soviet ideological spokespeople were explicitly challenging the geopolitical notion of Latin America as a natural part of the U.S. sphere of influence.[52]

In January 1960, Guevara's military aide, Major Emilio Aragonés, traveled to Mexico City to report to the Soviet embassy and KGB station on what the Communists around Fidel Castro were planning to do to obtain control of the revolution. Among other changes, Aragonés predicted a purge of the non-Communist wing of the 26th of July Movement, the creation of a new political party, and Fidel Castro's full participation in the coming "socialist revolution."[53] Mikoyan's subsequent visit to Cuba marked another qualitative step in the development of closer ties between the Soviet and Cuban governments. The visit was accompanied by the signing of a major trade agreement between the two countries, greatly increasing Washington's concern regarding the orientation of the Cuban leadership. Opposition to Communism also grew inside Cuba. Fidel Castro's perception of the changing foreign and domestic reaction may again have led him to behave in a more cautious manner. Castro's caution at this time did not escape the attention of the Soviet leadership, as Khrushchev noted in his memoirs.[54] Because of the Cuban leader's concerns, three months elapsed between Mikoyan's visit and the establishment of formal diplomatic relations between the two countries in May 1960.

A number of developments on the international scene in the spring of 1960 stimulated a greater aggressiveness in Soviet foreign policy, thereby facilitating the Soviet Union's political and material commitment to the Cuban revolutionary government. First, Chinese pressure on the Soviet Union for a more aggressive international posture increased. In April, a long editorial in the Chinese Communists' *Red Flag* published the first comprehensive critique of the Chinese view of Soviet foreign policy as conservative. This article specifically referred to Cuba's conflict with the United States as being incompatible with Khrushchev's policy of détente, which Mao Tse-tung opposed. Two months later, Khrushchev took advantage of the presence of the representatives of the Communist world at the Third Congress of the Romanian Workers' Party to denounce, in a closed-door session, Beijing's activity and to demand a conference of all Communist parties before the end of the year to isolate the Chinese leaders and force them to support, at least to a degree, Soviet foreign policy.[55] Perhaps most important, the downing of a U-2 spy plane flying over Soviet territory on May 1, 1960, eventually led to Khrushchev's cancellation of the summit meeting planned for that month in Paris.

The Cuban leadership began to take a more radical stance toward the U.S. government. At the end of June, the Cuban government seized Texaco's, Esso's, and Shell's refineries after they refused to process the crude oil Cuba had acquired from the Soviet Union. On July 6, the United States retaliated by cutting seven hundred thousand tons from the sugar it had committed itself to buy from Cuba, and Castro responded by nationalizing all U.S. firms in Cuba. Three days later, the Soviet Union announced that it would purchase the sugar that the United States had just refused to buy. The same day, Khrushchev made the famous speech threatening a missile defense of Cuba if it were attacked by the United States. While the Soviet leader originally emphasized the "metaphorical" nature of his threat, the Cuban government took it rather literally, and subsequent Soviet pronouncements on the issue consequently became rather ambiguous about the seriousness of the threat. The Soviet Union began to engage in a substantial program of military assistance shortly after Raúl Castro's July 1960 visit to Moscow. To minimize suspicions and concern in Washington, the Soviet government took steps to make it appear that this aid program was being carried out by Czechoslovakia rather than the Soviet Union, although that distinction may have made little difference to Washington.

Looking back on this short but critical period in the summer of 1960, French-Canadian scholar Jacques Lévesque acknowledged that the decisive impulse for radical action came from the Cuban leadership but noted that the leaders of the Soviet Union acted with surprising boldness, particularly in light of their previous caution. Lévesque pointed out that Cuba's importance to the Soviet Union grew during this period in terms of both a general concern for the fate of the revolutionary movement in Latin America as well as the push for a change in the world distribution of power. According to Lévesque, Khrushchev saw support for the Cuban Revolution as a convenient tool in his attempts to renovate Soviet society and foreign policy. Support for the new radical revolution could demonstrate the vitality of the Soviet system to its own people as well as to foreigners. Lévesque cited evidence from the Soviet press indicating that the Soviet Union encouraged the nationalization of the oil companies. While Lévesque thought that the Soviet Union might have preferred a slower pace for the nationalization of additional U.S. properties, he concluded that Fidel Castro knew that the overall situation was very favorable for eroding the Soviets' hesitation and getting them to go along with his actions. Lévesque noted that Khrushchev's "figurative" missile threat in defense of Cuba was also related to Cuba's extreme vulnerability to the United States and to the fact that the Soviet Union's commitment to Cuba was no longer limited and ambiguous, as witnessed by the Soviet pledge to become Cuba's most important sugar consumer. Khrushchev might have decided that he had to pull out all the stops to demonstrate his determination to Washington. At the same time, the missile threat was somewhat vague, leaving room for flexibility in case the U.S. government failed to take it as seriously as Khrushchev had intended.[56]

After this highly eventful summer, Soviet leaders continued to support Castro's radical course although they clearly expressed their preference for a more cautious Cuban policy on such matters as support of guerrilla movements in Latin America and the nationalization of Cuban businesses in the fall of 1960, an issue on which the Soviet Union joined the reservations expressed by the PSP leadership.[57] Thus, in December of that year, a communiqué signed by Guevara and Mikoyan after Moscow had stated that it was willing to buy more sugar expressed the hope that the United States would resume the purchase of Cuban sugar, in which case the Soviet Union would reduce its sugar purchases by an equivalent amount.[58] By the end of 1960, although Cuba had not officially declared itself "socialist," it had clearly become a close ally of the Soviet camp. Thus, with Cuba in mind, at the November 1960 conference of the Communist and Workers' Parties a new category, "national democratic states," was created for Third World countries that were considered closer to socialism than to capitalism. Such states maintained close cultural and economic ties with the Soviet bloc and pursued a pro-Soviet foreign policy. On the home front, they were to raise the people's standard of living and to engage in a process of "democratization," which implied the incorporation of the local Communist parties into the government. The national democratic states were also supposed to implement agrarian reform programs, nationalize foreign-owned industry, and establish a state sector of the economy.[59]

THE CONTRADICTORY NATURE OF SOVIET GOALS AT THE BEGINNING OF THE CUBAN REVOLUTION

The creation of the new category of national democratic states was a Soviet attempt to accommodate the "anomaly" of the Cuban Revolution and to address, even if inadequately, the contradictory nature of Soviet policy toward the island republic. The Soviet Union did not seem to have a strategically coherent approach to dealing with developments in Cuba even though Khrushchev pushed the Soviet Union into a proactive presence in the Third World and the international relation of forces seems to have favored the Soviet bloc. I am not merely referring to the fact that the Soviet Union was initially reluctant to grant Cuba full membership in the Communist bloc and did not want to assume full responsibility for the island's military and economic needs. The things for which the Soviet Union did push were incoherent and contradictory, in part because the Soviet Union's model of political intervention in the Third World was based on an Afro-Asian and Middle Eastern experience not applicable to the geopolitical realities of Latin America, particularly the Caribbean, which was literally the U.S. backyard.

The Soviet Union of the Khrushchev period typically supported Third World governments that broke with the West and adopted independent foreign policies, preferably tilting somewhat toward anti-imperialist, pro-Soviet positions.[60] Nehru's India seemed to have satisfied this criterion to a considerable degree, as did Nasser's Egypt. Thus, Nasser and his representatives for the most part supported the Soviet stand on international questions, including such critical issues as the recognition of the German Democratic Republic and the People's Republic of China, disarmament, and opposition to Western policies in Southeast Asia. Egypt still disagreed with the Soviet stand on the Congo and United Nations reorganization.[61] Following a similar logic, the Soviet Union strongly encouraged the development of the Cuban Revolution as a revolution of national liberation against Washington and supported Cuba's break with the traditional position of the Latin American republics in support of the United States in the Cold War.[62]

As mentioned earlier, Khrushchev's international strategy also expected that Third World nationalist governments would initiate domestic changes, moving those countries in the direction of a noncapitalist form of development if not adopting an outright Communist system. Therefore, the policies of agrarian reform and nationalization carried out in Third World countries such as Egypt were seen in a very positive light as progressive. Along the same lines, the Soviet Union strongly supported Cuba's radical May 1959 agrarian reform legislation. The Soviet press also took Cuba's side in the subsequent diplomatic clash with the United States that centered on the critical issue of prompt and effective compensation for property seized from U.S. nationals. Moreover, the Soviet Union saw agrarian reform as closely related to the national liberationist character of the Cuban Revolution, thereby helping the country get rid "of her semi-colonial economic system, her complete dependence . . . on the foreign (U.S.) market. [Agrarian reform] is bound to deal a blow to the reactionary big landlords who are the mainstay of the dominion of U.S. imperialism and its allies in Cuba."[63] Going further, the Soviet Union encouraged the nationalization of the U.S.- and British-owned refineries.

Khrushchev's Soviet Union was willing and ready to subordinate the fate of the local Communist parties to its alliances with Third World nationalist leaders, as witnessed by its toleration of Nasser's jailing of Egyptian Communist leaders. Of course, the Soviet Union much preferred that the nationalist leaders found a way to ally with local Communists and include them in ruling parties and governments. In this spirit, the Soviet press advocated during the first half of 1959 the inclusion of the Cuban Communists in the revolutionary government as a way of insuring that the revolution would constitute what the Soviets considered a real popular liberation movement.[64] Despite his radicalism, Fidel Castro delayed as much as possible the inclusion of open Communists in his government for both domestic and foreign policy reasons.

Unlike most Third World countries, Cuba had not been under the control of a European metropolis but instead had fallen under U.S. hegemony. Thus, the Soviet Union should have foreseen what the United States would do if faced with a revolution on its doorstep that broke with the United States and the West in the Cold War, carried out radical agrarian reform and nationalized oil refineries without properly compensating U.S. property owners, and—to add insult to injury—openly included Communists in its government. Although these changes by themselves would not have amounted to a Communist revolution in Cuba, they were radical enough to place into serious doubt Moscow's initial expectation that even such a relatively limited revolution could survive with only minimal Soviet involvement.[65] And these events occurred in 1959 and 1960, while the Cold War was still going on and only five years after a much less radical Guatemalan government had been overthrown in a Central Intelligence Agency–organized coup. Of course, Soviet Cuban policy in early 1959 might have simply been negligent and perhaps even cynical rather than incoherent and contradictory. The Soviet leadership may have been interested primarily in Latin American countries challenging the U.S. empire and less concerned about the viability and survival of the regimes carrying out the radical, anti-imperialist policies recommended by the Soviet Union.

THE ROLE OF THE CUBAN COMMUNISTS

Anarchist influence was strong in Cuban working-class circles at the beginning of the twentieth century, but the country had only a weak socialist presence. Despite major events such as World War I and the Russian Revolution of 1917, the Cuban Communist Party was not founded until 1925. Even in 1928 the Communist Party had no more than about one hundred members.[66] In addition, party's late founding meant that it was born almost Stalinized. The massive popular upheavals of the 1933 revolution against Machado and its aftermath greatly increased the party's membership and power, particularly in the union movement. Yet the sectarianism of the party during the critical 1928–35 period greatly hurt the chances for success of the 1933 revolution and divided the Cuban Left for many years to come. This situation prevented the party from building a popular front coalition with the nationalists it had so violently opposed a few years earlier. Instead, the Communists reached an agreement with Batista in 1938, exchanging political support for his government for control of the trade union movement and minor cabinet participation in 1940–44. The Communists had previously played a significant role in shaping the progressive 1940 constitution and subsequently in the electoral coalition that elected Batista that year. As followers of the "right-wing" line of U.S. Communist leader Earl Browder, the Cuban Communists took the name Partido Socialista Popular in 1944. After the Kremlin turned against Browder in 1945, the PSP leadership managed to reverse itself without any major purges, just as it generally managed to accommodate all the other twists and turns in the Kremlin's policies.

The Communists' deals with Batista and briefly with the liberal but corrupt Grau administration that succeeded Batista in 1944 both helped to cement Communist institutional power, particularly in the union movement, and reduced the Communists' ability to maintain political influence after the Cold War arrived and the party was cast into the political wilderness. As a result, the Cuban Communists found themselves with much reduced but still significant strength at the time of Batista's fall. Their influence on the Cuban working class and Cuban politics had sharply declined. A 1956 PSP report indicated that only 15 percent of the country's two thousand unions were led by Communists or by union leaders who supported collaboration with the PSP.[67]

The Communists' policies and tactics varied greatly during the Batista regime. Until 1957, the PSP's policies were closer to those of the moderate opposition. For a time the Communists maintained a position of electoral opposition to the Batista regime, even when the latter could not possibly have been expected to administer honest elections. At other times, the Communists made theoretically impeccable calls for a "mass struggle" against the Batista dictatorship that would culminate in another rebellion that would overthrow the government, as had been the case on August 12, 1933, when Machado was overthrown by a general strike. The "mass struggle" slogan was often counterposed with the "putschist" strategy and tactics of other revolutionary groups, such as the 26th of July Movement and the Directorio Revolucionario (Revolutionary Directorate), which were often referred to as "petty bourgeois." Thus, until late 1957, the PSP offered the strategy of mass action as an alternative rather than as a complement to armed struggle. Until the Communists realized that the 26th of July Movement's armed struggle represented the only show in town, they tended to act as if the Batista dictatorship was just a new episode—a downturn—in the cycle of reaction and progress they had witnessed for so many years. Probably counting on Batista being succeeded by some more liberal civilian or military regime, the party wanted to ensure that it would be in the strongest bargaining position and to avoid placing itself far out of the mainstream by adopting an insurrectionist attitude.

In late 1957, the PSP decided to fully support the armed struggle, and by the middle of the following year the party had reached an agreement with Fidel Castro, although it had much greater success in operating inside the guerrilla columns headed by Raúl Castro and Guevara than those under Fidel's direct control. The PSP also created its own guerrilla group of some sixty-five people under the command of Félix Torres in central Cuba.[68] An indicator of the PSP's new turn was the October 1957 meeting between Ursinio Rojas, a PSP leader and former official of the sugar workers' union, and Fidel Castro at which the two men explored the advantages and difficulties of an alliance between the PSP and Castro's movement.[69]

The PSP's ambiguous, relatively tardy role in the guerrilla movement helped to diminish its political influence at the beginning of 1959. Much of the populist Left perceived the PSP as a conservative force because of the Communists' electoral horse-trading and *politiquería* dating back to the late 1930s. The PSP thus was associated with the traditional political forces that the populist parties, such as the Auténticos and then the Ortodoxos, had been expected to eliminate from the political arena. Still, the PSP had important strengths. The organization was led by experienced and skilled politicians who had worked together for a long time and were considerably older than Fidel Castro and his associates. The PSP also had a cadre-type membership and a coherent political theory and program, which, although often shallow and superficial, were superior to the occasional, unsystematic, and programmatic pronouncements of the country's other political groups. Also, leftist intellectuals outside of the PSP had played little part in the struggle against Batista.[70] The PSP's organizational hardness and durability was remarkable, particularly in contrast to the traditional political groups, which had been completely discredited,[71] and the new revolutionary organizations such as the 26th of July Movement, which remained amorphous. PSP members were also active in nonparty organizations, where they were greatly outnumbered but nonetheless influential. In the trade unions, for example, the PSP had advantages over the more numerous members of the 26th of July Movement because unions were consistently the PSP's central priority. The PSP's trade-union cadres were typically older and far more experienced than workers who belonged to other parties or were unaffiliated. PSP unionists were well organized in party committees in many shops and industries, and the PSP's daily, *Hoy*, covered union affairs more extensively than did other Cuban newspapers.

The PSP was the only significant political force in Cuba that claimed to be socialist or Marxist and stressed the importance of a systematic ideology and program as the basis for the development of strategy and tactics.[72] Its ideology and program were tools used to win ideological support from radicalized Cubans seeking a systematic explanation of the country's situation. This aspect of the PSP is even more noticeable when contrasted with the 26th of July Movement's antitheoretical and antiprogrammatic stance.[73]

THE PSP'S PROGRAMS AND ANALYSES

Less than a month before the revolution's triumph, the PSP had rather defensively advocated the nationalization of foreign utilities and the "revision of colonialist concessions." The party also proposed an unspecified program of agrarian reform without mentioning the 1940 constitution's requirement for "previous payment" to dispossessed owners, a proviso that the Communists had criticized during the 1940 constitutional convention. This relatively cautious social program was nonetheless more anticapitalist than Castro's position in 1956–58. During this period, as we saw in chapter 4, Castro had sought to appeal to Cuban moderates and conservatives by setting aside the radical proposals of History Will Absolve Me, which were then little known to the great majority of Cubans. At this time, Castro even repudiated nationalization as a tool of public policy. The PSP also proposed that Batista's regime be replaced by a "democratic coalition" that would include "moderate elements," referring to leaders of traditional political organizations and former officeholders such as Carlos Prío Socarrás.[74] Fidel Castro had already abandoned this position, adopting a more radical political perspective that rejected corrupt pre-Batista politicians while welcoming nonparty notables such as prominent attorney José Miró Cardona and reputable Ortodoxos such as former presidential candidate Roberto Agramonte who had never held public office.

The PSP's programs and analyses in the early months following the Cuban Revolution demonstrated a great deal of flexibility and resilience. On the whole, the party kept pace with Fidel Castro in the radicalization of the revolution. From a programmatic point of view, the PSP remained significantly more anticapitalist than Castro in the first few months of 1959. With the passing of the May 1959 agrarian reform law, Castro began to catch up with the PSP, and by that fall the gap had been closed: Castro would soon surpass the PSP and turn against capitalism. But even when the PSP was more cautious than Castro, it always managed to support his measures, as in the matter of nationalizing firms owned by Cuban capitalists.

The positions staked out by the PSP in early January 1959 indicate the proximate goals of a party trying to end its political isolation and marginality. The PSP was also trying to advocate changes that would affect the society's social, economic, and class structure, injecting social content into what had thus far been a purely political revolution. At this point, the PSP had established a minimally radical program while trying to allay fears by insisting that socialism did not appear on the national agenda.[75] Although the PSP had adopted a very friendly stance toward Castro, it identified a right, center, and left in the revolutionary camp, which, it argued, existed at the top as well as among the rank and file. The PSP defined most of the early revolutionary cabinet in office before Castro became prime minister in mid-February 1959 as being on the right and criticized them for not acting in a revolutionary manner.[76] The general slogan of this period was "Defend the revolution and make it advance," or as top PSP leader Blas Roca said, "The revolution, to defend itself, must become more revolutionary."[77] Although at this earliest stage the PSP was perceived as being more anticapitalist than was Castro, its position did not imply that the PSP in any way wished to confront his control of the revolutionary process. The PSP essentially had developed the stance of a friendly leftist pressure group.

The PSP insisted that socialism was not on the agenda and initially defined the revolution as a "patriotic and democratic national liberation and agrarian revolution" required by the semifeudal nature of Cuban society.[78] The PSP's analysis of the revolutionary process was the most radical offered by any major political group in Cuba at this time. Moreover, as the revolution became radicalized in fact long before it did so in theory, the PSP was not to be left behind Fidel Castro's radical anticapitalist push. The party's analysis of the revolution proved to be very elastic and, taking advantage of the relaxation of Moscow's control under the conditions of an increasingly polycentric Communist world, went farther and faster than that of the Soviet Communist Party. At the important October 1959 plenum of the party's national committee, Roca reported that many of the revolution's national liberation tasks had already been accomplished. He continued, "There are stages in the revolutionary process, but they are not separated by Chinese walls. . . . [I]t is a process where one can advance from one stage to another." Roca further explained that the new PSP program would state the possibility "that the most advanced elements of the radical sector of the petty bourgeoisie, which today maintains revolutionary hegemony, evolve toward the proletariat, adopt its socialist point of view and continue to lead in the process of transition to socialism." Roca hedged his bets by cautioning that the absence of pure stages in a revolution did not mean that one could "in Cuba pass willy-nilly to the socialist stage of the revolution or even that this step is near." He nonetheless went on to make a statement that was surprising coming from such a veteran enemy of Trotskyism: "Marxism-Leninism teaches us as much that revolutions have stages as that they must develop uninterruptedly and pass from one stage to another."[79] By mid-March 1960, Roca continued his discourse on the nature of revolutionary stages, but he now unambiguously concluded that socialism "was the aspiration and next goal of the revolutionary forces," a perspective the Soviet leadership was not willing to entertain at that time. Four weeks later, another prominent PSP leader, Aníbal Escalante, compared the Egyptian and Cuban Revolutions and concluded that the main difference was that Cuba had pursued the road of "uninterrupted" revolution.[80] The PSP leaders also had reason to fear the establishment of strictly governmental relations between Moscow and Havana as had happened with Egypt and other nationalist regimes, leaving the local Communists exposed to the actual or potential hostility of the nationalist leaders.[81] At the PSP's Eighth National Congress, held in August 1960, Roca continued to characterize the Cuban Revolution as "national, emancipatory, agrarian, patriotic, and democratic," but he added that the "Cuban Revolution is radical, it uses radical methods, is developing in a rapid rhythm, and is advancing without interruption."[82] The PSP's concept of stages of development did not indicate the objective and subjective social factors that specifically accelerated or delayed the revolution's movement from one stage to the next.[83] As a result, the PSP's theory was in fact essentially descriptive and exclusively political, and because it was not based on a deeper analysis of underlying social realities, it lent itself more easily to ad hoc opportunistic uses determined by which way the political winds were blowing. In this kind of analysis, such factors as the extent of working-class consciousness and initiative and the nature of economic development played marginal roles at best.

THE PSP'S CLASS ANALYSIS OF THE REVOLUTION

During the early stages of the revolution, the PSP insisted that as long as Cuba was capitalist, the existence of classes and class struggle in Cuba could not be ignored.[84] The PSP took this position at a time when conservative opposition to Castro maintained that the existence of classes and the class struggle was a Communist myth. Furthermore, many populist supporters of Castro claimed that a popular, honest government could avoid eliminating social classes as such but instead make classes and the class struggle irrelevant.[85]

In early 1959, the PSP put forward a Cuban equivalent of Mao's "four-class" model accompanied by the recognition that the radical petty bourgeoisie rather than the national bourgeoisie led the revolution.[86] In the PSP's view, Cuba had four progressive classes: the working class, which, in the usual Stalinist fashion, expressed itself politically, by definition through the PSP; the peasantry; the urban petty bourgeoisie; and the national bourgeoisie, particularly its industrial sector.[87] Given this analysis, the PSP leaders sometimes tried to reconcile conflicting goals such as maintaining an appeal to the working class while arguing that the revolutionary ranks could accommodate the industrial national bourgeoisie.

For example, Carlos Rafael Rodríguez said that industrialists were entitled to profits but simultaneously proposed limiting them through an excess-profit tax to be used for the government's industrialization drive.[88] Rodríguez had previously insisted that the economic class struggle between workers and employers should not prevent them from working together to accomplish the political tasks of the revolution.[89] The PSP's repeated assurances that in China, unlike the Soviet Union, the Communists had welcomed many supportive bourgeois elements during the transition to socialism failed to carry much weight with the national industrial bourgeoisie or with a large part of the petty bourgeoisie, who chose the road to exile in Miami and elsewhere.[90]

Once again, the PSP's early caution did not prevent it from keeping up, in theory and practice, with the forward rush led by Fidel Castro. In early July 1959, Roca was still denying the anticapitalist character of the Cuban Revolution and asserting that the Cuban bourgeoisie could benefit from the anti-imperialist and antilandlord character of the revolution yet was also suggesting that the bourgeoisie could not be allowed to become the dominant class in the revolutionary process. For Roca, such a situation would mean the betrayal of the revolution because of the bourgeoisie's inclination toward moderation and reformism and its tendency to take advantage of the working class and the peasantry. Roca exhorted the national bourgeoisie to support the revolution and defeat the proimperialistic tendencies within the bourgeoisie. He clearly indicated, however, that his appeal for bourgeois support did not mean that the PSP would abandon its socialist program.[91] Even this kind of qualified appeal became less frequent in the PSP's pronouncements. By April 1960, the PSP's analysis and exhortations had undergone a noticeable change. In characterizing the class character of the revolution, the PSP now emphasized the "worker-peasant alliance."[92] This shift meshed with the PSP's new belief that in the uninterrupted development of the revolution, "socialism" had now become the next stage.

THE "UNITY" LINE

While the PSP grew in size during the early months of the revolution, its growing political influence resulted mainly from the strategic line put forward by the party and later supported by Fidel Castro. This line consisted of repeatedly stressing the need for "revolutionary unity." The specific programmatic bases for this unity were rather vague, but its organizational meaning clearly endorsed collaboration with those wings of the 26th of July Movement and lesser revolutionary organizations that, although not necessarily admirers of the PSP, were willing to refrain from criticizing the party's politics. The PSP skillfully pursued this particular strategy in numerous arenas such as the unions and the rebel army. The PSP's central leadership initially placed less emphasis on obtaining positions than on creating a favorable political milieu in each arena. Here the PSP partly was making a virtue out of necessity because Castro and his movement had refused to formally share power with other groups, including the PSP and the Directorio Revolucionario. Moreover, in the early stages of the revolution, any explicit PSP participation in governmental bodies would have created political difficulties for the government because Castro was still disassociating himself from Communism. Consequently, the top PSP leadership took an apparently patient and reasonable attitude toward not participating in the national government[93] or even in union leadership.[94] When the Communists became integrated into the revolutionary process in the early 1960s, the PSP aggressively developed large organizational ambitions that eventually provoked Fidel Castro's ire.[95]

Perhaps the greatest success of the PSP's "unity" line was the relationship it built with sectors of the 26th of July Movement that supported Communism. As far back as the summer of 1957, the PSP had sent a young but experienced Communist cadre to join Guevara in the Sierra Maestra and take charge of political indoctrination among the rebel troops under his command.[96] At the time, Communist militants had more freedom of action with the guerrillas under the command of Guevara and Raúl Castro than with other revolutionary commanders, and such remained the case in early 1959. By this time, a significant group of rebel army majors had become closely identified with the "unity" line. In addition to Guevara and Raúl Castro, this group included Majors Augusto Martínez Sánchez, William Gálvez, Demetrio Montseny (Villa), Manuel Piñeiro, and Faure Chomón from the Directorio Revolucionario.[97] This approach also met with some success in the trade unions. While the PSP had only a small influence in the unions, the PSP-influenced "unity" slates did better, and "prounity" forces dominated a few of the thirty-three industrial federations, including those of the textile, restaurant, and transport workers. In addition, proponents of "unity" controlled a number of locals in the sugar, tobacco, and maritime workers' federations.[98] Fidel Castro's intervention at the Tenth Congress of the Cuban Confederation of Workers in November 1959 paved the way for the confederation to be controlled by the minority "unity" unionists. Wholesale purges and neutralization of the anti-PSP majority soon followed this takeover, and then the PSP unionists quickly took over the confederation's top leadership positions, although Fidel Castro's ultimate control never came into question. The PSP thus helped create a political milieu that could not challenge Fidel Castro's power and prestige but could help legitimate the party's politics. At least part of the PSP's "unity" milieu might have become a source of opposition to Fidel Castro had he chosen to go in a different political direction.

The PSP had gained some distinct advantages by politically winning over many of the radicalized Fidelistas, particularly those who had been influenced by the more radical pronouncements of Raúl Castro and Guevara. Although both of these leaders enjoyed a great deal of prestige and were surpassed only by Fidel Castro and Major Camilo Cienfuegos, they were greatly limited by their dependence on Fidel Castro in a way that did not apply to the PSP. In other words, as representatives of the government, Guevara and Raúl Castro had to watch what they said; in contrast, the PSP had much more freedom to disseminate its worldview and thus could provide the only systematic explanation of events to its members and to radicalized Fidelistas. The PSP fully exploited its ideological monopoly as the one significant political force with a systematic methodology and the only Cuban voice speaking in the name of Marxism and socialism.[99] A number of informal political currents existed within the PSP (factions were forbidden by the Stalinist model of so-called democratic centralism). Rodríguez and some other PSP leaders were closer and more sympathetic to Fidel Castro and his associates and placed a high priority on getting along with the revolutionary leaders, even at the expense of what might have appeared to be the party's short-term organizational interests. Escalante stood at the other, far more sectarian end of the party's internal political spectrum.[100] These different orientations diverged over the existence of so-called Cuban exceptionalism.[101] The exceptionalist strategy involved a more aggressive party role, including an attempt to recruit leading revolutionaries into the PSP, but this course would have been dangerous. The fact that this approach did not prevail later made it easier for Rodríguez and the other PSP leaders on good terms with Castro to work closely with the revolutionary leadership without becoming a threat. The PSP leaders also became very valuable to Fidel Castro in enlisting Soviet support.[102] The beginning of polycentrism in the Communist world greatly facilitated the PSP's task of pressuring Moscow to commit itself to total support for Castro's revolution.

THE QUESTION OF ANTI-COMMUNISM

Early in the revolution, when Fidel Castro was systematically trying to avoid publicly taking a clear position on Communism, the PSP, as an established Communist party, carefully monitored anti-Communist pronouncements from all quarters. The PSP's organizational independence allowed it to name names at a time when doing so would have been difficult for Fidel Castro or even for Guevara and Raúl Castro.[103]

Typically, the right-wing and liberal opposition to Castro extensively employed the theme of anti-Communism at a very primitive level of know-nothing prejudice that had been greatly encouraged by the Cold War and McCarthyism. For the most part, eloquent defenses of civil liberties and democracy were unaccompanied by any understanding, let alone indictment, of capitalism and imperialism as a system. In combating these forces, the PSP's defense of the revolutionary government was joined by *Revolución*, the official organ of the 26th of July Movement, and several other publications. But the PSP and later Fidel Castro used the charge of anti-Communism to pressure supporters of the revolutionary camp to avoid criticizing existing Communist states or the PSP's political line. This accomplishment was notable because the PSP could propagandize freely on all of these issues. Consequently, the PSP could propagate Communist politics, but party opponents—whether moderate, radical, or conservative—found themselves characterized as part of an officially defined right-wing anti-Communist amalgam.

The use of this tactic in combination with the absence of a non-Communist Marxist or socialist tradition prevented any substantive discussion among those supporting radical change of the pros and cons of Communism as an economic, social, and political system. Perhaps the most important political casualties of this process were the persons associated with *Revolución*, edited by the former PSP member Carlos Franqui (who was allowed to resign and later to go to Italy in 1968). Euclides

Vázquez Candela, the non-Communist but radical chief theoretician of *Revolución*, closed the debate with the PSP in September 1959 by accusing the party of trying to portray the 26th of July Movement as a merely provisional formation as a means of preventing it from becoming a permanent organization. Vázquez Candela reiterated the need for such an organization and went on to specify the nature of his objections to the PSP's politics:

> To be a communist plain and simple is a way of confronting
> reality like many others and as such not at all shameful in itself. . . .
> To be a communist of a party of the Cominform is already, without
> doubt, to adopt a type of Marxism compromised with the interests
> and demands of a metropolis in which one blindly trusts in . . . the
> universal establishment of socialism. The open belligerence against
> these two forms of conduct and living is not at the center of our
> struggle. We have our own position, and we will defend it with the
> same right that all revolutions have defended their way of facing
> the restructuring of the society in which they must act.[104]

In conclusion, the Cuban Communists were quicker to respond to Fidel Castro's radicalization of the revolutionary process than were the Soviet leaders, notwithstanding the PSP's and the Soviets' common ideology and subordinate organizational ties. A Cuban Communist organization obviously had more potential gains and losses at stake in the development of the revolution than did the Soviet Union. In addition, the PSP had a vested interest in portraying the possibilities of the Cuban process in a very favorable light as a means of persuading Moscow to become more involved. This greater Soviet involvement in turn enhanced the PSP's importance in Fidel Castro's eyes.[105] The PSP's greater aggressiveness pointed to differences concerning tempo and short-term perspectives but did not by itself involve a major conflict with Moscow. This situation did not, however, mean the absence of potential conflicts between the two Communist entities. Cuban Communists were concerned about an Egypt-like situation in which Fidel Castro would establish friendly relations with the Soviet Union and ignore or even repress the PSP at home. The potential also existed for friction in connection with the relations between Washington and Moscow. While the PSP generally defended the Soviet policy of détente with the United States, party leaders worried to some degree about its possible implications. Thus, on January 9, 1960, the PSP's daily newspaper, *Hoy*, argued that the policy of "peaceful coexistence" did not mean the same thing for a highly vulnerable small country that had to be ready to face overwhelming U.S. power as it did for a major military power. The article concluded that "what for the USSR and Khrushchev is a disposition for peace and benevolence for us would be a dangerous venture."[106] In any case, the fact that the Cuban Revolution was taking place in the post-Stalin period, when Communist polycentrism was beginning to come into its own, created more elbow room in the Cuban PSP's relations with Moscow.

[EPILOGUE]

In this volume, I have tried to present a fresh view of the complex sequence of causes and consequences that culminated in the Cuban Revolution's eventual development to Communism. These events involved key aspects of the structure of Cuba's economy, politics, and society in the first six decades of the twentieth century; the impact of revolutionary populist political leadership; and the decisive role of outside powers such as the U.S. and the Soviet Union.

RECONSIDERING ECONOMICS, POPULISM, AND IMPERIALISM

The structure of Cuba's economy, society, and politics made a revolution possible—but not inevitable. The economics of U.S. imperial domination coupled with uneven development and the world depression of the 1930s produced serious economic crises that provoked strong working-class resistance and state regulation of the economy. These phenomena in turn created contradictory forces or "vicious circles" that led to overall economic stagnation.

While capitalism was the dominant economic system in prerevolutionary Cuba, the native capitalist class often could not exercise direct political rule on behalf of its own interests, particularly after the frustrated 1933 revolution.[1] This situation led to the rise of Bonapartist political leaderships such as that of Fulgencio Batista that constituted part of a social and political system that included politically inarticulate social classes, weak political parties, and a fundamentally mercenary army substantially different from the oligarchic, ideologically conservative armies common in Latin America.

Second, this social and political situation created an environment advantageous to the dominance of populist politics in terms of style, orientation, and content. This populism responded to the great sense of frustration and demoralization caused by the failures of struggles as far back as the fight for national independence at the end of the nineteenth century and the degeneration of most of the revolutionaries of the 1930s into practitioners of a thoroughly corrupt *politiquería* if not outright gangsterism. Cuba's neocolonial relationship with the United States led to a widespread sense of geopolitical fatalism among traditional and even nontraditional Cuban politicians, as expressed by the idea that nothing could be done in Cuba without U.S. consent.

Batista's coup and dictatorship in the 1950s threw into sharp crisis what proved to be a very precarious sociopolitical system. Batista's military regime never gained legitimacy in the eyes of the great majority of the population and was eventually blown apart by the rebels' 26th of July Movement. Fidel Castro's declassed political leadership, with few or no organizational or institutional ties either to the petty bourgeoisie or to any of the country's other major social classes, constituted the other side of the coin of Batista's decayed Bonapartism. In his fight against Batista, Fidel Castro allied himself with people supporting the interests of different social groups and classes at various times and did so by minimizing programmatic clarity and firm organizational commitments and maximizing his personal political control. Castro was also a masterful tactician who, while privately committed to the notion of pushing Cuba in a generally left-wing anti-imperialist direction, lacked a master plan. He was especially skilled at dealing with tactical situations, where he often managed to defeat his domestic enemies individually before they could unite against him. However, Castro was not merely a talented tactician, and he did have politics of a certain kind: a left-wing authoritarian populism that under existing circumstances evolved into a variety of Communist nationalism.

The characteristics of Castro's leadership and the movement he headed led to a revolution from above. This does not mean that the revolution was not popular or that it did not involve a radical social and political change. It does mean that although the great majority of the population was encouraged to participate, it was not allowed to control or direct the revolution. Manipulation; plebiscitary politics; virtually complete state control over political, social, and economic life; and—whenever the revolutionary leadership found it necessary—all-out repression and massive incarceration substituted for many years for genuine discussion and meaningful democratic decisions from below.

Third, outside powers had a great impact on the direction of the revolution. Notwithstanding the abolition of the Platt Amendment in 1934, U.S. imperial power weighed heavily on Cuba's economy, politics, and society. Although Fidel Castro relatively easily defeated internal opposition, such was not the case for the strong opposition put forward by U.S. interests. Although certainly hostile to the revolutionary leadership, U.S. business interests in Cuba were incapable of developing a united strategy to confront Castro on their own. The U.S. government was the only entity capable of devising a coherent strategy for overthrowing the revolutionary leadership, a policy that was structurally predetermined by the U.S. government's commitment to the defense of U.S. economic and geopolitical interests in Latin America and the Caribbean. Fidel Castro's political dissimulation prior to coming to power allowed him to take advantage of the element of surprise and to postpone a frontal clash with the United States. In addition, the rebels' total defeat of Batista's army and Castro's political skill in handling the liberal elements of his government in 1959 deprived the U.S. government of the sort of allies that had worked so well on behalf of U.S. interests in the rest of Latin America. Nevertheless, Castro and the other rebel leaders eventually came face to face with the tremendous U.S. economic, political, and military power over Cuba and chose to confront it in a bold and radical manner. This choice was dictated in part by the objective structural circumstances that confronted the Cuban leadership and in part by the leadership's political and ideological inclinations. I emphasize the agency of the revolutionary leaders. These leaders took advantage of highly favorable domestic circumstances to pursue independent political and ideological visions and not merely reacting to the policies of the Eisenhower and Kennedy administrations.

Fidel Castro and his close political associates took power at a time when the power of the Soviet Union relative to that of the United States seemed ascendant in the struggle for world supremacy. This made the Soviet leadership under Nikita Khrushchev feel confident about challenging the United States even in its Western Hemisphere backyard. At the same time, the growing rift between China and the Soviet Union and the spread of polycentrism in the Communist world helped Castro and his close associates retain a certain degree of autonomy from the Soviet leadership on which they subsequently came to depend for survival.

The international situation combined with unexpected opportunities that occurred at home as a result of the collapse of the traditional army and the political weakness of the upper and middle classes. In such an environment, Fidel Castro and his associates chose the Communist road for Cuba. Rather than the outcome, as some would have it, of a conspiracy hatched before January 1, 1959, Castro's—and Cuba's—eventual political direction was most likely the result of a conjunctural choice made by the fall of 1959. This choice was fostered first by the potentially high political cost that Fidel Castro would incur by breaking with the pro-Soviet and pro–Partido Socialista Popular wing of the 26th of July Movement headed by Raúl Castro and Che Guevara and second by the affinity of Castro's brand of authoritarian populism for the Soviet-type systems.[2]

THE CUBAN REVOLUTION IN HISTORICAL PERSPECTIVE

The Cuban Revolution was one of the most important events in twentieth-century Latin America and had a major impact well beyond the Western Hemisphere. The establishment of Cuban Communism resulted from a democratic, multiclass revolution against a rather typical Latin American dictatorship. Although distinctive in some ways, the initial opposition movement against the Batista dictatorship had many similarities to other struggles of the 1950s against tyrannical Latin American regimes such as those in Venezuela, Peru, and Colombia. The opposition movements in Cuba and in other Latin American countries saw themselves as part of the same political struggle against military dictatorships and for democracy and constitutional government. This was particularly true of Venezuela, where the democratic political movement that overthrew the Pérez Jiménez dictatorship in January 1958 provided substantial political and material support to the Cuban rebels in the Sierra Maestra.

Of course, the transformation of the Cuban multiclass democratic political revolution into a Communist social revolution and the development of a close alliance between Cuba and the Soviet bloc made this revolution unique. While subsequent political developments in such Western

Hemisphere countries as Chile, El Salvador, Grenada, and particularly Nicaragua were influenced by and in some ways even resembled the Cuban experience, they never approximated the singularity of the Cuban Revolution.

IDEOLOGY AND THE POLITICS OF TRANSITION

Many of the issues addressed in this volume have been debated since the beginning of the Cuban revolutionary process, but the new political climate in both Cuba and abroad created by the collapse of the Soviet bloc in the 1990s and the resulting impact on Cuba have given new life to these debates. That Cuba will eventually undergo a transition beyond the mere replacement of Fidel Castro as the head of the Cuban state is highly likely. Some observers predict that after a short period of continuity meant to reassure Cubans and foreigners about the system's stability, significant institutional changes in Cuban economic, social, and political life will occur. While much has been written about such likely changes in Cuba,[3] much less discussion has concerned the changes in the ideological and political landscape that are likely to accompany such institutional transformations. Historical revisionism, for example, will inevitably accompany any socioeconomic transition.[4] Any significant institutional change in Cuba will need to be supported and justified in political and ideological terms. This process will inevitably pose the question of why the revolution created the Cuba it did. In light of the strong procapitalist ideological tendencies that have developed in all post-Communist transitions and the existing tendencies in Cuban political thought that have been greatly strengthened since the 1990s, we can expect the renewed formulation of certain polemical positions regarding the background and early origins of the Cuban Revolution. Among the right and right-of-center opponents of the Cuban regime, this process has already involved a strong tendency to praise and exaggerate the supposed achievements of the prerevolutionary republic[5] and the claim that a radical social revolution was neither necessary nor justified in the Cuba of the late 1950s. In addition, the rejection of social revolution has been marked by the failure to make the fundamental analytical distinction between radical social revolution in general and the particular social revolution that took place in Cuba. Not surprisingly, in claiming that Fidel Castro's brand of Communism was the only possible alternative for Cuba, supporters of the Cuban regime fail to make the same distinction.

Fidel Castro's death will also have a major impact on Cuba's relations with the United States. A capitalist transition is highly likely to be led, as in the Soviet Union and China, by Cuban Communists and would restore, although not necessarily in the same form, much of the power that the United States lost in Cuba almost fifty years ago. Such renewed U.S. power would be ideologically and politically defended by procapitalist supporters of the transition and would likely include revisionist historical claims denying or at least minimizing the imperialist characteristics of U.S. policy before and during the revolution, with Cuban "moderate" supporters of the capitalist transition perhaps even rendering homage to U.S. Ambassador Philip Bonsal as a reasonable diplomat who could have resolved the conflict between the two countries. These interpretations will be challenged by those upholding the legacy of Fidel Castro as well as by those trying to create a new revolutionary and democratic Left in Cuba.

[NOTES]

INTRODUCTION

1. "Homenaje a la República" [Homage to the Republic], *Encuentro de la Cultura Cubana* (Madrid) 24 (Spring 2002): 5–151.

2. While the bulk of this work is brand-new, segments of this volume overlap with two of my previous publications on Cuba. I want to thank the publishers for their permission to use materials from those publications in this volume: Samuel Farber, *Revolution and Reaction in Cuba, 1933–1960: A Political Sociology from Machado to Castro* (Middletown, Conn.: Wesleyan University Press, 1976); Samuel Farber, "The Cuban Communists in the Early Stages of the Cuban Revolution: Revolutionaries or Reformists?" *Latin American Research Review* 18 (March 1983): 59–83; copyright © 1983 by the University of Texas Press; all rights reserved.

3. U.S. Department of State, *Foreign Relations of the United States, 1958–1960*, vol. 6, *Cuba* (Washington, D.C.: U.S. Government Printing Office, 1991).

4. *Confidential U.S. State Department Central Files: Cuba, 1955–1959: Internal Affairs and Foreign Affairs*, 25 reels (Frederick, Md.: University Publications of America, 1987).

5. Aleksandr Fursenko and Timothy Naftali, *"One Hell of a Gamble": Khrushchev, Castro, and Kennedy, 1958–1964* (New York: Norton, 1997).

6. See, for example, Luis Báez, *Secretos de Generales* (Havana: Editorial Si-Mar, 1996); William Gálvez, *Camilo: Señor de la Vanguardia* (Havana: Editorial de Ciencias Sociales, 1979); William Gálvez, *Frank: Entre el Sol y la Montaña*, 2 vols. (Havana: Ediciones Unión, 1991); Enrique Oltuski, *Vida Clandestina: My Life in the Cuban Revolution*, trans. Thomas Christensen and Carol Christensen (New York: Wiley, 2002).

7. Herbert Dinerstein, *The Making of a Missile Crisis: October 1962* (Baltimore: Johns Hopkins University Press, 1976), 1.

8. Fursenko and Naftali, *"One Hell of a Gamble,"* 11–15.

9. For a discussion of this issue, see Farber, *Revolution and Reaction*.

10. James O'Connor, *The Origins of Socialism in Cuba* (Ithaca: Cornell University Press, 1970), 11. While this work was published many decades ago, it remains the most sophisticated expression of the "objectivist" views discussed here.

11. Marifeli Pérez-Stable, *The Cuban Revolution: Origins, Course, and Legacy*, 2d ed. (New York: Oxford University Press, 1999), 61.

1. Norton Ginsberg, *Atlas of Economic Development* (Chicago: University of Chicago Press, 1961), 18.

2. Pedro C. M. Teichert, "Analysis of Real Growth and Wealth in the Latin American Republics," *Journal of Inter-American Studies* 1 (April 1959): 184–85.

3. Eugene Staley, *The Future of Underdeveloped Countries*, rev. ed. (New York: Harper, 1961), 16–17.

4. Louis A. Pérez Jr., *Cuba: Between Reform and Revolution* (New York: Oxford University Press, 1988), 285.

5. International Bank for Reconstruction and Development, *Report on Cuba* (Washington, D.C.: International Bank for Reconstruction and Development, 1951), 7.

6. Marifeli Pérez-Stable, *The Cuban Revolution: Origins, Course, and Legacy*, 2d ed. (New York: Oxford University Press, 1999), 15.

7. International Bank, *Report on Cuba*, 65.

8. Francisco López Segrera, *Cuba: Capitalismo Dependiente y Subdesarrollo (1510–1959)* (Havana: Editora de Ciencias Sociales, 1981), 158–59.

9. Ibid., 153.

10. Julio Le Riverend, *Historia Económica de Cuba* (Havana: Instituto Cubano del Libro, n.d.), 594–97.

11. Ibid., 626–27.

12. Jorge Ibarra, *Prologue to Revolution: Cuba, 1898–1958*, trans. Marjorie Moore (Boulder, Colo.: Rienner, 1998), 17.

13. Pérez, *Cuba*, 280–81.

14. Ibid., 252, 279–80.

15. U.S. Department of Commerce, Bureau of Foreign Commerce, *Investment in Cuba: Basic Information for United States Businessmen* (Washington, D.C.: U.S. Government Printing Office, 1956), 137.

16. Ismael Zuaznabar, *La Economía Cubana en la Década del 50* (Havana: Editorial de Ciencias Sociales, 1986), 22–23.

17. Jorge I. Domínguez, *Cuba: Order and Revolution* (Cambridge: Belknap Press of Harvard University Press, 1978), 74.

18. Carlos Rafael Rodríguez, *Cuba en el Tránsito al Socialismo, 1959–1963* (Havana: Editora Política, 1979), 24.

19. Le Riverend, *Historia Económica de Cuba* (n.d.), 650–53; López Segrera, *Cuba*, 197–99; Zuaznabar, *Economía Cubana*, 35–37; Dudley Seers, "The Economic and Social Background," in *Cuba: The Economic and Social Revolution*, ed. Dudley Seers (Chapel Hill: University of North Carolina Press, 1964), 11; Julio Le Riverend, *Historia Económica de Cuba* (Havana: Instituto Cubano del Libro, 1967), 252.

20. Andrés Bianchi, "Agriculture: The Pre-Revolutionary Background," in *Economic and Social Revolution*, ed. Seers, 83–84.

21. Julián Alienes y Urosa, *Características Fundamentales de la Economía Cubana* (Havana: Banco Nacional de Cuba, 1950), 113.

22. Bianchi, "Agriculture," 86.

23. López Segrera, *Cuba*, 158–59.

24. International Bank, *Report on Cuba*, 197–98; Bianchi, "Agriculture," 93.

25. Bianchi, "Agriculture," 91.

26. Carmelo Mesa-Lago, "Unemployment in Socialist Countries: Soviet Union, East Europe, China, and Cuba" (Ph.D. diss., Cornell University, 1968), 371–73.

27. Claes Brundenius, *Revolutionary Cuba: The Challenge of Economic Growth with Equity* (Boulder, Colo.: Westview, 1984), 13.

28. For an excellent discussion of the concept of uneven development (or "combined and uneven development"), see Leon Trotsky, "Peculiarities of Russia's Development," chap. 1 of *The History of the Russian Revolution*, trans. Max Eastman (Ann Arbor: University of Michigan Press, 1957); see also Leon Trotsky, *Results and Prospects* (New York: Merit, 1969). Sociologist Martin Murray, *The Development of Capitalism in Colonial Indochina (1870–1940)* (Berkeley: University of California Press, 1980), has utilized this concept in analyzing capitalist development in colonial Indochina. Writers outside the Marxist tradition such as Thorstein Veblen have also dealt with the significance of late economic development in social analysis; see Thorstein Veblen, *Imperial Germany and the Industrial Revolution* (Ann Arbor: University of Michigan Press, 1966). For a more contemporary analysis along these lines, see Alexander Gerschenkron, *Economic Backwardness in Historical Perspective: A Book of Essays* (Cambridge: Belknap Press of Harvard University Press, 1966).

29. Alienes y Urosa, *Características Fundamentales*, 12, 39–40; James O'Connor, *The Origins of Socialism in Cuba* (Ithaca: Cornell University Press, 1970), 13. The 1907 Cuban census tallied 2,048,980 persons; twelve years later, the census found a population of 2,889,004, including more than 245,000 Spanish-born persons (just over 8 percent of the total); and in 1931, 3,962,344 people were counted. For Spanish influence in Cuba, see Guillermo J. Grenier and Lisandro Pérez, *The Legacy of Exile: Cubans in the United States* (Boston: Allyn and Bacon, 2003), 36–37.

30. For an extensive discussion of these issues, see Samuel Farber, *Revolution and Reaction in Cuba, 1933–1960: A Political Sociology from Machado to Castro* (Middletown, Conn.: Wesleyan University Press, 1976).

31. López Segrera, *Cuba*.

32. Oscar Zanetti and Alejandro García, *Sugar and Railroads: A Cuban History, 1837–1959*, trans. Franklin W. Knight and Mary Todd (Chapel Hill: University of North Carolina Press, 1998), 33.

33. International Bank, *Report on Cuba*, 241.

34. For purposes of comparison, the United Kingdom is 847 miles long but much broader than the narrow island of Cuba. Cuba's total surface area is close to that of the state of Pennsylvania.

35. U.S. Department of Commerce, Bureau of Foreign Commerce, *Investment in Cuba*, 114.

36. Ernesto Che Guevara, "Sobre el Sistema Presupuestario de Financiamiento," in *Escritos Económicos* (Córdoba, Arg.: Cuadernos del Pasado y Presente, 1969), 41.

37. U.S. Department of Commerce, Bureau of Foreign Commerce, *Investment in Cuba*, 24.

38. K. Lynn Stoner, *From the House to the Streets: The Cuban Woman's Movement for Legal Reform, 1898–1940* (Durham: Duke University Press, 1991), 45.

39. Ibid., 46, 124; see also Lois M. Smith and Alfred Padula, *Sex and Revolution: Women in Socialist Cuba* (New York: Oxford University Press, 1996), 15, 19.

40. Stoner, *From the House*, 133.

41. Ibarra, *Prologue to Revolution*, 173.

42. Seers, "Economic and Social Background," 18.

43. Jose Luis Rodríguez, "La Economía Neocolonial Cubana," *Cuba Socialista* 37 (January–February 1989): 121.

44. Pérez, *Cuba*, 301.

45. Pérez-Stable, *Cuban Revolution*, 29.

46. Ibarra, *Prologue to Revolution*, 166.

47. Ibid., 162.

48. Agrupación Católica Universitaria, *Encuesta de Trabajadores Rurales, 1956–57*, reprinted in *Economía y Desarrollo* (Instituto de Economía de la Universidad de la Habana) (July–August 1972): 188–212.

49. Ibid., 191.

50. Ibid., 211.

51. Ibid., 206; Ibarra, *Prologue to Revolution*, 162.

52. Agrupación Católica Universitaria, *Encuesta*, 196–200.

53. Ibid., 201–2.

54. Ibid., 207–9.

55. López Segrera, *Cuba*, 270.

56. See Ibarra, *Prologue to Revolution*, 141–51. For a more extended discussion of blacks in Cuba during the period 1933–58, see Alejandro de la Fuente, *A Nation for All: Race, Inequality, and Politics in Twentieth-Century Cuba* (Chapel Hill: University of North Carolina Press, 2001), 175–255.

57. Seers, "Economic and Social Background," 25; International Bank, *Report on Cuba*, 138.

58. International Bank, *Report on Cuba*, 6.

59. Agrupación Católica Universitaria, *Encuesta*, 203–4.

60. Seers, "Economic and Social Background," 16.

61. Ibid., 15, 22.

62. International Bank, *Report on Cuba*, 7, 9, 146, 566–69.

63. This question is discussed at length in Farber, *Revolution and Reaction*, 235–37.

64. Le Riverend, *Historia Económica* (n.d.), 638–39.

65. O'Connor, *Origins of Socialism*, 66.

66. Seers, "Economic and Social Background," 88.

67. International Bank, *Report on Cuba*, 360.

68. U.S. Department of Commerce, Bureau of Foreign Commerce, *Investment in Cuba*, 4.

69. At about the same time, the Tribunal de Cuentas (Tribunal of Accounts) was established to attempt to audit and control the income and expenditures of governmental institutions.

70. International Bank, *Report On Cuba*, 630–35.

71. *Hispanic World Report* 2 (June 1949): 32; *Hispanic World Report* 2 (July 1949): 33.

72. *Business Week*, December 18, 1948, 117.

73. I am indebted to Dan Labotz for this formulation regarding how uneven development affected the Cuban working class.

74. International Bank, *Report on Cuba*, 66, 357–59, 525–27, 597, 779.

75. Ibid., 25, 386.

76. Ibid., 29.

77. Ibid., 119.

78. Ibid., 125.

79. Ibid., 357–89.

80. Ibid., 359.

81. I am indebted to Mel Bienenfield for the formulation regarding the economic consequences of uneven Cuban development.

82. Robin Blackburn, "Prologue to the Cuban Revolution," *New Left Review* 21 (October 1963): 71.

83. U.S. Department of Commerce, Bureau of Foreign Commerce, *Investment in Cuba*, 21.

84. Ibid., 19; see also Ibarra, *Prologue to Revolution*, 102.

85. United Nations, Department of Economic and Social Affairs, *Economic Survey of Latin America for 1953* (New York: U.N. Department of Economic and Social Affairs, 1954), 17.

86. United Nations, Department of Economic and Social Affairs, *Economic Survey of Latin America for 1954* (New York: U.N. Department of Economic and Social Affairs, 1955), 161.

87. José Luis Rodríguez, "Economía Neocolonial," 117.

88. United Nations, Department of Economic and Social Affairs, *Economic Survey of Latin America for 1957* (New York: U.N. Department of Economic and Social Affairs, 1959), 177.

89. Ibid., 183.

90. For the view that the Cuban economy grew at a very slow rate in the 1950s but promised to do better in the 1960s, see Carmelo Mesa-Lago, "Economic Policies and Growth," in *Revolutionary Change in Cuba*, ed. Carmelo Mesa-Lago (Pittsburgh: University of Pittsburgh Press, 1971), 277–338. For the view that the Cuban economy had stagnated since the depression, see, for example, Brundenius, *Revolutionary Cuba*, chap. 1; O'Connor, *Origins of Socialism*; Seers, "Economic and Social Background."

91. Seers, "Economic and Social Background," 12.

92. U.S. Department of Commerce, Bureau of Foreign Commerce, *Investment in Cuba*, 37.

93. Ibid., 16.

94. Juan F. Fuentes and Graciela Chailloux, "El Conflicto: Fuerzas Productivas y Relaciones de Producción como Causa Determinante del Triunfo de la Revolución Social en Cuba," *Economía y Desarrollo* 94 (September–October 1986): 64.

95. United Nations, Department of Economic and Social Affairs, *Economic Survey of Latin America for 1957*, 183.

96. Bianchi, "Agriculture," 72, 76–78.

97. Pérez-Stable, *Cuban Revolution*, 26.

98. U.S. Department of Commerce, Bureau of Foreign Commerce, *Investment in Cuba*, 140.

99. López Segrera, *Cuba*, 237–38.

100. Cuban Economic Research Project, *A Study on Cuba* (Coral Gables, Fla.: University of Miami Press, 1965), 620, 622.

CHAPTER 2

1. James H. Billington, *Fire in the Minds of Men: Origins of the Revolutionary Faith* (New York: Basic Books, 1980), 147–48.

2. Joan Casanovas, "La Nación, la Independencia, y las Clases," *Encuentro de la Cultura Cubana* (Madrid) 15 (Winter 1999–2000): 177–86.

3. Manuel Pedro González and Iván E. Schulman, *José Martí: Esquema Ideológico* (Mexico City: Publicaciones de la Editorial Cultura, 1961), 385–86; my translation. Unless otherwise noted, all translations from Spanish are my own.

4. Many Communist and populist activists and leaders of the 1930s began their involvement in politics in movements of the 1920s such as the Protest of the Thirteen, Minorismo, and the Veterans and Patriots movement (Louis A. Pérez Jr., *Cuba: Between Reform and Revolution* [New York: Oxford University Press, 1988], 236–48).

5. This decline appeared as early as the general elections of 1948, when Communist presidential candidate Juan Marinello obtained only 5.61 percent of the vote (Charles D. Ameringer, *The Cuban Democratic Experience: The Auténtico Years, 1944–1952* [Gainesville: University Press of Florida, 2000], 65).

6. Fidel Castro, *History Will Absolve Me*, in *Revolutionary Struggle, 1947–1958*, vol. 1 of *The Selected Works of Fidel Castro*, ed. Rolando E. Bonachea and Nelson P. Valdés (Cambridge: MIT Press, 1972), 183.

7. Andrés Suárez, *Cuba: Castroism and Communism, 1959–1966*, trans. Joel Carmichael and Ernst Halperin (Cambridge: MIT Press, 1967), 6–7.

8. Luis Báez, *Secretos de Generales* (Havana: Editorial Si-Mar, 1996), 20, 60, 112, 172, 258, 496.

9. Some of the defining features of Stalinist Marxism were a highly schematic view of the stages of historical development—that is, by definition, Latin American "feudalism" would be replaced by capitalism, and capitalism could in turn be followed only by socialism, ignoring, for example, the classical Marxist notion that capitalism could be replaced by either socialism or barbarism. Stalinist Marxist class analysis often tended to

be rigid as well as schematic—that is, Fidel Castro and his close associates represented the radical wing of the petty bourgeoisie even though Castro's group had no organic institutional connections to that class. Stalinism was also strongly "substitutionist," meaning first that the party defined itself as the representative of the working class regardless of the actually expressed views and wishes of that class and second that the party felt free to substitute its interests for those of the working class. This type of Marxism was also marked by an analytical opportunism where social analysis was developed in an ad hoc fashion to justify the numerous political twists and turns of the day. Finally, Stalinism meant a contempt for principled and consistent democratic practices whether inside the party (so-called democratic centralism) or in society at large (dismissing the need for civil liberties and democracy under socialism as a bourgeois notion).

10. Jorge G. Castañeda, *Compañero: The Life and Death of Che Guevara* (New York: Knopf, 1997), 103.

11. Ibid., 129; Jon Lee Anderson, *Che Guevara: A Revolutionary Life* (New York: Grove, 1997), 347. On the issue of bank robbery, see Che Guevara's letter to Enrique Oltuski [Sierra], November 3, 1958, in Enrique Oltuski, *Vida Clandestina: My Life in the Cuban Revolution*, trans. Thomas Christensen and Carol Christensen (New York: Wiley, 2002), 198–99.

12. K. Lynn Stoner, "Militant Heroines and the Consecration of the Patriarchal State: The Glorification of Loyalty, Combat, and National Suicide in the Making of Cuban National Identity," *Cuban Studies* 34 (2003): 92; Glen Caudill Dealy, *The Public Man: An Interpretation of Latin American and Other Catholic Cultures* (Amherst: University of Massachusetts Press, 1977); Glen Caudill Dealy, *The Latin Americans: Spirit and Ethos* (Boulder, Colo.: Westview, 1992).

13. William Ian Miller, *Humiliation and Other Essays on Honor, Social Discomfort, and Violence* (Ithaca: Cornell University Press, 1993), 83–87, 116–24.

14. Dealy views dignity primarily in terms of external matters such as dress and manners, not as the opposite of humiliation and disrespect; see Dealy, *Public Man*, 98–107.

15. William Gálvez, *Camilo: Señor de la Vanguardia* (Havana: Editorial de Ciencias Sociales, 1979), 357–58.

16. The value of loyalty also applied to sports. Even though winter league professional baseball teams were not, during the 1940s and 1950s, locally based, loyalty to one's chosen team was taken very seriously. There was no worse person than a *cambia casaca* (turncoat) who had changed his or her team loyalties. A *cambia casaca* who had changed loyalties from a losing to a winning team was, if anything, even more strongly repudiated.

17. Craig Calhoun, "The Problem of Identity in Collective Action," in *Macro-Micro Linkages in Sociology*, ed. Joan Huber (Newbury Park, Calif.: Sage, 1991), 64, 68.

18. Edward González, "Castro's Revolution, Cuban Communist Appeals, and the Soviet Response," *World Politics* 21 (October 1968): 43.

19. Lois M. Smith and Alfred Padula, *Sex and Revolution: Women in Socialist Cuba* (New York: Oxford University Press, 1996), 21.

20. Ibid., 22–23.

21. Ibid., 27, 30. See also Tiffany A. Thomas-Woodard, "'Towards the Gates of Eternity': Celia Sánchez Manduley and the Creation of Cuba's New Woman," *Cuban Studies* 34 (2003): 154–80.

22. Lois M. Smith and Padula, *Sex and Revolution*, 32.

23. Carlos Moore, *Castro, the Blacks, and Africa* (Los Angeles: Center for Afro-American Studies, University of California at Los Angeles, 1988), 48–50.

24. Maida Donate-Armada and Zoila Macías, *El Suicidio en Miami y en Cuba* (Miami, Fla.: Consejo Nacional Cubanoamericano, 1998), 7.

25. I thank historian Louis A. Pérez, who is currently working on the topic of suicide in Cuba, for this insight and information.

26. Émile Durkheim, *Suicide* (Glencoe, Ill.: Free Press, 1958), 217–40. According to historian Louis A. Pérez, Cuba has had a high suicide rate since even before the twentieth century. See also Donate-Armada and Macías, *Suicidio*, 13–18.

27. Ameringer, *Cuban Democratic Experience*, 39–40, 87, 148.

28. For a further discussion of this generational theme in Cuban politics, see Maurice Zeitlin, *Revolutionary Politics and the Cuban Working Class* (New York: Harper Torchbooks, 1970), chap. 9.

29. Here I differ from Edward González, who many years ago addressed many of the issues discussed in this chapter. González saw the generation of 1953 as "committed to nationalism, anti-imperialism and revolutionary change" without noting the important changes in Cuban political culture that had taken place since the early 1940s (*Cuba under Castro: The Limits of Charisma* [Boston: Houghton Mifflin, 1974], 32).

30. The literal translation of *vergüenza* is "shame," but that constitutes an unclear and awkward rendition of what Chibás and the Ortodoxo Party had in mind.

31. Luis Conte Agüero, *Eduardo Chibás: El Adalid de Cuba* (Mexico City: Editorial JUS, 1955), 729, 688–89, 602–3.

32. Marifeli Pérez-Stable, "El Patriotismo Autonomista," *El Nuevo Herald* (Miami), July 31, 2000.

33. Marifeli Pérez-Stable, "Mayo de 1902: La Marcha Cívica de Tomás Estrada Palma," *El Nuevo Herald* (Miami), May 20, 1999, A15.

34. Marifeli Pérez-Stable, "Tribuna del Lector: Elogio de Carlos Márquez Sterling," *El Nuevo Herald* (Miami), September 8, 1998, A10. This is also the view of another prominent advocate of the new Cuban liberalism; see Rafael Rojas, "Precursores," *El Nuevo Herald* (Miami), January 18, 2005, A21. For Márquez Sterling's recommendation, through attorneys Mario Lazo (Márquez Sterling's cousin) and Jorge Cubas, to the U.S. government, see "Telegram from the Embassy in Cuba to the Department of State," Havana, November 6, 1958, 5 P.M., in U.S. Department of State, *Foreign Relations of the United States, 1958–1960*, vol. 6, *Cuba* (Washington, D.C.: U.S. Government Printing Office, 1991), 251.

35. See, for example, the collection "Dossier Europa del Este," with articles by Adam Michnik, Vladimir Tismaneanu, Elzbetia Matynia, Miguel Angel Centeno and Tania Rands, and Marcin Krol, in *Encuentro de la Cultura Cubana* (Madrid) 25 (Summer 2002): 181–257; Adam Michnik, "La Lógica del Compromiso," *Encuentro de la Cultura*

Cubana (Madrid) 32 (Spring 2004): 271–75, warning Cubans against the "utopia" of the third way or road, which in his view can lead only to the Third World.

36. I experienced this personally as a political activist in my public high school near Havana in the mid-1950s. The budgets of the student groups had so routinely been stolen by their successive leaders that I and my associates faced deeply entrenched mistrust when our slate, with myself as cotreasurer, was elected to run the graduating committee for the academic year 1955–56. This committee, elected after a strongly fought political campaign, organized and raised funds to finance and organize the graduation ceremony and served as intermediaries in our classmates' purchases of graduation rings. We literally had to go out of our way not only to be honest but also to appear to be honest. In the end—to the amazement of students, faculty, and staff—the unprecedented occurred: we not only covered several thousand dollars in normal graduation expenses but produced a surplus with which we bought books for the high school's library.

37. Marifeli Pérez-Stable, "Democracia y Soberanía: La Nueva Cuba a la Luz de Su Pasado," *Encuentro de la Cultura Cubana* (Madrid) 6–7 (Fall–Winter 1997): 195.

38. Hugh Thomas, "Middle Class Politics and the Cuban Revolution," in *The Politics of Conformity in Latin America*, ed. Claudio Véliz (London: Oxford University Press, 1967), 261.

39. Crecencio Pérez, one of Fidel Castro's few early supporters in the Sierra Maestra, who had a long record of leading peasant struggles, played virtually no leadership role in the revolutionary government after victory.

40. Báez, *Secretos de Generales*.

41. Gálvez, *Camilo*, 99. See also Carlos Franqui, *Camilo Cienfuegos* (Barcelona: Seix Barral los Tres Mundos, 2001).

42. Moore, *Castro, the Blacks, and Africa*, 16.

43. Leslie Dewart, *Christianity and Revolution: The Lesson of Cuba* (New York: Herder and Herder, 1963), 103–5.

44. Hugh Thomas, *Cuba: The Pursuit of Freedom* (New York: Harper and Row, 1971), 982–83.

45. Dewart, *Christianity and Revolution*, 105–7.

46. Wyatt MacGaffey and Clifford R. Barnett, *Twentieth-Century Cuba: The Background of the Castro Revolution* (Garden City, N.Y.: Doubleday Anchor, 1965), 243.

47. Mateo Jover Marimón, "The Church," in *Revolutionary Change in Cuba*, ed. Carmelo Mesa-Lago (Pittsburgh: University of Pittsburgh Press), 400–402.

48. Marcos A. Ramos, *Protestantism and Revolution in Cuba* (Coral Gables, Fla.: Research Institute for Cuban Studies, Institute for Interamerican Studies, Graduate School for International Studies, University of Miami, 1989), 139–40.

49. MacGaffey and Barnett, *Twentieth-Century Cuba*, 245.

50. Ramos, *Protestantism and Revolution*, 48.

51. Ibid., 53, 166, 49–50.

52. Among those who studied at Protestant schools were Armando Hart and Pepín Naranjo; the teachers included José Antonio Portuondo, an important intellectual in Castro's Cuba (Ramos, *Protestantism and Revolution*, 36).

53. Ibid., 37.

54. Ibid.

55. MacGaffey and Barnett, *Twentieth-Century Cuba*, 245.

56. Ibid.

57. While Fidel Castro's official birth date is August 13, 1926, he was actually born on August 13, 1927. His father had Fidel's original birth certificate changed so that he could enroll at the Belén high school (Claudia Furiati, *Fidel Castro: La Historia Me Absolverá*, trans. Rosa S. Corgatelli [Barcelona: Plaza Janés, 2003], 48–49, 81).

58. Ibid., 89–90; Katiuska Blanco, *Todo el Tiempo de los Cedros: Paisaje Familiar de Fidel Castro Ruz* (Havana: Casa Editorial Abril, 2003), 208.

59. Fidel Castro, *My Early Years*, ed. Deborah Shnookal and Pedro Alvarez Tabío (Melbourne, Aus.: Ocean Press, 1998), 70.

60. Cited in Georgie Anne Geyer, *Guerrilla Prince: The Untold Story of Fidel Castro* (Boston: Little, Brown, 1991), 38.

61. Gabriel García Márquez, prologue to Gianni Mina, *Habla Fidel* (Mexico City: Edivisión Compañía Editorial, 1988), 18.

62. Suárez, *Cuba*, 13.

63. Nelson P. Valdés and Rolando E. Bonachea, "Fidel Castro y la Política Estudiantil de 1947 a 1952," *Aportes* (Paris) 22 (October 1971): 33, 35.

64. While casting Castro's student activism in a favorable light, Mario Mencía, "Fidel Castro en el Bogotazo," *Bohemia* (Havana) 15 (April 14, 1978): 50–59; 16 (April 21, 1978): 50–57, conveys the flavor of student politics at the University of Havana in this period; see also Blanco, *Todo el Tiempo*, 223–44.

65. Charles D. Ameringer, *The Caribbean Legion: Patriots, Politicians, Soldiers of Fortune, 1946–1950* (University Park: Pennsylvania State University Press, 1996).

66. For a favorable view and details of Fidel Castro's participation in the Bogotazo, see Mencía, "Fidel Castro."

67. The exception was the several volumes of *Capital* that Castro kept in his cell, of which he read only a relatively small part; see Mario Mencía, *The Fertile Prison: Fidel Castro in Batista's Jails* (Melbourne, Aus.: Ocean Press, 1993), 40–41; Thomas, *Cuba*, 1375.

68. See Fidel Castro to Angel Castro, April 3, 1948, in Blanco, *Todo el Tiempo*, 247–51.

69. Suárez, *Cuba*, 15–16.

70. See Robert E. Quirk, *Fidel Castro* (New York: Norton, 1993), 618–29.

71. René Dumont, *Cuba, Est-Il Socialiste?* (Paris: Seuil, 1970).

72. Geyer, *Guerrilla Prince*, 51.

73. Castro, *My Early Years*, 75.

74. Ibid., 98.

75. Ibid., 126–27.

76. Ibid., 134.

77. Ibid.

78. Anderson, *Che Guevara*, 294.

79. Carlos Franqui, *Diario de la Revolución Cubana* (Paris: Ruedo Ibérico, 1976), 362.

80. Rufo López Fresquet, *My 14 Months with Castro* (New York: World, 1966), 111–12. Felipe Pazos, another important Cuban functionary who traveled to the United States with Fidel Castro, told a similar story to Edward González. González also described several incidents indicating political tensions between Fidel Castro and Raúl Castro and Che Guevara in April and May 1959. See Edward González, "The Cuban Revolution and the Soviet Union, 1959–1960" (Ph.D. diss., University of California at Los Angeles, 1966), 376–79.

81. Aleksandr Fursenko and Timothy Naftali, *"One Hell of a Gamble": Khrushchev, Castro, and Kennedy, 1958–1964* (New York: Norton, 1997), 18, 359.

82. Anderson, *Che Guevara*, 417.

83. Tad Szulc, *Fidel: A Critical Portrait* (New York: Morrow, 1986).

84. Ibid., 473.

85. Ibid., 475.

86. Both of these documents can be found in Rolando E. Bonachea and Nelson P. Valdés, eds. *Revolutionary Struggle, 1947–1958*, vol. 1 of *The Selected Works of Fidel Castro* (Cambridge: MIT Press, 1967), 164–220, 259–70.

87. According to Mencía, *Fertile Prison*, 110–11, the original plan was to print and distribute 100,000 copies of *History Will Absolve Me*. In the end, 27,500 copies were actually printed. Mencía mentions the names of several distributors of the pamphlet in various Cuban provinces but provides no figures on how many copies actually circulated.

88. Bonachea and Valdés, *Revolutionary Struggle*, 343–48.

89. Franqui, *Diario*, 473.

90. Luis Conte Agüero, *26 Cartas del Presidio* (Havana: Editorial Cuba, 1960), 73. These letters were published before Conte Agüero's break with Castro.

91. Franqui, *Diario*, 611.

92. William Gálvez, *Frank: Entre el Sol y la Montaña* (Havana: Ediciones Unión, 1991), 2:542–49; see also Bonachea and Valdés, *Revolutionary Struggle*, 98–101.

CHAPTER 3

1. This assessment is based on my exposure to liberal opinion over more than forty years of teaching and public speaking about Cuba to educational, union, and political groups.

2. Richard E. Welch Jr., *Response to Revolution: The United States and the Cuban Revolution, 1959–1961* (Chapel Hill: University of North Carolina Press, 1985), 47.

3. Ibid.

4. The idea that Castro aimed to turn Cuba into a Communist country even before Eisenhower moved against the Cuban leader is central to Alan H. Luxenberg's thesis that the United States was on the whole blameless for Castro's move toward Communism; see Alan H. Luxenberg, "Did Eisenhower Push Castro into the Arms of the Soviets?" *Journal of Interamerican Studies and World Affairs* 30 (Spring 1988): 37–71.

5. For a comprehensive historical account of nineteenth-century U.S. interest in annexing the island, see Oscar Pino Santos, "De la Habana al Mississippi: La Isla Estratégica y la Teoría de la Anexión, 1800–1898," *Temas* (Havana) 37–38 (April–September 2004): 146–58.

6. The complete text of the Platt Amendment can be found in Wyatt MacGaffey and Clifford R. Barnett, *Twentieth-Century Cuba* (Garden City, N.Y.: Doubleday Anchor, 1965), 17.

7. "Cuba's Great Expectations," *Business Week*, December 18, 1948, 117–18; U.S. Department of Commerce, Bureau of Foreign Commerce, *Investment in Cuba* (Washington, D.C.: U.S. Government Printing Office, 1956), 124. For an overall discussion and analysis of the period between the 1933 and 1959 revolutions, see Samuel Farber, *Revolution and Reaction in Cuba, 1933–1960: A Political Sociology from Machado to Castro* (Middletown, Conn.: Wesleyan University Press, 1976).

8. Morris H. Morley, *Imperial State and Revolution: The United States and Cuba, 1952–1986* (Cambridge: Cambridge University Press, 1987), 48. Although Morley looked at virtually all the same declassified U.S. documents as I did, we have reached somewhat different conclusions.

9. Former *New York Times* reporter Tad Szulc (*Fidel: A Critical Portrait* [New York: Morrow, 1986], 427–30) maintained that the CIA supplied funds to Fidel Castro's 26th of July Movement, perhaps without Castro's knowledge, between the fall of 1957 and the middle of 1958. So far, neither Szulc nor anyone else has supplied the requisite evidence to confirm this claim. On the Cuban government's side, General Fabián Escalante has made numerous claims about Central Intelligence Agency activities within the opposition to Batista. These claims are even harder to evaluate because they are for the most part based on information that Escalante claimed to have obtained from Cuban state security files; see Fabián Escalante, *The Secret War: CIA Covert Operations against Cuba 1959–62*, ed. Mirta Muñiz, trans. Maxine Shaw (Melbourne, Aus.: Ocean Press, 1995).

10. See, for example, Morley, *Imperial State*, 61–68.

11. Szulc, *Fidel*, 448–50.

12. However, the U.S. ambassador to Havana's consultative group of business executives from the local American community thought in late 1958 that the "Castro movement is Communist-inspired and dominated." It is interesting to note that conservative and pro-Batista U.S. Ambassador Earl E. T. Smith refrained from endorsing that assessment (U.S. Embassy in Cuba to Department of State [telegram], December 2, 1958 [secret], in U.S. Department of State, *Foreign Relations of the United States, 1958–1960*, vol. 6, *Cuba* [Washington, D.C.: U.S. Government Printing Office, 1991] [hereafter cited as *FRUS*], 276–77).

13. Cited in Thomas G. Paterson, *Contesting Castro* (New York: Oxford University Press, 1994), 252.

14. R. R. Rubottom to Christian A. Herter, October 23, 1959 (confidential), *FRUS*, 633–35.

15. R. R. Rubottom, to Christian A. Herter through S/S, December 30, 1959, in *Confidential U.S. State Department Central Files: Cuba, 1955–1959: Internal Affairs and*

Foreign Affairs, reel 25, internal affairs nos. 737, 837, 937; foreign affairs nos. 637, 611.37 (Bethesda, Md.: University Publications of America, 1987) (hereafter cited as *Central Files*).

16. Lester D. Mallory to C. Douglas Dillon, February 24, 1960 (confidential), *FRUS*, 808–10.

17. Memorandum of discussion at the 429th meeting of the National Security Council, Washington, D.C., December 16, 1959 (top secret, eyes only), *FRUS*, 703–6.

18. Memorandum of discussion at the 432d meeting of the National Security Council, January 14, 1960 (top secret), *FRUS*, 740–46.

19. Arleigh Burke to secretary of defense, July 10, 1958 (top secret), *Central Files*, reel 3.

20. Memorandum of discussion at the 396th meeting of the National Security Council, Washington, D.C., February 12, 1959 (top secret, eyes only), *FRUS*, 397–98.

21. Memorandum of discussion of the 429th meeting of the National Security Council, Washington, D.C., December 16, 1959, *FRUS*, 705.

22. Richard Nixon, *Six Crises* (New York: Warner, 1979), 416.

23. Luxenberg, "Did Eisenhower Push Castro," 47–49.

24. Welch, *Response to Revolution*, 48.

25. Morley, *Imperial State*, 75–76.

26. Memorandum of conversation, Washington, D.C., March 12, 1959 (confidential), *FRUS*, 424–28.

27. William Appleman Williams, *The United States, Cuba, and Castro: An Essay on the Dynamics of Revolution and the Dissolution of Empire* (New York: Monthly Review Press, 1962), 39.

28. Tad Szulc and Karl E. Meyer, *The Cuban Invasion: The Chronicle of a Disaster* (New York: Ballantine, 1962), 35.

29. On May 3, 1960, the Senate Internal Security Subcommittee went even further and held a hearing featuring former Batista army officers, including the former chief of staff and the onetime commander of the military prison whom Batista had removed from office after the prisoners protested inhumane treatment.

30. Welch, *Response to Revolution*, 114.

31. I thank an anonymous reader for the University of North Carolina Press for bringing this fact to my attention.

32. Williams, *United States, Cuba, and Castro*, 127.

33. Morley, *Imperial State*, 83.

34. Harry R. Turkel, memorandum, Washington, D.C., July 1, 1959 (confidential), *FRUS*, 546–51.

35. Jules R. Benjamin, *The United States and the Origins of the Cuban Revolution: An Empire of Liberty in an Age of National Liberation* (Princeton: Princeton University Press, 1990), 188.

36. For a discussion of the U.S. sugar quota, see chap. 1.

37. Memorandum of a conversation, Washington, D.C., June 1, 1959 (official use only), *FRUS*, 517–19.

38. Welch, *Response to Revolution*, 106.

39. Foreign Secretary Selwyn Lloyd to Christian A. Herter, October 30, November 12, 1959, Herter to Lloyd, November 4, 17, 1959, *FRUS*, 647–48, 653–56, 663–65, 669–71.

40. Benjamin, *United States*, 188–89.

41. Assistant Secretary of State for Inter-American Affairs' Special Assistant John C. Hill to R. R. Rubottom, Washington, D.C., December 10, 1959 (secret), *FRUS*, 697–98.

42. Department of State memorandum of telephone conversation between General Nathan B. Twining and Livingston T. Merchant, December 29, 1959 (official use only), *Central Files*, reel 7.

43. Benjamin, *United States*, 189.

44. Memorandum of a conference with the president, Washington, D.C., February 17, 1960, attended by General Andrew Goodpaster and Gordon Gray, special assistant to the president for national security affairs (top secret), *FRUS*, 789–90.

45. "A Program of Covert Action against the Castro Regime," paper prepared by the 5412 Committee, Washington, D.C., March 16, 1960 (secret, eyes only), *FRUS*, 850–51.

46. Benjamin, *United States*, 189.

47. Morley, *Imperial State*, 88.

48. Philip Bonsal, *Cuba, Castro, and the United States* (Pittsburgh: University of Pittsburgh Press, 1971), 149–50.

49. Ibid., 151.

50. Morley, *Imperial State*, 122.

51. Welch, *Response to Revolution*, 57–58.

52. Ibid., 77–79.

53. Dwight Eisenhower to Christian A. Herter, June 27, 1959, R. R. Rubottom to Herter (confidential), July 2, 1959, Herter to Eisenhower, July 7, 1959, concerning recommendations by Robert Kleberg, *Central Files*, reel 6; memorandum of conversation between Lawrence Crosby and Rubottom and R. A. Stevens, June 29, 1959 (limited official use), *Central Files*, reel 6.

54. Statement of United States Inter-American Council, June 2, 1959, William F. Combs, executive director of United States Inter-American Council, to Christian A. Herter, July 1, 1959, R. R. Rubottom to Combs, October 2, 1959, *Central Files*, reel 17.

55. Department of State memorandum of telephone conversation between Harold S. Geneen and R. R. Rubottom, December 14, 1959 (official use only), *Central Files*, reel 7.

56. Department of State memorandum of conversation between Al Nehmer, consultant on sugar to bottlers, bakers, and confectioners, and Jean H. Mulliken, November 30, 1959 (official use only), *Central Files*, reel 18.

57. U.S. Embassy in Cuba to Department of State (telegram), December 2, 1958 (secret), *FRUS*, 276–77.

58. U.S. Embassy in Cuba to Department of State (telegram), January 6, 1959 (confidential), *FRUS*, 345–46.

59. Robert A. Stevenson to R. R. Rubottom, December 17, 1959 (official use only), *Central Files*, reel 18. A similar concern that particular U.S. business interests in Cuba might be sacrificed in the pursuit of larger policy goals was expressed by Eugene

LeBaron, vice president of International Telephone and Telegraph, when U.S. financial assistance to Cuba was considered during a brief moment when an agreement was thought possible between the two countries. LeBaron objected to the United States providing aid to Cuba in light of the fact that his company had been negatively affected by Cuban government policies (Department of State memorandum of conversation between LeBaron and William Snow, August 7, 1959 [official use only], *Central Files*, reel 15).

60. Morley, *Imperial State*, 82.

61. Department of State to U.S. Embassy in Cuba (telegram), May 22, 1959 (confidential), *FRUS*, 510–11.

62. Department of State memorandum of conversation, Washington, D.C., September 24, 1959 (limited official use), *FRUS*, 605–11.

63. Department of State memorandum of conversation between Lawrence Crosby and R. R. Rubottom and R. A. Stevenson, June 29, 1959 (limited official use), *Central Files*, reel 6.

64. Department of State memorandum of conversation, Washington, D.C., September 24, 1959, *FRUS*, 605–11.

65. Department of State memorandum of conversation, Washington, D.C., June 30, 1960 (secret), *FRUS*, 973–75.

66. Van Gosse, *Where the Boys Are: Cuba, Cold War America, and the Making of a New Left* (London: Verso, 1993), 216–22.

67. Robert L. Beisner, *Twelve against Empire: The Anti-Imperialists, 1898–1900* (New York: McGraw-Hill, 1968), 225.

68. Gosse, *Where the Boys Are*, 216–22.

69. Williams, *United States, Cuba, and Castro*, 158.

70. Welch, *Response to Revolution*, 167–68.

71. Gosse, *Where the Boys Are*, 67–81, 118–19.

72. Welch, *Response to Revolution*, 161.

73. It is important to distinguish between these early executions of Batista henchmen and the later use of executions as the maximum penalty for common and "counterrevolutionary" political crimes.

74. Szulc and Meyer, *Cuban Invasion*, 32.

75. Ibid., 33.

76. Piero Gleijeses, *Shattered Hope: The Guatemalan Revolution and the United States, 1944–1954* (Princeton: Princeton University Press, 1991).

77. For an analysis that stresses the importance of the "long arm" of U.S. power and influence in Cuba and Latin America and its impact on Cuban revolutionary developments, see Jorge Domínguez, *Cuba: Order and Revolution* (Cambridge: Belknap Press of Harvard University Press, 1978), 1–133; Jorge Domínguez, *To Make a World Safe for Revolution* (Cambridge: Harvard University Press, 1989), 8–133.

78. Here I disagree with Morley's assertion (*Imperial State*, 128–29) that there was no such thing as a moderate U.S. government position vis-à-vis Cuba, although I agree with his overall thesis of U.S. hostility to authentic revolutionary change, which includes the position taken by moderates such as Bonsal.

79. While discussing the early period of the revolution, Morley described the U.S. officials' overt hostility to "the Castro faction" of the Cuban government, thus failing to note the clear distinction that the U.S. government (as well as many other people) made between Raúl Castro and Che Guevara on one hand and Fidel Castro on the other; see Morley, *Imperial State*, 128.

80. Bonsal, *Cuba, Castro, and the United States*, 39, 61.

81. U.S. Embassy in Cuba to Department of State (telegram), May 6, 1959 (confidential), *FRUS*, 503–4.

82. Memorandum of discussion at the 400th meeting of the National Security Council, Washington, D.C., March 26, 1959 (top secret), FRUS, 440–42.

83. U.S. Embassy in Cuba to Department of State (telegram), April 14, 1959 (secret), FRUS, 456–57.

84. Philip Bonsal to R. R. Rubottom, September 1959 (confidential), *FRUS*, 615.

85. Bonsal, *Cuba, Castro, and the United States*, 41–42.

86. Ibid., 41.

87. For a useful and detailed account of the U.S. military embargo policy vis-à-vis Cuba, see Paterson, *Contesting Castro*, 59, 135–37, 159, 174, 187.

88. Bonsal, *Cuba, Castro, and the United States*, 98.

89. Ibid., 99.

90. U.S. Embassy in Cuba to Department of State (telegram), July 31, 1959 (secret), *FRUS*, 578.

91. Department of State to Philip Bonsal (telegram), August 1, 1959 (secret), *Central Files*, reel 25.

92. U.S. Embassy in Cuba to Department of State, March 9, 1959 (confidential), *FRUS*, 421–24.

93. Ibid., 469–70.

94. Morley, *Imperial State*, 78–80.

95. Bonsal, *Cuba, Castro, and the United States*, 42.

96. Ibid., 135, 156.

97. Ibid., 160.

98. Ibid., 161.

99. Robert Alexander, *Bolivia: Past, Present, and Future of Its Politics* (New York: Praeger, 1982), 80–81; James M. Malloy, *Bolivia: The Uncompleted Revolution* (Pittsburgh: University of Pittsburgh Press, 1970), ix.

100. Malloy, *Bolivia*, 95–110.

101. Ibid., 115–16, 144, 149; James M. Malloy, "Revolutionary Politics," in *Beyond the Revolution: Bolivia since 1952*, ed. James M. Malloy and Richard S. Thorn (Pittsburgh: University of Pittsburgh Press, 1971), 112–18.

102. Malloy, *Bolivia*, 219–20.

103. Ibid., 164, 211, 214, 240, 334.

104. Ibid., 149, 216–35.

105. Alexander, *Bolivia*, 93.

106. Malloy, *Bolivia*, 172–75.

107. Cole Blasier, "The United States and the Revolution," in *Beyond the Revolution*, ed. Malloy and Thorn, 100.

108. Ibid., 63.

109. Ibid., 64.

110. Ibid., 65.

111. Alexander, *Bolivia*, 93.

112. Ibid., 98; James W. Wilkie, *The Bolivian Revolution and U.S. Aid since 1952* (Berkeley: University of California Press, 1969), 8.

113. James Dunkerley, *Rebellion in the Veins: Political Struggles in Bolivia, 1952–1982* (London: Verso, 1984), 113.

114. Blasier, "United States and the Revolution," 80–82.

115. Dunkerley, *Rebellion*, 105.

116. Ibid., 106.

117. Ibid., 108–11.

118. Malloy, *Bolivia*, 179–82; Blasier, "United States and the Revolution," 93.

119. Blasier, "United States and the Revolution," 93–94.

120. Alexander, *Bolivia*, 94.

121. Blasier, "United States and the Revolution," 94–95.

CHAPTER 4

1. Morris H. Morley, *Imperial State and Revolution: The United States and Cuba, 1952–1986* (Cambridge: Cambridge University Press, 1987), 127.

2. On the basis of a study conducted in the archives of the Instituto Nacional de Reforma Agraria (National Institute of Agrarian Reform), Juan and Verena Martínez Alier conclude that the rural working class demanded land or work, thus creating a great deal of class pressure on the revolutionary government and bringing about its radicalization. Although it is plausible that the rural workers demanded land or work, it is impossible to assess how representative these cases were of the rural proletariat, particularly if we make the reasonable assumption that only the most discontented would complain to the Instituto Nacional de Reforma Agraria. A more important objection is that, again, the researchers did not say anything about whether the rural complainants were demonstrating impatience with, discontent with, or distrust of the Cuban government's policies and actions; see Juan Martínez Alier and Verena Martínez Alier, "'Tierra ó Trabajo': Notas Sobre el Campesinado y la Reforma Agraria, 1959–1960," in *Cuba: Economía y Sociedad* (Paris: Ruedo Ibérico, 1972), 109–208.

3. Aleksandr Fursenko and Timothy Naftali, *"One Hell of a Gamble": Khrushchev, Castro, and Kennedy, 1958–1964* (New York: Norton, 1997), 18.

4. Paco Ignacio Taibo II, *Ernesto Guevara También Conocido como el Che* (Mexico City: Editorial Joaquín Mortiz, 1996), 354.

5. I am using the term "hegemony" in the sense given to it by Italian Marxist Antonio Gramsci. John M. Cammett, a Gramsci scholar, describes hegemony as "the 'spontaneous'

loyalty that any dominant social group obtains from the masses by virtue of its social and intellectual prestige and its supposedly superior function in the world of production" (*Antonio Gramsci and the Origins of Italian Communism* [Stanford, Calif.: Stanford University Press, 1967], 204).

6. For a more elaborate discussion of these issues, see Samuel Farber, *Revolution and Reaction in Cuba, 1933–1960: A Political Sociology from Machado to Castro* (Middletown, Conn.: Wesleyan University Press, 1976), 16–27.

7. Ibid., esp. 235–37.

8. Herbert Matthews, *Fidel Castro* (New York: Simon and Schuster, 1969), 112.

9. Julia E. Sweig, *Inside the Cuban Revolution* (Cambridge: Harvard University Press, 2002), 51.

10. Ibid., 105.

11. Ibid., 173.

12. Farber, *Revolution and Reaction*, 72–77, 168–72.

13. For a translation of this letter, see Rolando Bonachea and Nelson P. Valdés, eds., *Revolutionary Struggle, 1947–1958*, vol. 1 of *The Selected Works of Fidel Castro* (Cambridge: MIT Press, 1972), 351–63. For a more detailed discussion of this incident, see Sweig, *Inside the Cuban Revolution*, 63–71.

14. Farber, *Revolution and Reaction*, 198–99, 203.

15. This analysis resembles that of James O'Connor, a U.S. economist sympathetic to the Castro regime, in "On Cuban Political Economy," *Political Science Quarterly* 79 (June 1964): 233–47.

16. Fidel Castro, *Discursos Para la Historia*, books 1–2 (Havana: Imprenta Emilio Gall, 1959), 137.

17. Marcelo Fernández, "Zona Rebelde," *Revolución* (Havana), February 16, 1959, 1.

18. Marifeli Pérez-Stable, *The Cuban Revolution: Origins, Course, and Legacy*, 2d ed. (New York: Oxford University Press, 1999), 72–73.

19. Fursenko and Naftali, *"One Hell of a Gamble,"* 33–34.

20. Alfred Padula, "Financing Castro's Revolution, 1956–1958," *Revista/Review Interamericana* 8 (Summer 1978): 234–46.

21. Taibo, *Ernesto Guevara*, 354.

22. K. S. Karol, *Guerrillas in Power: The Course of the Cuban Revolution*, trans. Arnold Pomerans (New York: Hill and Wang, 1970), 466–76.

23. Farber, *Revolution and Reaction*, 28–92.

24. Ibid., 156–61.

25. Fidel Castro, *My Early Years*, ed. Deborah Shnookal and Pedro Alvarez Tabío (Melbourne, Aus.: Ocean Press, 1998), 81.

26. Carlos Rafael Rodríguez, "Reflexiones ante un Aniversario," *Hoy*, July 29, 1959, 1.

27. Louis A. Pérez Jr., *On Becoming Cuban: Identity, Nationality, and Culture* (Chapel Hill: University of North Carolina Press, 1999).

28. Carlos Alberto Montaner, *Cuba: Claves para una Conciencia en Crisis* (Madrid: Biblioteca Cubana Contemporánea, Editorial Playor, 1982).

29. The movements of the 1960s made an important contribution to Left politics by

suggesting that no "Chinese wall" separates the personal from the political and that issues arising in one of these areas are relevant to the other. Nevertheless, this important insight was sometimes converted or perverted into the idea that political priorities do not exist and that every issue is, by definition, as important as everything else. Thus, the essence of politics and morality (which is about choices and priorities) is thereby abolished.

30. "Proclama del Escambray," in Enrique Rodríguez Loeches, *Bajando del Escambray* (Havana: Editorial Letras Cubanas, 1982), 189.

31. Buró Obrero del II Frente Oriental, "Frank País," in *Unidad y Acción* (Havana: Ediciones Verde Olivo, 1999), 55.

32. Farber, *Revolution and Reaction*, 215.

33. See Felipe Pazos, "Comentarios a dos Artículos sobre la Revolución Cubana," *El Trimestre Económico* (Mexico City), 29 (January–March 1962): 1–18.

34. Farber, *Revolution and Reaction*, 219.

35. For example, in a sensitively written article, Carlos Luis casts serious doubt on the veracity of Castro's charges that bombings by U.S.-based planes, rather than Cuban antiaircraft fire, had caused a number of civilian casualties in an important episode that took place in October 1959; see Carlos Luis, "Notes of a Cuban Revolutionary in Exile," *New Politics* 2 (Fall 1963): 143–47.

CHAPTER 5

1. Harold R. Isaacs, *The Tragedy of the Chinese Revolution*, 2d rev. ed. (New York: Atheneum, 1966).

2. Jerry F. Hough, *The Struggle for the Third World: Soviet Debates and American Options* (Washington, D.C.: Brookings Institution, 1986), 226–27.

3. Harry Gelman, "The Soviet Union in the Less Developed World: A Retrospective View and Prognosis," in *The Soviet Union and the Third World: The Last Three Decades*, ed. Andrzej Korbonski and Francis Fukuyama (Ithaca: Cornell University Press, 1987), 276.

4. Carol R. Saivetz and Sylvia Woodby, *Soviet–Third World Relations* (Boulder, Colo.: Westview, 1985), 23–25.

5. Ibid., 25.

6. Joseph S. Berliner, *Soviet Economic Aid: The New Aid and Trade Policy in Underdeveloped Countries* (New York: Praeger, 1958), 14.

7. Hough, *Struggle*, 227.

8. Karen Dawisha, *Soviet Foreign Policy towards Egypt* (New York: St. Martin's, 1979).

9. Francis Fukuyama, "Soviet Strategy in the Third World," in *Soviet Union*, ed. Korbonski and Fukuyama, 26.

10. By the early 1960s, the Soviet Union had also begun to institutionalize the study of the Third World. Thus, the Institute of Africa and the Institute of Latin America were created in 1960 and 1961, respectively (Hough, *Struggle*, 37).

11. Fukuyama, "Soviet Strategy," 26–27.

12. Edward González, "The Cuban Revolution and the Soviet Union, 1959–1960" (Ph.D. diss., University of California at Los Angeles, 1966), 52; Edward González, "Castro's Revolution, Cuban Communist Appeals, and the Soviet Response," *World Politics* 21 (October 1968): 47n.

13. Wayne Smith, ed., *The Russians Aren't Coming: New Soviet Policy in Latin America* (Boulder: Rienner, 1992), 2; see also Robert Alexander, *Communism in Latin America* (New Brunswick, N.J.: Rutgers University Press, 1957).

14. Wayne Smith, *Russians Aren't Coming*, 5.

15. Ibid., 7.

16. Ibid., 8.

17. For a detailed account of the Guatemalan events, see Piero Gleijeses, *Shattered Hope: The Guatemalan Revolution and the United States, 1944–1954* (Princeton: Princeton University Press, 1991); Herbert S. Dinerstein, *The Making of a Missile Crisis: October 1962* (Baltimore: Johns Hopkins University Press, 1976), chap. 1.

18. Edward González, "Cuban Revolution," 24.

19. Dinerstein, *Making of a Missile Crisis*, 1.

20. Edward González, "Cuban Revolution," 45–46.

21. Roger Phillip Hamburg, "The Soviet Union and Latin America, 1953–1963" (Ph.D. diss., University of Wisconsin–Madison, 1965), 109–10.

22. Aleksandr Fursenko and Timothy Naftali, *"One Hell of a Gamble": Khrushchev, Castro, and Kennedy, 1958–1964* (New York: Norton, 1997), 77. However, as Dinerstein pointed out (*Making of a Missile Crisis*, 55–56), it eventually became evident that the fear of a missile gap was unfounded, the Soviet attainment of rough parity in strategic weapons did not dramatically alter the balance of power, the Soviet economy began to decline, and the Communist world was about to splinter irremediably.

23. Hough, *Struggle*, 120.

24. William Taubman, *Khrushchev: The Man and His Era* (New York: Norton, 2003), 402.

25. Dinerstein, *Making of a Missile Crisis*, 113.

26. Hough, *Struggle*, 120.

27. Jean Lacouture, *Nasser: A Biography* (New York: Knopf, 1973), 230–35, 244.

28. Hough, *Struggle*, 120.

29. At about the same time as Khrushchev's visit to Washington, the PSP leaders were cultivating the Chinese to increase the Cuban party's leverage with Moscow (Edward González, "Castro's Revolution," 54–55).

30. Nikita Khrushchev, *Khrushchev Remembers*, trans. and ed. Strobe Talbott (Boston: Little, Brown, 1970), 492. Khrushchev's recollections in this context are generally supported by the existing literature.

31. Edward González, "Cuban Revolution," 246.

32. Ibid., 250.

33. Yuri Pavlov, *Soviet-Cuban Alliance, 1959–1961* (Miami, Fla.: University of Miami North-South Center, 1994), 4.

34. See, for example, the conspiratorial interpretations put forward by Tad Szulc in *Fidel: A Critical Portrait* (New York: Morrow, 1986), chap. 3.

35. Taubman, *Khrushchev*, 492.

36. Khrushchev, *Khrushchev Remembers*, 488.

37. Ibid., 489.

38. Fursenko and Naftali, *"One Hell of a Gamble,"* 12.

39. Ibid., 13.

40. Ibid.

41. Ibid., 11–12.

42. Ibid., 13.

43. Edward González, "Castro's Revolution," 46–47.

44. Cited in Jacques Lévesque, *The USSR and the Cuban Revolution: Soviet Ideological and Strategical Perspectives, 1959–1977*, trans. Deanna Drendel Leboeuf (New York: Praeger, 1978), 11.

45. Fursenko and Naftali, "One Hell of a Gamble," 23–24; Taubman, *Khrushchev*, 532.

46. Cited in John Lewis Gaddis, *We Now Know: Rethinking Cold War History* (Oxford: Clarendon, 1997), 181.

47. Fursenko and Naftali, *"One Hell of a Gamble,"* 28–29.

48. Ibid., 33–34.

49. Edward González, "Cuban Revolution," 621–23.

50. Fursenko and Naftali, *"One Hell of a Gamble,"* 63.

51. Cited in Edward González, "Cuban Revolution," 570.

52. Lévesque, *USSR and the Cuban Revolution*, 12; Edward González, "Cuban Revolution," 573.

53. At this time, Alekseev did not have access to direct and secure communications with Moscow (Fursenko and Naftali, *"One Hell of a Gamble,"* 35, 361).

54. Khrushchev, *Khrushchev Remembers*, 489.

55. Lévesque, *USSR and the Cuban Revolution*, 16–17.

56. Ibid., 15–18, 21.

57. Andrés Suárez, *Cuba: Castroism and Communism, 1959–1966*, trans. Joel Carmichael and Ernst Halperin (Cambridge: MIT Press, 1967), 107.

58. Lévesque, *USSR and the Cuban Revolution*, 21–22.

59. Ibid., 24; Saivetz and Woodby, *Soviet–Third World Relations*, 9.

60. Hough, *Struggle*, 232.

61. Dawisha, *Soviet Foreign Policy*, 151–65.

62. Edward González, "Cuban Revolution," 438–59.

63. Cited in Edward González, "Cuban Revolution," 446.

64. Lévesque, *USSR and the Cuban Revolution*, 51.

65. Edward González, "Castro's Revolution," 48.

66. Comrade Marín (Cuba), "Report to the Seventh World Congress of the Communist International," *International Press Correspondence* 15 (October 10, 1935): 1301.

67. Jorge Ibarra, *Prologue to Revolution: Cuba, 1898–1958*, trans. Marjorie Moore (Boulder, Colo.: Rienner, 1998), 170.

68. C. Fred Judson, *Cuba and the Revolutionary Myth: The Political Education of the Rebel Army, 1953–1963* (Boulder, Colo.: Westview, 1984), 213.

69. Jon Lee Anderson, *Che Guevara: A Revolutionary Life* (New York: Grove, 1997), 297.

70. For analyses of the political role of intellectuals in prerevolutionary Cuba, see Roberto Fernández Retamar, "Hacia una Intelectualidad Revolucionaria en Cuba," and Ambrosio Fornet, "Revaluaciones del Movimiento Cultural del 30," in *Casa de las Americas* 7 (January–February 1967).

71. For a fuller discussion of this matter, see Samuel Farber, *Revolution and Reaction in Cuba, 1933–1960: A Political Sociology from Machado to Castro* (Middletown, Conn.: Wesleyan University Press, 1976), chaps. 7, 8.

72. Traditional, union-oriented social democracy was never a significant force in Cuba. Anarchism had been important until the 1920s but declined sharply thereafter. Trotskyism had some influence during the 1930s, but most of its adherents eventually merged and disappeared into the populist Auténticos in the late 1930s. By the time of the 1959 revolution, Cuban Trotskyism had been reduced to a little-known, tiny sect (Robert Alexander, *Trotskyism in Latin America* [Stanford, Calif.: Hoover Institution Press, 1973], 215–35).

73. For a good rendition of this mood, see C. Wright Mills, *Listen Yankee* (New York: Ballantine, 1960); see also Granma, "Hechos, No Palabras," *Revolución* (Havana), May 16, 1959; Cesar Leante, "Tiene la Revolución Cubana una Ideología," *Revolución* (Havana), September 2, 1959.

74. *La Solución Que Conviene a Cuba* (Havana: Partido Socialista Popular, 1958). This fifteen-page mimeographed pamphlet was produced clandestinely; a copy is held by the New York Public Library.

75. Blas Roca, "Qué Clase de Revolución Es Ésta?" *Hoy*, April 11, 1959, 1.

76. Blas Roca, continuation of report to PSP January Plenum, published in *Hoy*, January 28, 1959, 1.

77. *Hoy*, January 27, 1959, 1.

78. Roca, "Qué Clase de Revolución," 1.

79. Blas Roca, "Informa Blas Roca ante el Pleno del Comité Nacional del Partido Socialista Popular sobre el Programa del PSP," *Hoy*, October 7, 1959, 1.

80. Aníbal Escalante, "El Marxismo-Leninismo y la Revolución Cubana," *Hoy Domingo* (Sunday supplement), April 10, 1959.

81. Edward González, "Castro's Revolution," 60.

82. Quoted in Suárez, *Cuba*, 101.

83. This observation holds true for even the PSP's most important theoretical documents. See, for example, Blas Roca on *socialismo* in his *Fundamentos del Socialismo en Cuba*, rev. ed. (Havana: Imprenta Nacional de Cuba, 1961).

84. See, for example, Raúl Valdés Vivó, "En el Frente de las Ideas," *Hoy*, April 19, 1959, 1.

85. Argos, "Con Cien Ojos," *Hoy*, June 19, 1959, 1, criticized Minister of Labor Manuel Fernández for saying that the class struggle had been laid off (*cesante*). A couple of weeks later, Argos criticized Nasser for saying that classes could coexist even as nations could coexist (*Hoy*, July 5, 1959, 2).

86. Edward González, "Castro's Revolution," 45.

87. Valdés Vivó, "En el Frente," 1.

88. Carlos Rafael Rodríguez, "Los Industriales, los Obreros, y la Revolución," *Hoy*, December 10, 1959, 1.

89. Carlos Rafael Rodríguez, "Unidad Revolucionaria, Unidad Popular, y Lucha de Clases," *Hoy*, May 24, 1959, 1.

90. Ibid. See also Blas Roca, "Consideraciones sobre lo Dicho por Aguilar León," *Hoy*, July 8, 1959, 1; Roca, "Informa," 1.

91. Roca, "Consideraciones," 1.

92. See, for example, "Llamamiento del Partido Socialista Popular al 1ero de Mayo," *Hoy*, April 28, 1960, 1; Blas Roca, "Bases y Fundamentos de la Alianza Obrero-Campesina," *Hoy*, June 26, 1960, 1.

93. See, for example, the report of a televised interview with Blas Roca, *Hoy*, May 8, 1959, 8.

94. See, for example, Lázaro Peña's comments on Ursinio Rojas's report on "La Lucha por la Unión Obrera y la Democracia Sindical," at the May 1959 PSP plenum in "Terminó la Reunión del Comité Ejecutivo Nacional del PSP," *Hoy*, May 27, 1959, 1.

95. This ambition was the context of the first major dispute between Aníbal Escalante and Fidel Castro in 1962; see Maurice Halperin, *The Rise and Decline of Fidel Castro: An Essay in Contemporary History* (Berkeley: University of California Press, 1972), 149–59.

96. Anderson, *Che Guevara*, 296–97.

97. See, for example, the report of the May Day celebrations in "La Unidad Fue el Centro de los Discursos del Primero de Mayo," *Hoy*, May 3, 1959. Montseny and Gálvez gave "prounity" speeches in Santa Clara, and on the same day, Raúl Castro and Guevara gave "prounity" speeches in Havana and Santiago de Cuba.

98. For a listing of some of the unions under "unity" leadership, see the account of the labor rally at Parque Trillo in Havana during the summer of 1959 in "Denunció Jesús Soto el Mujalismo Que Aún Perdura en el Movimiento Obrero: Mitin en Parque Trillo," *Hoy*, July 16, 1959, 1.

99. Carlos Rafael Rodríguez revealed that Major Guillermo Jiménez of the Directorio Revolucionario consulted with him for political orientation and that Major Faure Chomón, also from the Directorio, studied Marxist texts with PSP leader Raul Valdés Vivó (cited in Maurice Halperin, *The Taming of Fidel Castro* [Berkeley: University of California Press, 1981], 53).

100. For a very detailed although sometimes speculative account of political differences within the PSP, see Suárez, *Cuba*.

101. Escalante elaborated the exceptionalist thesis, maintaining that the Cuban Revolution had not taken the classical road but had developed first in the countryside and ultimately surrounded the cities. Escalante claimed that the PSP had assisted this process

and helped open the way for the "Chinese road." He concluded that the party should recruit aggressively and even usher these recruits toward positions of leadership (Edward González, "Cuban Revolution," 343–46).

102. Edward González, "Castro's Revolution," 67.

103. See, for example, the indirect and strange polemic between Raúl Castro and Guevara with various 26th of July Movement leaders after May 1, 1959. At the May Day rallies, Raúl Castro and Guevara called for "unity" and attacked those opposed to it; in response, all of the 26th of July Movement's provincial coordinators except Oriente's published statements in *Revolución* arguing for "unity from below" and against "unity from above." Neither side identified those being criticized. See *Revolución* (Havana), May 4, 6, 7, 8, 12, 1959.

104. Euclides Vázquez Candela, "Saldo de una Polémica," *Revolución* (Havana), September 14, 1959, 1.

105. Edward González, "Cuban Revolution," 309.

106. Ibid., 602.

EPILOGUE

1. For an in-depth discussion of this issue, see Samuel Farber, *Revolution and Reaction in Cuba, 1930–1960: A Political Sociology from Machado to Castro* (Middletown, Conn.: Wesleyan University Press, 1976).

2. I am indebted to an anonymous reader for the University of North Carolina Press for raising many of the issues addressed in this epilogue.

3. See, for example, Carmelo Mesa-Lago and Horst Fabian, "Analogies between East European Socialist Regimes and Cuba: Scenarios for the Future," in *Cuba after the Cold War*, ed. Carmelo Mesa-Lago (Pittsburgh: University of Pittsburgh Press, 1993); Mark Falcoff, *Cuba the Morning After: Confronting Castro's Legacy* (Washington, D.C.: AEI Press, 2003); and the many volumes of the Association for the Study of the Cuban Economy's *Cuba in Transition* (Miami, Fla.: Florida International University, 1992–).

4. The case of the former Soviet Union is instructive in this context. The collapse of Communism in 1991 greatly accentuated the already existing disillusionment and disenchantment with revolution in general and the Bolshevik Revolution in particular; see, for example, Orlando Figes and Boris Kolonitskii, *Interpreting the Russian Revolution: The Language and Symbols of 1917* (New Haven: Yale University Press, 1999). In addition, former Russian Communists violently turned against Lenin with the same vulgarity with which they had previously defended him. See Dimitri Volkogonov, *Lenin: A New Biography*, trans. and ed. Harold Shukman (New York: Free Press, 1994).

5. See, for example, the collection of articles "Homenaje a la República" [Homage to the Republic], *Encuentro de la Cultura Cubana* (Madrid) 24 (Spring 2002): 5–151.

[SELECTED BIBLIOGRAPHY]

BOOKS AND PAMPHLETS

Agrupación Católica Universitaria. *Encuesta de Trabajadores Rurales, 1956–57*. Reprinted in *Economía y Desarrollo* (Instituto de Economía de la Universidad de la Habana) (July–August 1972): 188–212.

Alienes y Urosa, Julián. *Características Fundamentales de la Economía Cubana*. Havana: Banco Nacional de Cuba, 1950.

Anderson, Jon Lee. *Che Guevara: A Revolutionary Life*. New York: Grove, 1997.

Báez, Luis. *Secretos de Generales*. Havana: Editorial Si-Mar, 1996.

Benjamin, Jules R. *The United States and the Origins of the Cuban Revolution: An Empire of Liberty in an Age of National Liberation*. Princeton: Princeton University Press, 1990.

Blanco, Katiuska. *Todo el Tiempo de los Cedros: Paisaje Familiar de Fidel Castro Ruz*. Havana: Casa Editora Abril, 2003.

Bonachea, Rolando E., and Nelson P. Valdés, eds. *Revolutionary Struggle, 1947–1958*. Vol. 1 of *The Selected Works of Fidel Castro*. Cambridge: MIT Press, 1967.

Bonsal, Philip. *Cuba, Castro, and the United States*. Pittsburgh: University of Pittsburgh Press, 1971.

Castañeda, Jorge G. *Compañero: The Life and Death of Che Guevara*. New York: Knopf, 1997.

Castro, Fidel. *History Will Absolve Me*. In *Revolutionary Struggle, 1947–1958*. Vol. 1 of *The Selected Works of Fidel Castro*, ed. Rolando E. Bonachea and Nelson P. Valdés. Cambridge: MIT Press, 1967.

———. *My Early Years*. Ed. Deborah Shnookal and Pedro Alvarez Tabío. Melbourne, Aus.: Ocean Press, 1998.

Conte Agüero, Luis. *Eduardo Chibás: El Adalid de Cuba*. Mexico City: Editorial JUS, 1955.

Cuban Economic Research Project. *A Study on Cuba*. Coral Gables, Fla.: University of Miami Press, 1965.

de la Fuente, Alejandro. *A Nation for All: Race, Inequality, and Politics in Twentieth-Century Cuba*. Chapel Hill: University of North Carolina Press, 2001.

Dewart, Leslie. *Christianity and Revolution: The Lesson of Cuba*. New York: Herder and Herder, 1963.

Dinerstein, Herbert. *The Making of a Missile Crisis: October 1962*. Baltimore: Johns Hopkins University Press, 1976.

Domínguez, Jorge I. *Cuba: Order and Revolution*. Cambridge: Belknap Press of Harvard University Press, 1978.

———. *To Make a World Safe for Revolution*. Cambridge, Mass.: Harvard University Press, 1989.

Dumont, René. *Cuba, Est-Il Socialiste?* Paris: Seuil, 1970.

Dunkerley, James. *Rebellion in the Veins: Political Struggles in Bolivia, 1952–1982*. London: Verso, 1984.

Farber, Samuel. *Revolution and Reaction in Cuba, 1933–1960: A Political Sociology from Machado to Castro*. Middletown, Conn.: Wesleyan University Press, 1976.

Franqui, Carlos. *Diario de la Revolución Cubana*. Paris: Ruedo Ibérico, 1976.

Fursenko, Aleksandr, and Timothy Naftali. *"One Hell of a Gamble": Khrushchev, Castro, and Kennedy, 1958–1964*. New York: Norton, 1997.

Gálvez, William. *Camilo: Señor de la Vanguardia*. Havana: Editorial de Ciencias Sociales, 1979.

———. *Frank: Entre el Sol y la Montaña*. 2 vols. Havana: Unión de Escritores y Artistas de Cuba, 1991.

Gerschenkron, Alexander. *Economic Backwardness in Historical Perspective: A Book of Essays*. Cambridge: Belknap Press of Harvard University Press, 1966.

González, Edward. *Cuba under Castro: The Limits of Charisma*. Boston: Houghton Mifflin, 1974.

Gosse, Van. *Where the Boys Are: Cuba, Cold War America, and the Making of a New Left*. London: Verso, 1993.

Halperin, Maurice. *The Rise and Decline of Fidel Castro: An Essay in Contemporary History*. Berkeley: University of California Press, 1972.

———. *The Taming of Fidel Castro*. Berkeley: University of California Press, 1981.

Ibarra, Jorge. *Prologue to Revolution: Cuba, 1898–1958*. Trans. Marjorie Moore. Boulder, Colo.: Rienner, 1998.

Karol, K. S. *Guerrillas in Power: The Course of the Cuban Revolution*. Trans. Arnold Pomerans. New York: Hill and Wang, 1970.

Lacouture, Jean. *Nasser: A Biography*. New York: Knopf, 1973.

Le Riverend, Julio. *Historia Económica de Cuba*. Havana: Instituto Cubano del Libro, 1967.

Lévesque, Jacques. *The USSR and the Cuban Revolution: Soviet Ideological and Strategical Perspectives, 1959–1977*. Trans. Deanna Drendel Leboeuf. New York: Praeger, 1978.

López Fresquet, Rufo. *My 14 Months with Castro*. New York: World, 1966.

López Segrera, Francisco. *Cuba: Capitalismo Dependiente y Subdesarrollo (1510–1959)*. Havana: Editora de Ciencias Sociales, 1981.

MacGaffey, Wyatt, and Clifford R. Barnett. *Twentieth-Century Cuba*. Garden City, N.Y.: Doubleday Anchor, 1965.

Malloy, James M. *Bolivia: The Uncompleted Revolution*. Pittsburgh: University of Pittsburgh Press, 1970.

Matthews, Herbert. *Fidel Castro*. New York: Simon and Schuster, 1969.

Mencía, Mario. *The Fertile Prison: Fidel Castro in Batista's Jails*. Melbourne, Aus.: Ocean Press, 1993.

Mills, C. Wright. *Listen Yankee*. New York: Ballantine, 1960.

Moore, Carlos. *Castro, the Blacks, and Africa*. Los Angeles: Center for Afro-American Studies, University of California at Los Angeles, 1988.

Morley, Morris H. *Imperial State and Revolution: The United States and Cuba, 1952–1986*. Cambridge: Cambridge University Press, 1987.

O'Connor, James. *The Origins of Socialism in Cuba*. Ithaca: Cornell University Press, 1970.

Oltuski, Enrique. *Vida Clandestina: My Life in the Cuban Revolution*. Trans. Thomas Christensen and Carol Christensen. New York: Wiley, 2002.

Paterson, Thomas G. *Contesting Castro*. New York: Oxford University Press, 1994.

Pavlov, Yuri. *Soviet-Cuban Alliance, 1959–1961*. Miami, Fla.: University of Miami North-South Center, 1994.

Pérez, Louis A. *Cuba: Between Reform and Revolution*. New York: Oxford University Press, 1988.

———. *On Becoming Cuban: Identity, Nationality, and Culture*. Chapel Hill: University of North Carolina Press, 1999.

Pérez-Stable, Marifeli. *The Cuban Revolution: Origins, Course, and Legacy*. 2d ed. New York: Oxford University Press, 1999.

Quirk, Robert E. *Fidel Castro*. New York: Norton, 1993.

Ramos, Marcos A. *Protestantism and Revolution in Cuba*. Coral Gables, Fla.: Research Institute for Cuban Studies, Institute for Interamerican Studies, Graduate School of International Studies, University of Miami, 1989.

Roca, Blas. *Fundamentos del Socialismo en Cuba*. Rev. ed. Havana: Imprenta Nacional de Cuba, 1961.

Rodríguez, Carlos Rafael. *Cuba en el Tránsito al Socialismo, 1959–1963*. Havana: Cuba Editora Política, 1979.

Rodríguez Loeches, Enrique. *Bajando del Escambray*. Havana: Editorial Letras Cubanas, 1982.

Seers, Dudley, ed. *Cuba: The Economic and Social Revolution*. Chapel Hill: University of North Carolina Press, 1964.

Smith, Lois M., and Alfred Padula. *Sex and Revolution: Women in Socialist Cuba*. New York: Oxford University Press, 1996.

Smith, Wayne, ed. *The Russians Aren't Coming: New Soviet Policy in Latin America*. Boulder, Colo.: Rienner, 1992.

Stoner, K. Lynn. *From the House to the Streets: The Cuban Woman's Movement for Legal Reform, 1898–1940*. Durham: Duke University Press, 1991.

Suárez, Andrés. *Cuba: Castroism and Communism, 1959–1966*. Trans. Joel Carmichael and Ernst Halperin. Cambridge: MIT Press, 1967.

Sweig, Julia. *Inside the Cuban Revolution*. Cambridge: Harvard University Press, 2002.

Szulc, Tad. *Fidel: A Critical Portrait*. New York: Morrow, 1986.

Szulc, Tad, and Karl E. Meyer. *The Cuban Invasion: The Chronicle of a Disaster*. New York: Ballantine, 1962.

Taibo, Paco Ignacio, II. *Ernesto Guevara También Conocido como el Che*. Mexico City: Editorial Joaquín Mortiz, 1996.

Thomas, Hugh. *Cuba: The Pursuit of Freedom*. New York: Harper and Row, 1971.

Trotsky, Leon. *The History of the Russian Revolution*. Trans. Max Eastman. Ann Arbor: University of Michigan Press, 1957.

————. *Results and Prospects*. New York: Merit, 1969.

Welch, Richard E., Jr. *Response to Revolution: The United States and the Cuban Revolution, 1959–1961*. Chapel Hill: University of North Carolina Press, 1985.

Williams, William Appleman. *The United States, Cuba, and Castro: An Essay on the Dynamics of Revolution and the Dissolution of Empire*. New York: Monthly Review Press, 1962.

Zanetti, Oscar, and Alejandro García. *Sugar and Railroads: A Cuban History, 1837–1959*. Trans. Franklin W. Knight and Mary Todd. Chapel Hill: University of North Carolina Press, 1998.

Zuaznabar, Ismael. *La Economía Cubana en la Década del 50*. Havana: Editorial de Ciencias Sociales, 1986.

ARTICLES AND ESSAYS

Bianchi, Andrés. "Agriculture: The Pre-Revolutionary Background." In *Cuba: The Economic and Social Revolution*, ed. Dudley Seers. Chapel Hill: University of North Carolina Press, 1964.

Blackburn, Robin. "Prologue to the Cuban Revolution." *New Left Review* 21 (October 1963): 52–91.

Blasier, Cole. "The United States and the Revolution." In *Beyond the Revolution: Bolivia since 1952*, ed. James M. Malloy and Richard S. Thorn. Pittsburgh: University of Pittsburgh Press, 1971.

Calhoun, Craig. "The Problem of Identity in Collective Action." In *Macro-Micro Linkages in Sociology*, ed. Joan Huber. Newbury Park, Calif.: Sage, 1991.

Casanovas, Joan. "La Nación, la Independencia y las Clases." *Encuentro de la Cultura Cubana* (Madrid) 15 (Winter 1999–2000): 177–86.

Draper, Hal. "The Two Souls of Socialism." *New Politics* 5 (Winter 1966): 57–84.

Enzensberger, Hans Magnus. "Bildnis Einer Partei: Vorgeschichte, Struktur und Ideologie der PCC." *Kursbuch* (Berlin), October 18, 1969. Translated into English as "Portrait of a Party: Background, Structure, and Ideology of the PCC." *International Socialism* 44 (July–August 1970): 11–19.

Farber, Samuel. "The Cuban Communists in the Early Stages of the Cuban Revolution: Revolutionaries or Reformists?" *Latin American Research Review* 18 (March 1983): 59–83.

————. "The Resurrection of Che Guevara." *New Politics* 7 (Summer 1998): 108–16.

Fernández Retamar, Roberto. "Hacia una Intelectualidad Revolucionaria en Cuba." *Casa de las Américas* 7 (January–February 1967): 4–18.

Fornet, Ambrosio. "Revaluaciones del Movimiento Cultural del 30." *Casa de las Américas* 7 (January–February 1967).

Fuentes, Juan F., and Graciela Chailloux. "El Conflicto: Fuerzas Productivas y Relaciones de Producción como Causa Determinante del Triunfo de la Revolución Social en Cuba." *Economía y Desarrollo* 94 (September–October 1986): 43–67.

Fukuyama, Francis. "Soviet Strategy in the Third World." In *The Soviet Union and the Third World: The Last Three Decades*, ed. Andrzej Korbonski and Francis Fukuyama. Ithaca: Cornell University Press, 1987.

Gelman, Harry. "The Soviet Union in the Less Developed World: A Retrospective View and Prognosis." In *The Soviet Union and the Third World: The Last Three Decades*, ed. Andrzej Korbonski and Francis Fukuyama. Ithaca: Cornell University Press, 1987.

González, Edward. "Castro's Revolution, Cuban Communist Appeals, and the Soviet Response." *World Politics* 21 (October 1968):39–68.

"Homenaje a la República." *Encuentro de la Cultura Cubana* (Madrid) 24 (Spring 2002): 5–151.

Jover Marimón, Mateo. "The Church." In *Revolutionary Change in Cuba*, ed. Carmelo Mesa-Lago. Pittsburgh: University of Pittsburgh Press, 1971.

Luis, Carlos. "Notes of a Cuban Revolutionary in Exile." *New Politics* 2 (Fall 1963): 143–47.

Luxenberg, Alan H. "Did Eisenhower Push Castro into the Arms of the Soviets?" *Journal of Interamerican Studies and World Affairs* 30 (Spring 1988): 37–71.

Malloy, James M. "Revolutionary Politics." In *Beyond the Revolution: Bolivia since 1952*, ed. James M. Malloy and Richard S. Thorn. Pittsburgh: University of Pittsburgh Press, 1971.

Mencía, Mario. "Fidel Castro en el Bogotazo." *Bohemia* (Havana) 15 (April 14, 1978): 50–59; 16 (April 21, 1978): 50–57.

Mesa-Lago, Carmelo. "Economic Policies and Growth." In *Revolutionary Change in Cuba*, ed. Carmelo Mesa-Lago. Pittsburgh: University of Pittsburgh Press, 1971.

———. "La Seguridad Social." *Encuentro de la Cultura Cubana* (Madrid) 25 (Summer 2002): 313–24.

O'Connor, James. "On Cuban Political Economy." *Political Science Quarterly* 79 (June 1964): 233–47.

Padula, Alfred. "Financing Castro's Revolution, 1956–1958." *Revista/Review Interamericana* 8 (Summer 1978): 234–46.

Pazos, Felipe. "Comentarios a dos Artículos sobre la Revolución Cubana." *El Trimestre Económico* (Mexico City) 29 (January–March 1962): 1–18.

Pino Santos, Oscar. "De la Habana al Mississippi: La Isla Estratégica y la Teoría de la Anexión, 1800–1898." *Temas* (Havana) 37–38 (April–September 2004): 146–58.

Rodríguez, José Luis. "La Economía Neocolonial Cubana." *Cuba Socialista* 37 (January–February 1989): 105–23.

Seers, Dudley. "The Economic and Social Background." In *Cuba: The Economic and*

Social Revolution, ed. Dudley Seers. Chapel Hill: University of North Carolina Press, 1964.

Teichert, Pedro C. M. "Analysis of Real Growth and Wealth in the Latin American Republics." *Journal of Inter-American Studies* 1 (April 1959): 173–202.

Thomas, Hugh. "Middle Class Politics and the Cuban Revolution." In *The Politics of Conformity in Latin America*, ed. Claudio Véliz. London: Oxford University Press, 1967.

Valdés, Nelson, and Rolando E. Bonachea. "Fidel Castro y la Política Estudiantil de 1947 a 1952." *Aportes* (Paris) 22 (October 1971): 24–40.

PUBLIC DOCUMENTS

Confidential U.S. State Department Central Files: Cuba, 1955–1959: Internal Affairs and Foreign Affairs. 25 reels. Frederick, Md.: University Publications of America, 1987.

International Bank for Reconstruction and Development. *Report on Cuba*. Washington, D.C.: International Bank for Reconstruction and Development, 1951.

U.S. Department of Commerce, Bureau of Foreign Commerce. *Investment in Cuba: Basic Information for United States Businessmen*. Washington, D.C.: U.S. Government Printing Office, 1956.

U.S. Department of State. *Foreign Relations of the United States, 1958–1960*. Vol. 6, *Cuba*. Washington, D.C.: U.S. Government Printing Office, 1991.

UNPUBLISHED MATERIAL

González, Edward. "The Cuban Revolution and the Soviet Union, 1959–1960." Ph.D. diss., University of California at Los Angeles, 1966.

Hamburg, Roger Phillip. "The Soviet Union and Latin America, 1953–1963." Ph.D. diss., University of Wisconsin–Madison, 1965.

Mesa-Lago, Carmelo. "Unemployment in Socialist Countries: Soviet Union, East Europe, China, and Cuba." Ph.D. diss., Cornell University, 1968.

[I N D E X]

Acción Democrática government, Venezuela, 57
Agrarian Reform Law (May 1959), 4, 121, 135; and liberals, 124; and Soviet Union, 146; United States business reactions to, 87, 91; United States policy after, 80–84
Agrarian reform law (1958, Sierra Maestra), 120
Agricultural experiments under Castro, 58
Alekseev, Aleksandr, 3, 147–48
Alvarez Díaz, José R., 32
American Society of Newspaper Editors, 60
American Sugar Refining Company, 92
Amoedo, Julio A., 85, 148
Anarchism, 154, 194 (n. 72)
Anderson, Robert B., 85, 89
Anfuso, Victor, 79
Anti-Communism, 121, 164–66
Anti-imperialism, 129–31, 136
Aragonés, Emilio, 149
Aramayo family, 106
Arbenz, Jacobo, 3, 84, 142
Argentina, 40, 41, 103, 107
Ariel (Rodó), 46
Arteaga, Manuel, 52
Association for the Study of the Cuban Economy, 1
Atatürk, Mustafa Kemal, 139
Auténtico Party, 25, 29, 117, 124, 131
Autonomistas, 47

Baggett, Sam H., 91
BANFAIC (Banco de Fomento Agrícola e Industrial de Cuba, Cuban Bank for Agricultural and Industrial Development), 25

Bank robbery: as revolutionary action, 41
Barrientos, René, 108
Batista, Fulgencio: Castro's movement against, 64–65, 75, 116–17, 144, 155–56, 168; and Catholic Church, 52–53; and control of press, 41; coup d'état (1952), 25, 28, 32, 52, 73, 148, 168; and Cuban Communist Party, 38, 141, 155, 157–58; Cuban women's movement and, 44; economic legacy of, 32, 102–3; execution of supporters (1959), 79, 96, 134, 185 (n. 29), 187 (n. 73); failed assassination attempt (1957), 117; failed coup against (1956), 117; fall of (January 1959), 3, 32, 33, 61, 75, 89, 113, 133; fraudulent 1958 elections, 47–48; and Grau San Martín government, 37, 38; groups struggling against (1950s), 115–17, 120, 128; lack of alliances in regime of, 28–29; and *politiquería*, 47–48, 49; and public works projects, 31; rise of, 37, 38, 167–68; and union activities, 73–74, 115; United States support for, 73–75, 96–97
Bay of Pigs invasion, 45, 75, 84, 86; U.S. left-wing protests against, 94, 95
Belén (Bethlehem) High School, 54, 55, 58
Bender, Frank, 61
Beria, Lavrenty, 139
Bianchi, Andrés, 13
Billington, James H., 35, 36
Blackburn, Robin, 28–29
Blanqui, Auguste, 35
Bogotazo riots, Colombia, 56, 59, 66
Bohemia, 65
Bolivian Revolution (1952), 2, 98, 104–11, 124, 135–36; Bolivian Communists

and, 105, 107, 111; miners'/peasants' militias, 109–10; overthrow of MNR government (1964), 110

Bolsheviks, 64, 147

Bonapartism, 116, 167

Bonsal, Philip, 76, 77, 81, 91, 95, 172; Castro's avoidance of, 83, 99, 136; role in U.S. policy toward Cuban Revolution, 98–104, 111, 187 (n. 78); and Urrutia, 146–47; and U.S. restrictions on Cuban sugar, 85–86

Braddock, Daniel M., 89, 90

Braga, B. Rionda, 91

Browder, Earl, 155

Bulganin, Nikolay, 140

Buonarroti, Filippo, 35

Burke, Arleigh, 78

Burma, 143

Business Advisory Council, 93

Business Week, 25–26

Cabell, C. P., 83

Calhoun, Craig, 43–44

Caral, Oscar Fernández, 55

Caribbean Legion, 56

Casanovas, Joan, 36

Castro, Fidel: and anti-Communism, 121, 164; birth, 182 (n. 57); vs. Communist revolutionary leaders, 99, 126–27, 134, 154, 156, 162–63; and Cuban Communist Party, 4, 37–38, 57, 59–63, 121, 126–27, 154, 156, 158, 162–63, 195 (n. 95); and Cuban economic climate (1959), 33; and Directorio Revolucionario (Revolutionary Directorate), 124–25; and honor, as value, 44, 54; as leader of revolution, 110–11, 114, 115–19, 120–23, 138, 168–69; life (1940s to 1950s), 54–56; and Miami Pact, 60, 120–21; Moncada army barracks attack, 49–50, 57, 64, 129; murder charges (1948), 55; meeting with Nixon, 78; and Ortodoxo Party, 47; political ideology, intentions after taking power, 5, 60–61, 66–68, 69–71, 111, 170, 183 (nn. 4, 80); political ideology, roots of, 34, 39–41, 54–59, 178–79 (n. 9), 182 (n. 67); political

moves prior to revolution, 132–33; political moves following revolution, 59–66, 123–27, 133–36, 168–69; political skills (early 1950s), 55–56, 182 (n. 64); and populism, 40–41, 50, 56–58; in prison, 57, 182 (n. 67); revolutionary strategy of stages, 59–66; self-proclaimed expertise of, 57–58; and Sierra Maestra revolutionaries, 50, 51, 60, 65; "socialist revolution" declaration, 1, 86, 143; and Soviet Union, 62–63, 145–46, 148–49; Spanish background of, 54–55; tactical genius of, 40–41, 63, 66–67, 134, 138, 168; United States business view of, 89–90, 93; United States plans for assassination of, 84; United States view of (late 1950s), 74–75, 79–80, 184 (n. 12); United States visit (April 1959), 60–61, 78, 79–80, 100, 102–3, 183 (n. 80). *See also* Castro regime

Castro, Manolo, 55

Castro, Raúl, 40, 50; and Batista henchmen executions, 134; and Communism, 57, 145, 164; and Fidel Castro's political intentions, 60–61; as pro-Communist leader in 26th of July Movement, 3, 62, 68, 99, 114, 126, 156, 162, 196 (n. 103); and Second Front revolutionaries, 118, 132; and Soviet Union, 146, 150; and U.S. hostages, 74, 78

Castro regime: agricultural experiments during, 58; and Cuban liberalism, 123–24; deterioration through 1990s, 1, 58; disbanding of independent organizations, 44; and middle-class opposition, 65–66, 135; nationalization of industries, 3, 23–24, 81, 106; and Soviet Union, 2, 3–4, 62–63, 69, 84, 85, 143–54, 165; suicide among leaders in, 44–45; and denouncement of United States imperialism, 107; United States military activities developing against, 78, 82, 83–86, 103

Catholic association at University of Havana, 21

Catholic Worker Action organization, 53

Catholic Worker Youth organization, 53
Cayo Confites expedition (1947), 56, 58–59, 66
Celler, Emanuel, 79
Central Highway, 18
Central Intelligence Agency, U.S. (CIA), 61, 95, 142; Cuban activities (late 1950s), 76, 78, 82, 83–84, 184 (n. 9)
Charter of the Organization of American States, 101
Chávez, Nuflo, 108
Chiang Kai-shek, 139
Chibás, Eduardo, 45, 46–47, 65, 120, 131
Chibás, Raúl, 65, 67, 120
Chibasismo, 131
Chinese Communism, 150, 192 (n. 29); coming to power (1949), 139; defeat of, in Chinese Revolution (1927), 139; rift with Soviet Union, 3, 150, 169
Chomón, Faure, 162
Cienfuegos, Camilo, 42–43, 50–51, 62, 163
Cienfuegos, Osmani, 51
Cienfuegos, Ramón, 51
Class structure: during Batista rule, 22–23, 115–16, 128; bourgeoisie, 18; bourgeoisie, after revolution, 123–25, 134–35; Cuban Communist Party analysis, in light of revolution, 160–61; middle-class opposition to Castro, 65–66, 135; multiclass nationalism, 131, 170; multiracial working class (1930s), 17–18; and populism, 49–52; after revolution (1933), 115, 167–68; ruling classes and army, 115, 119; rural population, 24, 50; sugar workers, 14, 17–18, 23–24, 26–27, 29–30, 156; white rural middle class, 24; working class (early twentieth century), 154–55; working class (1950s), 22–23, 50–51, 128–29, 131; working class influences after revolution, 114, 189 (n. 2)
Cold War: Cuba at end of, 58; and Cuban Communist Party, 38, 178 (n. 5); Latin America, consequences for, 141–42; Soviet Union and Third World activities, 140, 191 (n. 10); Soviet/U.S. relations (late 1950s to early 1960s), 137, 142–43, 169–70, 192 (n. 22); U.S.

foreign policy and, 69, 73, 76, 129
Colombia, 170; Bogotazo riots, 56, 59, 66
Comibol (Corporación Minera de Bolivia), 106, 109
Committees for the Defense of the Revolution, 133
Communications, mid-twentieth-century Cuba, 17–19
Communist and Workers' Party conference (1960), 152
Communist International, 37, 141
Communist Party of the Soviet Union, 140, 145, 159
Compensation for expropriated property, 106, 107
Confidential State Department Central Files, 2
Conte Agüero, Luis, 66
Corporación Minera de Bolivia (Comibol), 106, 109
Costa Rica, 126, 145
Coup d'état (1952), 25, 28, 32, 52, 73, 148, 168
Crosby, Lawrence, 87–88, 90, 91, 92
Cuba in the Struggle for Freedom and Independence (Obyden), 149
Cuban Americans. *See* Cuban exiles, Florida
Cuban American Sugar Company, 91
Cuban army: class changes in, 115, 119; collapse (1958), 119, 169
Cuban bourgeoisie, 18; after revolution, 123–25, 134–35
Cuban Catholicism. *See* Roman Catholic Church: and Cuban revolution
Cuban Communist Party, 1, 51, 99, 114, 116; and anti-Communism, 121, 164–66; and Batista rule, 38, 141, 155, 157–58; and Castro, 4, 57, 59–63, 121, 126–27, 154, 156, 158, 162–63, 195 (n. 95); Castro unifying (1965), 37–38, 63, 105; and Chinese Communism, 192 (n. 29); and Cuban blacks, 52; development of, before revolution, 154–57, 178 (n. 4), 194 (n. 72); development through Cuban Revolution, 4–5, 159–64, 195–96 (n. 101); founding of (1925), 37, 154; populism, compared with,

124, 135–36; and Bolivian militias, 109–10; overthrow of (1964), 110

Naftali, Timothy, 2
Nasser, Gamal Abdel, 139, 140, 143, 153
National Bank of Cuba, 65, 76
National Catholic Congress (Havana, 1959), 123, 148
National City Bank, 9
Nationalism: multiclass nature of Cuban, 131, 170
National revolutionaries, 35
National Security Council, 75, 78, 83, 87, 93, 100
Neutrality Act, 78
Ne Win, U., 143
Nicaragua, 73, 136, 171; Cuban exile air raid from (April 1961), 86
Nichols, John A., 91–92
1917 April Theses, 64
Nixon, Richard, 78, 86
North Atlantic Treaty Organization (NATO), 100
Novins, Stuart, 99

Obyden, Konstantin M., 149
Ocho Vias, 57
Oil: Cuban government seizure of U.S. refineries, 85, 86, 150, 153; demand by Cuban government for U.S. refineries to process Soviet oil, 85, 89, 127, 150
Oliver, William F., 92
Oltuski, Enrique, 114, 125, 126
Organization of American States, 93
Ortodoxo Party, 45, 46–47, 65, 116, 117, 124, 158

País, Frank, 50, 53, 67, 132
Partido Socialista Popular (PSP). See Cuban Communist Party
Pavlov, Yuri, 144
Paz Estenssoro, Víctor, 106, 108, 109
Pazos, Felipe, 65, 67, 76, 98, 120
Peña, Felix, 45
Peña, Lázaro, 52, 146
Pérez, Faustino, 50, 53, 114, 117, 125, 126
Pérez, Louis A., 130
Pérez Jiménez, Marcos, 52, 73, 97, 170

Pérez-Stable, Marifeli, 122
Perón, Juan, 52, 107
Peru, 170
Philippines, 71
Piñeiro, Manuel, 162
Pitaluga, Gustavo, 58
Platt Amendment, 9, 129; abolition of (1934), 10, 72, 130, 169; titles of, 71
Politiquería, 116, 168; rejection of, 38, 46, 47–49, 128, 181 (n. 36)
Popular Front stage, Communist International, 141
Popular music, 19
Populism: and Castro, 40–41, 50, 56–58; class, race, national origin and, 49–52; and Cuban economy, 167–68; generational consciousness of, in Cuba, 45–47, 180 (n. 29); tradition in Cuba, 34, 37, 39–52, 56–58, 178 (n. 4); values, 41–45
Porter, Charles, 79
Portuondo, José Antonio, 181 (n. 52)
Poverty (1950s), 20–22, 128
Powell, Adam Clayton, 79
Prío Socarrás, Carlos, 25, 29, 32, 45, 117, 158
Protestantism, 53–54, 181 (n. 52)
Public morality (late 1940s), 131–32, 190–91 (n. 29)
Puerto Rico, 71

Quevedo, Angel, 45

Race: and Cuban revolution, 44, 51–52
"Race war" of 1912, 52
Racism (1950s), 22
Radicalization of Cuban Revolution, 4, 135–36, 159, 170–71
Radical nationalism, 5
Radio, 19; Radio Rebelde, 118, 119
Railroads, 18
Ramos, Marcos A., 54
Rent Reduction Act (1959), 65, 80–81, 135
Report on Cuba (IBRD), 8, 23, 25, 26–27, 33
Revolución, 62, 79, 122, 125, 164–65
Rice production, 31–32
Rio Treaty (1947), 101

ENVISIONING CUBA

Samuel Farber, *The Origins of the Cuban Revolution Reconsidered* (2006).

Lillian Guerra, *The Myth of José Martí: Conflicting Nationalisms in Early Twentieth-Century Cuba* (2005).

Rodrigo Lazo, *Writing to Cuba: Filibustering and Cuban Exiles in the United States* (2005).

Alejandra Bronfman, *Measures of Equality: Social Science, Citizenship, and Race in Cuba, 1902–1940* (2004).

Edna M. Rodríguez-Mangual, *Lydia Cabrera and the Construction of an Afro-Cuban Cultural Identity* (2004).

Gabino La Rosa Corzo, *Runaway Slave Settlements in Cuba: Resistance and Repression* (2003).

Piero Gleijeses, *Conflicting Missions: Havana, Washington, and Africa, 1959–1976* (2002).

Robert Whitney, *State and Revolution in Cuba: Mass Mobilization and Political Change, 1920–1940* (2001).

Alejandro de la Fuente, *A Nation for All: Race, Inequality, and Politics in Twentieth-Century Cuba* (2001).